Virtue and Knowledge

This book focuses on the concept of virtue, and in particular on the virtue of wisdom or knowledge, as it is found in the epic poems of Homer, some tragedies of Sophocles, selected writings of Plato, Aristotle, and the Stoic and Epicurean philosophers.

The key questions discussed are the nature of the virtues, their relation to each other, and the relation between the virtues and happiness or well-being.

Thanks, among others, to the work of Alasdair MacIntyre and Philippa Foot, there has been renewed interest recently in the concept of virtue. The value of William Prior's book is that it provides the background and interpretive framework to make classical works on ethics, such as Plato's *Republic* and Aristotle's *Nicomachean Ethics*, accessible to readers with no training in the classics. Moreover, it does so in a style that is lucid and well-presented, while offering a fresh approach to the familiar story.

Virtue and Knowledge will appeal to everyone interested in Greek ethics, but especially to the new student in philosophy.

William J. Prior is Associate Professor of Philosophy and Director of the University Honors Program at Santa Clara University, California.

VIRTUE AND KNOWLEDGE

An Introduction to Ancient Greek Ethics

William J. Prior

London and New York

First published 1991
by Routledge
11 New Fetter Lane, London EC4P 4EE

Simultaneously published in the USA and Canada
by Routledge
a division of Routledge, Chapman and Hall, Inc.
29 West 35th Street, New York, NY 10001

Printed in England by Clays Ltd, St Ives plc

British Library Cataloguing in Publication Data
Prior, William J.
   Virtue and knowledge: and introduction to Ancient Greek
   ethics.
   1. Ethics. Ancient Greek theories
   I. Title
   170'.938

Library of Congress Cataloguing in Publication Data
Prior, William J.
   Virtue and knowledge: an introduction to ancient Greek
   ethics/William J. Prior.
     p. cm.
     1. Ethics, Greek. I. Title.
   BJ161.P72 1991
   170'.938–dc20   89–49680

ISBN 0-415-02470-6
ISBN 0-415-05324-26 pbk

This book is dedicated to my children.

CONTENTS

Preface   ix
Acknowledgements   xi
Introduction: virtue, knowledge, and happiness   1

1 BEFORE PHILOSOPHY: SOME LITERARY
  PORTRAITS OF VIRTUE   5
  The Homeric hero   7
  Greek tragedy   21
  Conclusion   36

2 THE SOPHISTS AND SOCRATES   38
  The crisis in values: the Sophists   38
  The life of Socrates   43
  Socrates and Plato   46
  Socrates on trial   49
  The moral philosophy of Socrates: the *Crito*   67
  The Socratic quest: method and paradox   74

3 PLATO'S MORAL PHILOSOPHY: THE *REPUBLIC*   91
  Book I: what is justice?   92
  The challenge of Glaucon and Adeimantus   97
  The just state   99
  Justice in the individual   105
  The philosopher-king   114
  Defective states and individuals: the comparison of lives   126
  The critique of literature and education   133

4 ARISTOTLE'S *NICOMACHEAN ETHICS*   144
  Aristotle's life and works   144
  The structure of the *Nicomachean Ethics*   145
  Aristotle's methodology   146
  The good: *eudaimonia*   148
  Arete: moral excellence or virtue   155
  The particular virtues: courage and temperance   163

Contents

Justice and friendship   167
Deliberation, choice and practical wisdom   175
Moral weakness   182
The lives of theoretical and practical wisdom   188
Conclusion   192

5 EPICUREANISM AND STOICISM   194
The Hellenistic World   194
Epicureanism   198
Stoicism   207
Stoicism, Epicureanism and the classical tradition   219

FURTHER READING   225
INDEX OF PASSAGES CITED   229
GENERAL INDEX   237

PREFACE

There has been a recent revival of interest among philosophers in the ethics of virtue. Alasdair MacIntyre, Philippa Foot and others have argued that an ethical theory based on the concept of virtue is superior to its main modern competitors. This revival has led to renewed interest in the works of the ancient philosophers such as Plato, Aristotle, the Stoics and the Epicureans, who originated "virtue ethics" and remain among its finest exponents. Unfortunately, however, the contemporary reader is apt to lack an understanding of the cultural context in which these works were written. I have written this book to bridge the gap between the contemporary student and the ancient texts.

This is not a book for scholars. The reader will find in it no footnotes, no discussion of scholarly controversies, no extensive bibliography. I wrote it instead for beginners in philosophy who want to understand some of the great classical works on ethics. I have aimed it specifically at my own students in introductory philosophy courses, but I hope it will prove useful to the general reader as well. I am aware that some of the things I say are controversial in scholarly circles, and in particular that I draw a more "intellectualist" picture of Aristotle's view of happiness than do most scholars. I felt, though, that engaging in scholarly debate would not be profitable for the intended audience of the book. To put matters succinctly, those scholars of ancient philosophy who read the book will know where my interpretations differ from those of others; non-scholars will appreciate having a straightforward interpretation that does not digress into such matters.

I have limited my discussion to the most important and widely read ancient works on the subject. I have not tried to discuss every aspect of these works, rather, I have focused on the concepts of virtue, knowledge and happiness. The question of the relation among these concepts is a central theme of ancient ethical thought, and it is also one that any theory of virtue, ancient or modern, must consider. No other topic is so well suited, I think, to bring out both the continuity and the specific differences in ancient ethics.

Preface

My decision to write a book on ancient ethics is based on personal convictions. Since the reader will not find a defense of these beliefs in the book, I think it only fair that I should state them here. I agree with those contemporary philosophers who find in the ethics of virtue a superior way of thinking about moral philosophy. I also believe in the enduring merit of the writings of the ancient philosophers on this subject. I do not think that they have had the last word; I believe that the ancient approach to ethics is overly rationalistic and needs to be supplemented by a greater appreciation of the positive role the emotions play in ethics. None the less, it seems to me that the study of ancient philosophical ethics is an indispensible part of liberal education.

Ancient Greece produced some of the greatest philosophers who ever lived. Their writings on ethics are unsurpassed in philosophical merit. Moreover, their central theme is of interest to every thoughtful person. Though they sometimes contain abstract philosophical discussions that can confuse or intimidate the novice, their primary focus is on practical questions that everyone needs to reflect on. Though the modern world differs in many respects from the ancient society for which these thinkers wrote, their works can still provide a practical guide to living the good life. For this reason alone every educated person ought to read them.

I would like to express my gratitude to Malcolm Schofield for his helpful comments on an earlier draft of this book, and to my research assistant, Douglas Gabbard, for his careful proofreading of the manuscript.

Santa Clara, California
July, 1989

ACKNOWLEDGEMENTS

The material quoted from Aristotle's *Nichomachean Ethics*, translated by Martin Ostwald, is reprinted with permission of Macmillan Publishing Company. Copyright © 1962; renewed © 1986 by Macmillan Publishing Company. The quotations from *The Iliad of Homer*, translated with an introduction by Richard Lattimore, are reprinted with permission of the University of Chicago Press. Copyright 1951 by the University of Chicago. The lines from Sophocles' *Antigone*, translated by Elizabeth Wyckoff, are reprinted with permission of the University of Chicago Press. Copyright 1954 University of Chicago. The lines from Sophocles' *Oedipus the King*, translated by David Grene, are reprinted with permission of the University of Chicago Press. Copyright 1942 by the University of Chicago. The selections from *The Manual of Epictetus*, translated by P. E. Matheson, are reprinted with permission of Oxford University Press. The selected passages from Diogenes Laertius' *Lives of Eminent Philosophers*, vol. 2, translated by R. D. Hicks, in the Loeb Classical Library (first published 1925) are reprinted with permission of Harvard University Press.

INTRODUCTION: VIRTUE, KNOWLEDGE, AND HAPPINESS

When we think about ethics, we are apt to think about right and wrong, morality and immorality, and universal, objective standards of conduct. This way of thinking is in large part a legacy of the Judaeo-Christian tradition, and its influence on the Western intellectual tradition is so great that we tend to identify ethics with these concepts and think that there is no other way to think about the subject than in terms of them.

Greek ethics speaks to us in a different voice. Although the concepts above are not entirely absent from it, they are not of central importance. Rather than right and wrong, the ancient Greeks thought primarily in terms of good and bad. Their notions of goodness and badness were not exclusively moral notions, but embraced every aspect of human life. A common Greek phrase of commendation for a person was *kalos k'agathos*, "beautiful and good," in which what we would call moral and aesthetic notions are combined into a single ideal of noble character. The focus of Greek ethical thought was not on universal principles of conduct, but on ideal types of human life. The primary question the Greeks sought to answer was not, "What actions are universally morally right?" but "What is the best sort of life for human beings to live?"

Because Greek thought has been only slightly less influential in Western intellectual history than the Judaeo-Christian tradition, later moral philosophers have not entirely lost sight of this question; nonetheless, it has in general been of secondary importance in moral philosophy. Like many others writing today on ethics, I believe that this is unfortunate; concentration on the issues in Greek ethics can correct many of the problems that arise from thinking of ethics primarily in terms of universal principles of moral right and wrong.

In Chapter 1 I shall argue that the ancient Greek focus on the ideal human life has its origin in the portrayal of the hero in Greek epic and tragic literature. Before I begin the story of the

1

development of this theme in literature and philosophy, however, I want to discuss in a general way the framework shared by all the Greek writers on ethics. If we see at the outset the areas of agreement among the ancient Greek thinkers, we shall be better able to understand the differences among them, on which later chapters will focus.

As I have already noted, Greek thinkers based their ethical thinking on the ideal of an exemplary human life. They saw the attainment of a good life as the *telos*, the end or goal, of human existence. For most Greek philosophers, this end is *eudaimonia*. This term is usually translated "happiness," and I shall in general follow this convention. The reader should be aware, however, that the end sought by the Greek thinkers differs considerably from happiness as we understand it. By "a happy life" we tend to mean a life filled with pleasant experiences, one in which one's desires are generally satisfied. We think of happiness as a rather subjective psychological property which may not correspond to one's objective circumstances. One might be happy, we think, while living in poverty or even in prison; more controversially, perhaps, a morally evil person could be happy if only his or her desires were satisfied.

Though some later Greek thinkers, in particular the Stoics, anticipated the separation of psychological state from external situation, no Greek thinker saw happiness as divorced entirely from objective considerations. To achieve the end of human existence was for the Greeks not merely to experience pleasure or satisfaction, but to attain to some objectively good status, whether that of the Homeric hero, the Platonic philosopher-king, or the Stoic sage. The end of human existence, then, for all the Greek thinkers, is not a state of subjective satisfaction, but one of objective achievement, of excellence. It would be perhaps less misleading to refer to this goal as "the good life" or "human flourishing" than as "happiness."

The good life, then, is the life of excellence. The Greek word for excellence is *arete*, the customary translation of which is "virtue." Again, I shall follow the convention of the translators, and speak throughout this book of virtue and the virtues; but again I must warn the reader of the misleading connotations of the term. Despite the resurgence of interest in the concept of virtue among philosophers, it remains a somewhat archaic term, with connotations of sexual chastity. *Arete* had for the Greeks no such limitations: it was not primarily sexual, or even moral in its meaning. The *aretai*, the "excellences" or "virtues" were simply the qualities that made a life admirable or excellent. Homer regards physical attributes such as speed and strength as virtues, and Aristotle lists ambition, pleasantness and wit among the virtues. Thus, while the claim that the best human life is the life of virtue would seem to an English speaker to be a substantive moral claim, the corresponding Greek claim that the life of *eudaimonia* is a life of *arete* has the feel of an analytical, tautological statement: an excellent life requires excellence.

The Greeks did think of characteristics we regard as moral virtues, such as courage, justice, and temperance, as among the most important human excellences, though they did not sharply separate these virtues from others we think of as non-moral. Another human characteristic which the Greeks generally thought of as a virtue is wisdom (*sophia*) or knowledge (*episteme*).

Two kinds or aspects of wisdom are particularly important for ethics. One is the practical ability to determine the correct course of action in a particular situation. This sort of wisdom is like the ability of a skilled craftsman to make the best use of material in creating an artistic product; it is a kind of "know-how," a skill. The second is more general, more abstract. It is a kind of perspective on the human condition, one which tells us who we are, what human life is like, and what our place is in the overall scheme of things. It is from this sort of wisdom that our understanding of the nature of the good life comes. Both kinds of wisdom contribute to the living of the good life: it helps to know both the end to aim at and the best means of reaching it.

The Greek thinker who first focused on wisdom as the virtue of central importance to ethics was Socrates. Socrates in fact identified virtue with knowledge, and treated knowledge as equivalent to wisdom. Again, there are difficulties with translation for the reader to bear in mind. It is helpful to recall when considering Socrates' view or the views of other philosophers on the relation between virtue and knowledge that these philosophers are not thinking of knowledge in general but knowledge of the end of human existence and the means to achieve it. We might call this knowledge "practical wisdom" (*phronesis*).

Most Greeks did not accept Socrates' identification of virtue with knowledge, but all would agree with the claim that wisdom or knowledge of the sort just described was an important virtue and a great aid to the living of the good life. In fact, all the writers on Greek ethics that we shall examine would agree on the following framework of ethical theory. First of all, there is an ideal form of human existence, which individuals strive to attain and which it is possible for them to achieve. Second, the virtues are necessary to the attainment of this ideal. Third, wisdom or knowledge is at least one of the virtues needed for its attainment.

Within the general framework of the good life with its attendant virtues, including wisdom, there is much room for disagreement about the correct answer to the following questions. First, what is the good life; what does the goal of human existence look like when described in detail? Second, what are the virtues; in what do justice, temperance and the like consist? What makes them virtues? Third, what are the relations among the virtues; are some more important than others? Do they form a harmonious whole, or can one conflict with another? Can one have one of the virtues but lack others? Fourth, how does wisdom fit into the picture? Is it a virtue on a par with the others? What is its nature? Are the two aspects of wisdom inseparable, or can one be wise in one respect but not in the other? Fifth and finally, what is the relation between the virtues and the good life; are the virtues all equally important for living the good life? Are some dispensable? Do some even impede one in the search for the good life? Granted that at least some of the virtues are necessary for the good life; are they sufficient? That is, can one possess the virtues and still fail to lead the good life? The writers we shall consider in this book disagreed with each other on all of these questions; the debate among them constitutes the subject of the book.

1

BEFORE PHILOSOPHY:
SOME LITERARY PORTRAITS
OF VIRTUE

Greek thought about virtue, knowledge, and the good life begins,
not with philosophy, but with literature. Understanding the
historical origin of a concept is often vital to understanding its
meaning; it is particularly important in this case, for at the
beginning of Greek literature and thought stand the two great
Homeric epic poems, the *Iliad* and the *Odyssey*, whose influence on
later Greek thought is unparalleled.

When the ancient Greeks thought about virtue, they were
more likely to think of examples of virtuous individuals than
abstract principles or rules of virtuous conduct. These examples
may have been drawn from history, but they were more often taken
from poetry. The poetic examples which would have sprung first
and foremost to the mind of the ordinary Greek were those of the
great heroes of the Homeric poems: Achilles in the *Iliad* and
Odysseus in the *Odyssey*. We may say, in fact, that these characters
serve as *paradigms* of virtuous conduct for the Greeks: they are
primary examples of virtue, and any theory of virtue would have to
consider them seriously and not simply dismiss them.

The *Iliad* and the *Odyssey* are among the classics of Western
literature. The Greeks regarded these poems, and in particular the
Iliad, as the greatest literary works their culture had produced.
They did not, however, simply look on these poems as literary
masterpieces. They used them as the primary texts in the education
of their youth, and drew from them much of their theology, their
ethics, and their understanding of their culture.

The ancient Greeks never attained national political unity. The
main unit of social organization in classical times was the self-
governing city-state, or *polis*. These Greek city-states were fiercely

5

independent; they were often, as in the case of Athens and Sparta, political rivals. Despite this fragmented political situation, however, the ancient Greeks shared a common culture. Consider religion: though each city had its own protective deity (in Athens it was Athena, the goddess of wisdom), all Greeks recognized the same twelve Olympian gods, today the still-familiar subjects of books and courses on "Greek mythology."

The Homeric poems give definitive form to this Olympian religion. These poems present to the reader a world in which the gods interact with humans and display many human qualities. The gods get angry with people and with each other, they take sides in human conflicts, such as the Trojan War, they seduce and deceive both mortals and immortals, and they cause human deaths. Though they are also shown as responsive to human needs on occasion, the portrait of the gods in these poems is not a flattering one. They seem, to the modern reader at any rate, less noble and admirable than the great human heroes of the poems, Achilles and Odysseus and the Trojan prince Hector.

Despite the fact that these poems do not depict the gods in the most favorable light, they formed the basis of much later Greek religious thought. Most Greeks, it seems safe to say, accepted Homer's picture of the gods as true, and thought of these poems as in some sense divinely inspired. (Homer invokes the muses, Greek goddesses of poetry and art, at the start of each poem.) Nor was the influence of Homer limited to theology. It is often said that the *Iliad* and *Odyssey* were regarded much as the Bible has been regarded throughout most of Western civilization: as the source of knowledge about human conduct and the world in general as well as about the divine. There are of course differences: the Greeks were not concerned to establish the authority of Homer as a sacred text as Christians were in the case of the Bible. If, however, one thinks of the way in which the people and stories of the Bible became for centuries the common coin of Western civilization, structuring our view of our origins, nature and history, one will have a fairly close analog of the influence of Homer on the ancient Greeks. As Adam and Eve, Noah, Moses and David shaped the imaginations even of non-believers, so Achilles, Odysseus and Agamemnon provided models of human conduct for the Greeks.

About Homer we know virtually nothing. The Greeks regarded him as the composer of both the *Iliad* and the *Odyssey*, but they also possessed little information about him as a person. Scholars in this century have discovered that the poems were the last stage in a long tradition of oral composition, to which many poets may have contributed. The *Iliad* and *Odyssey* achieved their present form sometime in the eighth century BC, but they contain material that is centuries older than that; some of it may date back to the Trojan War itself, which probably took place in the twelfth or even the thirteenth century. How much of these poems is based on historical occurrence and how much is invention, how much is due to a single poet who put them into final form and how much to his many predecessors who contributed material to the final synthesis, and even whether the two poems are the work of the same final composer — these are things we shall never know with certainty. Fortunately, our uncertainty about the authorship of the poems has little effect on our evaluation of their content.

The Homeric hero

The Homeric poems are set in the period of the Trojan War. This war, which the ancient Greeks at any rate regarded as an historical event, provided the material for much later Greek literature. According to tradition, the cause of the war was the abduction of Helen, the wife of the Spartan king Menelaus, by Paris, the son of the Trojan king Priam. Menelaus and his brother, Agamemnon, king of Mycenae, assembled an armada of ships from other Greek cities and led a vast army against Troy (a city on the coast of Asia Minor). This combined force besieged Troy for a decade. Unable to capture it by force, the Greeks resorted to the deception of the Trojan horse to gain entry to the city, which they then destroyed. Their return to Greece was marked by more tribulations; Odysseus, the last to reach home, took another ten years to do so.

Homer does not attempt to tell the full story of the war or its aftermath. Instead, he focuses in the *Iliad* on a brief period in the last year of the war, and in the *Odyssey* on the final days of Odysseus' wanderings and his return home. In the course of describing these brief episodes, however, Homer gives us a picture of the life of an entire civilization.

Society, as depicted in the Homeric poems, is highly stratified. At the top are the great kings, Agamemnon among the Greeks and Priam among the Trojans. They are the leaders of loose alliances

7

with other states; the kings of these states are independent, yet honor the authority of Agamemnon or Priam, whom they treat as "first among equals." Beneath the great kings and their noble allies are the mass of ordinary soldiers (in the *Iliad*) and citizens (in the *Odyssey*), about whom we hear very little from Homer. At the bottom of the social order are slaves, who often are women of free or even noble birth who had the misfortune to be captured in war. Homer devotes a good deal of attention to the portrayal of female characters in the two poems; this should not conceal from us, however, the fact that women in Homeric society derive their social status from that of their fathers and husbands. People who perform certain valuable ceremonial, religious or socially useful functions, such as heralds, prophets and doctors hold an intermediate rank, not honored as the kings or nobles, but having privileges not possessed by ordinary men. Between individuals of whatever rank there are rules of conduct which are derived from their respective status. Heroes must behave in a certain way toward their king, in another toward heralds and prophets, and in a third toward ordinary men. These standards of conduct are sanctified by tradition and are well known to everyone in Homeric society.

The heroes of the Homeric poems live for one thing above all else, glory. In war, the primary means of attaining glory is through success in combat. The measure of glory is the honor one receives from one's fellow nobles, and honor is not simply an abstract concept, but something reflected concretely in the distribution of the spoils of war. The pursuit of glory is what unites the heroes on both sides in the Trojan War. Homer is not unaware of the fact that the Greeks are at war with the Trojans because of Paris' theft of Helen, and he makes it clear in Book VI of the *Iliad* that Hector, the greatest of the Trojan warriors, is fighting in defense of his home and family, but one feels that such motives, important as they are, are less important to the Homeric hero than the pursuit of glory. If combat is the arena in which the heroes of the *Iliad* win glory, it is also the arena of death. Death and glory go hand in hand, and one of the surest ways to win glory is to die in heroic combat. The heroes of the *Iliad* are aware of this relationship, but in general they accept the goal as worth the risks; their attitude is exemplified by the hero Sarpedon, a Trojan ally, when he says to his companion Glaukos

> Glaukos, why is it you and I are honoured before others
> with pride of place, the choice meats and the filled wine
>   cups
> in Lykia, and all men look on us as if we were
>   immortals . . . ?
> Man, supposing you and I, escaping this battle,
> would be able to live on forever, ageless, immortal
> so neither would I myself go on fighting in the foremost
> nor would I urge you into the fighting where men win glory.
> But now, seeing that the spirits of death stand close about us
> in their thousands, no man can turn aside nor escape them,
> let us go on and win glory for ourselves, or yield it to others.
> (*Iliad* XII, 310—12, 322—8; Lattimore's translation)

The hero is expected to display certain virtues in his pursuit of glory. The virtues of primary importance are those characteristics that lead to success in combat, and these include physical strength and speed as well as courage. Since war is not merely an arena for solitary combat, however, loyalty to the cause for which one is fighting is also a virtue, and so is wisdom, here manifested in the concern of the wise man for maintaining the unity of the army and conducting the war well. In the *Iliad* Nestor and Odysseus manifest this kind of wisdom on the Greek side, while Poulydamas offers sage advice to the Trojans. Achilles, Hector and Agamemnon bring tragedy on themselves as a direct result of ignoring this wise advice. For the most part, however, wisdom plays a fairly minor role in the attainment of heroic status. No one attains this status by virtue of wisdom alone, and no hero in the prime of life, not even wily Odysseus, is known entirely for wisdom and not for the martial virtues as well. It is no accident that Nestor, the character in the *Iliad* most closely associated with this virtue, is beyond fighting age, and even he notes that he was the equal or superior of the current generation of heroes in his youth.

From these remarks there emerges a picture of the typical Homeric hero: he is a person of noble rank who functions in a highly stratified society according to a strict code of conduct. He lives for glory, which he achieves by the display of virtue or excellence, particularly excellence in combat, and which is accorded to him by his fellow heroes in the form of gifts and renown. Wisdom, reflected in military counsel, is one form of virtue, though not the primary one for a hero in the prime of life. We can already see functioning here the general framework of Greek ethics I spoke of in the Introduction: a goal (the heroic life or the life of glory) to which the virtues, including wisdom in its own way, contribute.

Achilles

Achilles, the preeminent hero of the *Iliad*, is far from the typical hero. He is unique among the Homeric heroes in that he manages to violate most, if not all of the traditions in his society; yet he does not lose the status of a hero by so doing. Achilles is the finest warrior among the Greek and Trojan armies. This is a fact recognized by everyone, including Achilles himself; only Hector at times questions Achilles' prowess, and this is a sign of Hector's self-deception. Despite his superior physical strength, speed of foot (he is customarily referred to as "swift-footed Achilles"), military skill and courage, however, he is not the military leader of the Greeks, that position is reserved for Agamemnon, in his capacity as king. From this fact stem all the troubles of the *Iliad*.

The *Iliad* begins with a quarrel between Achilles and Agamemnon. Agamemnon has refused the request of a priest of Apollo to return his daughter Chryseis, who has become Agamemnon's "prize of war" or concubine. Apollo has accordingly stricken the Greek army with a plague. Achilles has called an assembly to discover the cause of the plague. When the prophet Calchas, with Achilles' promise of protection, has revealed that Agamemnon is responsible, Agamemnon finally agrees to give back the girl, but demands another as compensation. When Achilles quarrels with Agamemnon over this demand, Agamemnon threatens to remove Achilles' "prize," Briseis. Achilles is so furious that he considers killing Agamemnon on the spot, but on the advice of the goddess Athena, who offers him "shining gifts" to compensate for his humiliation, he instead withdraws from the fighting.

This unfortunate series of events is only possible because of the division of power between Achilles and Agamemnon. Had Agamemnon been the greatest warrior among the Greeks as well as king, no one would have dared to stand up to him. Certainly no other hero of the Greek army would have taken it upon himself, as Achilles does, to call the assembly, offer his protection to Calchas, and upbraid Agamemnon in public. Even Achilles, however, finally balks at murdering Agamemnon, showing the power the office of king and the traditions of his society have even over a warrior powerful enough to kill with impunity. Agamemnon no doubt reacts harshly to Achilles because he sees his actions as a threat to his royal power; in a sense, Achilles brings his punishment upon himself. Yet because Achilles is the greatest Greek warrior, Agamemnon cannot simply kill him or expel him from the army, as he might a lesser warrior; Achilles is too powerful to kill, and the army needs him.

Without Achilles to aid them, the Greeks are defeated by the Trojans under Hector. In Book IX Agamemnon, at the prompting of Nestor, agrees to send an embassy to Achilles, apologizing and offering many gifts, including the return of Briseis, if he will return to battle. This was the result predicted by Athena in Book I, the conventional wisdom suggests that Achilles should accept Agamemnon's offer. As I noted above, the glory of a Greek hero is measured by the gifts with which he is honored. Agamemnon had dishonored him by taking away his female companion, he now attempts to restore and in fact to increase his honor by the return of his lost prize and more.

As he did in Book I when he challenged Agamemnon, however, Achilles again behaves unconventionally. When Odysseus relates Agamemnon's offer, Achilles treats it with contempt. He refuses the gifts and rejects Agamemnon's apology: "I hate his gifts. I hold him light as the strip of a splinter" (IX, 378). Why does he do so? In part it is because his anger at Agamemnon still burns within him. Briseis, he says, was more to him than a prize; he loved her (340—3). When Aias chides Achilles for the hardness of his heart in refusing compensation in this case, whereas others accept it even in cases of murder (632—8), Achilles acknowledges the wisdom of Aias' recommendation, but also reveals the grip anger has on him

> Son of Telamon, seed of Zeus, Aias, lord of the people:
> all that you have said seems spoken after my own mind.
> Yet still the heart in me swells up in anger, when I remember
> The disgrace that he wrought upon me before the Argives,
> the son of Atreus, as if I were some dishonoured vagabond.
>
> (*Iliad* IX, 644—8)

11

In other words, Achilles knows that Aias and the others in the embassy are correct, but he is driven by his anger to act against his better judgment.

There is, however, another reason for Achilles' refusal. The theft of Briseis has caused Achilles to call into question the fairness of the entire system in terms of which heroic conduct is recognized and rewarded. His anger has turned to something more radical: disillusionment. Agamemnon's action has caused Achilles to look at the entire basis on which heroic life is conducted: honor. What he has found disturbs him profoundly.

> Fate is the same for the man who holds back, the same if he
>   fights hard.
> We are all held in a single honour, the brave with the
>   weaklings.
> A man dies still if he has done nothing, as one who has done
>   much.
> Nothing is won for me, now that my heart has gone through its
>   afflictions,
> in forever setting my life on the hazard of battle.
>
> (*Iliad* IX, 317—22)

In conventional terms, what Achilles says is false: though Agamemnon had dishonored him, he was in general held in the highest honor by the Greek army, and precisely because of his bravery and accomplishments. Achilles, however, is no longer speaking in conventional terms. He has imposed a new standard, that of death, on that of honor, and honor has been found wanting. What Achilles says is quite unheroic, in fact it is a betrayal of the heroic code, manifested in the speech of Sarpedon quoted above. Only Achilles, among the Homeric heroes, is allowed this awareness of the limitations of the heroic code. Book IX shows him to be a hero of insight as well as of uncontrollable anger.

The difficulty Achilles faces is this, he can no longer unthinkingly accept the values of his society, but neither can he live outside society, governed by his own rules alone. When his companion Patroclus has been killed by Hector, and anger with Hector has supplanted his anger toward Agamemnon, Achilles seems for a time to exist on a superhuman, or perhaps a subhuman, plane. Warned by his mother that he must die shortly after Hector, he none the less pursues his enemy with single-minded fury. Refusing food and drink, he cuts a swath through the Trojan army, doing battle even with the river-god Scamander. When he has caught and killed Hector, he remains merciless. Hector, in his death throes, asks Achilles to return his body to the Trojans and not despoil it. Achilles replies

No more entreating of me, you dog, by knees or parents.
I only wish that my spirit and fury would drive me
to hack your meat away and eat it raw for the things that
you have done to me. So there is no one who can hold the dogs
    off
from your head, not if they bring here and set before me ten
    times
and twenty times the ransom, and promise more in addition,
not if Priam son of Dardanos should offer to weigh out
your bulk in gold; not even so shall the lady your mother
who herself bore you lay you on the death-bed and mourn you;
no, but the dogs and the birds will have you all for their
    feasting.

(Iliad XXII, 345–54)

Yet even Achilles finds it impossible in the end to sustain the rage toward Hector that led to this outburst. His attempts to despoil the body outrage the gods, who order him to return it to Priam. When Priam comes to Achilles' tent with ransom for the body of his son, Achilles' recollection of his own father leads to a tearful reconciliation. As in Book IX, Achilles is motivated by a knowledge of the human condition which is far removed from the heroic code

Such is the way the gods spun life for unfortunate mortals,
that we live in unhappiness, but the gods themselves have no
    sorrows.
There are two urns that stand on the door-sill of Zeus. They
    are unlike
for the gifts they bestow; an urn of evils, an urn of blessings.
If Zeus who delights in thunder mingles these and bestows
    them

on man, he shifts, and moves now in evil, again in good
   fortune.
But when Zeus bestows from the urn of sorrows, he makes a
   failure
of man, and the evil hunger drives him over the shining
earth, and he wanders respected neither of gods nor mortals.

(Iliad XXIV, 525—33)

His reconciliation with Priam and the return of Hector's body
mark Achilles' return to the human community. The *Iliad* ends
with the burial of Hector, during a truce arranged by Achilles,
himself facing imminent death.

Two features of Achilles' character stand out in the *Iliad*. The
first is his wrath, which the poet mentions in the very first line of
the poem, and which is the primary theme of the work. The second
is his insight into his own and the general human condition. Most
of the *Iliad*'s plot develops as a result of Achilles' inability to
contain his anger, first toward Agamemnon and then toward
Hector. Homer, who does not often directly judge his characters,
makes it clear that Achilles gives in to his anger more than is wise,
and that he suffers as a result. Homer is of course not a
philosopher, and did not depict Achilles' uncontrollable wrath for
the sake of a philosophical lesson. Later philosophers could hardly
be blamed, however, for thinking of Achilles' conduct as
representative of what happens to people who lack the practical
wisdom necessary to restrain their emotions.

If Achilles were merely a very strong person who went awry
because he could not use reason to curb his emotions, he would
have been a great object lesson for philosophers but not a great
tragic hero. What gives tragic stature to Achilles is his
understanding of man's fate. He sees, more clearly than any other
hero of classical literature, the universality of human suffering and
the futility of human existence. He does not merely grasp death as
an abstract end of all human life, however; he sees, thanks to his
mother's warning, that his own death will follow upon his killing of
Hector. In the face of this clear knowledge, he chooses the course
of action which will lead to his death.

Achilles possesses a form of wisdom, an understanding of at
least some of the contours of human existence. The wisdom he
possesses is not, however, wisdom of the sort that can help him to

lead a good life. It leads him to reject the only standard of the good life known to heroic society, that of glory, but gives him nothing to substitute for that standard. (It is perhaps because he can see no life worth living that he is able to choose death.) It leads him to violate virtually every norm of conduct in his society and eventually brings ruin on himself and his closest friend. His insight is of no benefit to him, it alienates him from his culture, and makes it impossible for him to desire the only kind of life that the culture recognizes as good. Unaccompanied by practical reason, it leads him to disaster. At the same time, however, it makes him admirable to the reader in a way quite different from anyone else in the story.

The *Iliad* presents a tragic picture of human life. People, even heroes, may possess the virtues in different degrees, or lack some altogether, but no amount of virtue is sufficient to guarantee the possessor a good life. Moreover, the virtues may conflict with one another: the course of practical wisdom may lead to safety, whereas the path of courage may lead to doom. The absence of practical wisdom repeatedly leads to disaster, not only for Achilles but also for Agamemnon and for Hector, who suffer the consequences of failing to listen to good advice. What would be the fate, however, of a hero who possessed practical wisdom in addition to the other heroic virtues? To find the answer to that question, we must turn to the *Odyssey* and Homer's portrait of Odysseus.

Odysseus

Odysseus is a hero of a very different sort from Achilles, and the *Odyssey*, the epic poem of which he is the hero, is quite different from the *Iliad*. Whereas the *Iliad* is set in the midst of the Trojan war, and accordingly deals primarily with situations involving combat, the *Odyssey* is set in the war's aftermath and treats more often of peaceful, domestic, situations (though it has its share of violence, too). The *Odyssey* is the story of Odysseus' return home from the war, after ten years of wanderings and adventures. Unlike the *Iliad*, which is tragic, the *Odyssey* is a romance with a happy ending. Odysseus overcomes many obstacles, including the wrath of the god Poseidon, to reach home and be reunited with his wife and son, whom he has not seen for twenty years.

Though Odysseus and Achilles are different, many of the differences between them are differences of degree rather than of kind. Both are members of the Greek nobility, and preeminent among that group. Both conform to the heroic ideal formulated by Phoenix in *Iliad* IX, when he says that he raised Achilles to be "a speaker of words and one who accomplished in action" (443). Though Odysseus is superior to Achilles in his speaking ability, Achilles is no mean speaker himself; we need only recall his response to the embassy in Book IX, which silenced the ambassadors, and his remarks to Priam about human suffering in Book XXIV, to see that. Likewise, though Achilles is clearly superior to Odysseus as a warrior and man of action, Homer makes it clear that Odysseus is outstanding in this respect also. For example, when Odysseus is challenged by the Phaeacian Euryalus to participate in an athletic competition in *Odyssey* VIII, he throws a heavy discus farther than the Phaeacians are able to throw their lighter ones, and convincingly claims preeminence with the bow and spear as well (186—229). Both Achilles and Odysseus are "speakers of words and ones who accomplish in action."

In two respects, however, Odysseus and Achilles are absolutely different. Odysseus lacks the critical perspective on the life of the Homeric hero that Achilles displayed in the *Iliad*, but he possesses, in the highest degree, the practical wisdom, the ability to know and do what the occasion demands, that eludes Achilles. Odysseus is completely at home in Homeric society; Achilles' alienation is not a possibility for him. At the start of the *Odyssey* he is stranded on Calypso's island. Calypso is a goddess, she loves Odysseus and would like to make him immortal; but all Odysseus desires is to return to his own wife. Here is his response to her offer

> Goddess and queen, do not be angry with me. I myself know
> that all you say is true and that circumspect Penelope
> can never match the impression you make for beauty and
>   stature.
> She is mortal after all, and you are immortal and ageless.
> But even so, what I want and all my days I pine for
> is to go back to my house and see my day of homecoming.
> And if some god batters me far out on the wine-blue water,
> I will endure it, keeping a stubborn spirit inside me,
> for already I have suffered much and done much hard work
> on the waves and in the fighting. So let this adventure follow.
>   (*Odyssey* V, 215—24)

Faced with physical alienation from his home and family of a sort Achilles might have welcomed in the *Iliad* (though life on an island with a beautiful goddess would have accorded him no opportunity to display his martial prowess), Odysseus desires only to return home and be reintegrated into the society from which circumstance has removed him. Odysseus' wanderings give him a familiarity with other forms of society that the heroes of the *Iliad* lack, but throughout the work his single-minded determination to return to Ithaca rarely flags.

This single-minded determination, this ability to keep his mind fixed on a single goal, is one of Odysseus' most striking characteristics. If practical wisdom is the ability to discern the right thing to do in a given situation, it requires this clear perception of the end of action as a part: one cannot know the right thing to do if one does not know what one aims to accomplish. Other heroes lose sight of the aim of the war from time to time, but not Odysseus. He alone always keeps in mind that the object of the war is the destruction of Troy, not the pursuit of glory. It is no accident that Odysseus devises the ruse of the Trojan horse, by which Troy is finally taken. This objective, however, is not one Odysseus devised for himself, it was the aim of Agamemnon, and Odysseus embraced it only when he became part of the Greek army. Legend has it that Odysseus did not want to join the expedition to Troy, and feigned madness to avoid service. His acceptance of this goal in which he has no personal stake is indicative of his integration into Homeric society. Although Homer shows Odysseus as a victim of occasional lapses of concentration on the objective of returning to Ithaca in the *Odyssey* (he stays with Circe for a year, and only the prompting of his crew reminds him to think of homecoming), for the most part he shows the same dedication to this goal, which after all is one his own heart desires, as to victory in the war.

Practical wisdom of the sort for which Odysseus is distinguished requires not only a clear perception of one's end, but an ability to find the best means to achieve it. Here Odysseus excels, and his excellence is reflected in the epithets by which Homer knows him. As the first line of the *Iliad* speaks of the wrath of Achilles, the first line of the *Odyssey* describes Odysseus as "the man of many ways." *Polutropos*, the Greek adjective used here, has the dual meaning of "much traveled" and "versatile, ingenious";

17

both senses fit Odysseus perfectly. He also bears the epithet *polumetis*, which means "having many ingenious plans or stratagems." Throughout the two epics Odysseus shows an ability to find a clever means to an end that is far beyond that of any other Homeric hero.

The most famous example of a stratagem devised by Odysseus is the Trojan horse (described by Menelaus at *Odyssey* IV, 271—89, and by the Phaeacian bard Demodocus at VIII, 492—520) and two other examples illustrate his cunning as well. When captured by the Cyclops Polyphemus (*Odyssey* IX, 105 to end), Odysseus devises an elegant plan to blind the giant, conceal his own identity, and escape with his crew on the underside of the Cyclops' sheep. When he finally returns to Ithaca, Odysseus develops and executes an elaborate scheme to return to his own house in disguise and kill Penelope's suitors, a plan he describes to Telemachus at *Odyssey* XVI, 270—307 and carries out between Books XVII and XXIII. The execution of this grand scheme is in fact the main plot of the latter part of the *Odyssey*.

In order to carry out his plans, Odysseus needs more than intelligence. He also needs, and possesses, control of his passions. Menelaus describes how, when he and Odysseus were shut up along with others in the horse, Helen came by calling their names, her voice imitating the voices of their wives. Only Odysseus has the presence of mind to keep silent and restrain the others, thus ensuring the success of the plan

> Now I myself and the son of Tydeus and great Odysseus
> were sitting there in the middle of them and we heard you
>   crying
> aloud, and Diomedes and I started up, both minded
> to go outside, or else to answer your voice from inside,
> but Odysseus pulled us back and held us, for all our eagerness.
> Then all the other sons of the Achaians were silent;
> there was only one, it was Antiklos, who was ready to answer,
> but Odysseus, brutally squeezing his mouth in the clutch of his
>   powerful
> hands, held him, and so saved the lives of all the Achaians
> *(Odyssey* IV, 280—8)

In a second incident, at the start of Book XX, Odysseus, in his own home but disguised as a beggar, overhears several of the household servants laughing and talking with each other on their way to the beds of the suitors. He is vexed by their conduct, and considers killing them on the spot, which would ruin his plans to kill the suitors; but he thinks better of it

> He struck himself on the chest and spoke to his heart and
>   scolded it:
> 'Bear up, my heart. You have had worse to endure before this
> on that day when the irresistible Cyclops ate up
> my strong companions, but you endured it until intelligence
> got you out of the cave, though you expected to perish.'
>
> (Odyssey XX, 18-21)

In addition to self-control, Odysseus makes extensive use of the techniques of concealment. He lies freely and skillfully to everyone he encounters about his identity. Among those he lies to are his wife Penelope, in Book XIX, and his father Laertes in Book XXIV. His concealment of his identity from Penelope is justified, perhaps, by his fear that she would inadvertently give away his plan if she knew who he was; but when he conceals his identity from his father, the suitors have been killed and there is no further point in deception. Odysseus' actions here seem pointless and cruel, and he seems to be following a practice of deception out of habit, or for its own sake. To be fair to Odysseus, we must recall that most of his troubles on the voyage home were caused when he revealed his name to the Cyclops Polyphemus after escaping from him, thus identifying himself to Poseidon, the Cyclops' father. In any case, however, Odysseus' practical wisdom does not include as a matter of course the moral virtue of truthfulness. When Achilles says to Odysseus in *Iliad* IX, "as I detest the doorways of Death, I detest that man, who/ hides one thing in the depths of his heart, and speaks forth another" (312–13), he may not have Odysseus, whom he certainly does not detest, in mind, but he could hardly distinguish his own approach to life more clearly from that favored by Odysseus.

If Odysseus' practical wisdom distinguishes him from Achilles, it also distinguishes him from the typical Homeric hero. When he reveals himself to the suitors and, with the help of his son and some loyal servants, kills them in open combat, he acts as a hero of the *Iliad* might act, though the largely faceless throng of suitors does not constitute an adversary as worthy as Achilles' foe Hector. Such action, however, is rare for him. He does not lack courage, or strength, or skill in combat, all traits that mark the typical hero, nor does he lack the heroic virtue of loyalty. He cares for his men; as *Odyssey* I, 5—9 tells us, it was their folly and not his that caused their deaths. It is in the addition of wisdom to his character, not in the absence of other virtues, that Odysseus differs from the heroic norm. As Penelope says of him in *Odyssey* IV, 725, he "surpassed in all virtues."

Odysseus finds practical wisdom such a valuable tool that he prefers to live by it rather than by the virtues typical of the Homeric hero: he prefers brains to brawn, though he has both. Nor does he live for glory, as the typical hero does. Odysseus in the *Odyssey* is motivated by a desire to return to his home and family; as he says to the Phaeacian princess Nausicaa in *Odyssey* VI, "nothing is better than this, more steadfast than when two people, a man and his wife, keep a harmonious household" (182—4). It may be because this end is more solid and substantial than the end of glory that motivates the heroes of the *Iliad* that Odysseus never becomes disillusioned with it.

Three features of his wisdom that I noted above will figure prominently in later accounts of practical wisdom: the clear perception of the end sought; identification of the best means to that end; and control of conflicting passions. Though Homer is, as I have said before, a poet and not a philosopher, his Odysseus is in some ways the archetype of philosophical accounts of practical wisdom.

A Greek philosopher reflecting on the stories of Achilles and Odysseus would naturally look for some general significance in them, some universal moral lesson that went beyond the individual tales themselves. It could hardly escape his notice that Achilles, despite his unique perspective on heroic life, is led to a tragic end because of his inability to control his anger, and because of a general lack of practical wisdom. Odysseus, on the other hand, survives countless perils at sea and at home to achieve his desired end — return to Ithaca and reunion with his family — precisely because of his practical wisdom. This suggests, at the very least, that wisdom deserves a higher position among the virtues than Homeric society in general accorded it. It may not be the only virtue, but it might be the most important.

The Homeric poems suggest, in fact, that wisdom of the sort possessed by Odysseus is a necessary part of the good life. Is it also, when combined with the other virtues, sufficient? Odysseus, despite his wisdom, undergoes many trials and suffers great misfortune; in addition to being *polutropos*, "of many ways," and *polumetis* "of many counsels," he is called by Homer *polutlas*, "much-suffering." Clearly, Homer did not think that practical wisdom could enable Odysseus to avoid all sorrow; but did he think that wisdom could ensure that its possessor would eventually find happiness? This is what happens in the case of Odysseus but, as every philosopher knows, it is dangerous to construct a general theory on the basis of a single case. We must consider some additional examples, which Greek tragedy can provide.

Greek tragedy

Homer had many successors among the poets, and educated Greeks would have been familiar with them all. None surpassed him in reputation or influence, but Athens in the fifth century BC produced some worthy competitors in a trio of tragic poets: Aeschylus, Sophocles and Euripides. These three produced dramas for the annual Athenian religious festival in honor of the god Dionysus. A good number of their plays survive (though the majority have been lost, due to the ravages of time) and they are among the finest tragedies in Western literature.

Since the plays were written for a religious festival, they portray, as did Homer, the interaction of the gods and men. Though the three playwrights disagree with each other as well as with Homer on the questions of the nature of the gods, their relation to humans and the nature of human excellence, they all draw for their dramas on a stock of legendary stories dating back at least to Homer's time, including many of Homer's own. This makes some of these plays, in effect, commentaries on the Homeric poems, and there is no better way to compare the religious and moral attitudes of the fifth century with those of Homer's time than to read these plays in light of the Homeric originals.

Though many changes separate fifth-century Athens from Homer's time, the surviving plays reveal that Athenian culture was rooted in tradition. The playwrights do not hesitate to introduce innovations in theology, and Euripides in particular often views the gods more as forces of nature than as individuals, but they still deal with theological questions in terms of the Homeric framework of the Olympian gods. They reinterpret the heroes of ancient legend: Sophocles, in his *Philoctetes*, is particularly hard on Odysseus, turning the cunning hero of Homer into a disreputable schemer, and Euripides is fond of making anti-heroes out of the heroes of antiquity, but they do not reject the legends themselves. Though new intellectual currents are flowing in fifth-century Athenian tragedy (currents we shall consider in Chapter 2) the surviving tragedies indicate that Athenian civilization of the fifth century was the high point of traditional Greek culture, and the tragic poets brought the ideals of this culture to their highest literary expression. It is in part because of their writing that this period is known as the "Golden Age" of Greek civilization.

The theme of Greek tragedy is the downfall of noble people and noble families. The typical tragedy (and not all the serious plays of the Greek theater are typical tragedies) shows us a person or persons of high birth or position led to ruin. The cause of this misfortune may be the choices or characteristics of the persons who suffer, or it may be the actions of another person, who could be divine or human, a character in the drama or a remote ancestor. Some sufferers are innocent of wrongdoing, others contribute to their own fate. It was a commonly held view in the post-Homeric Greek world that the gods sought out and punished cases of *hubris*. Sometimes *hubris* stands for arrogance or excessive pride, but often it seems that elevated social standing or great wealth itself brings on the vengeance of the gods. When Aeschylus has the chorus in the *Agamemnon* say that only impiety, not wealth, brings divine punishment (744—54), he is consciously opposing this common belief.

Widespread acceptance of the view that the gods punish *hubris*, and that even those innocent of wrongdoing may incur the envy of the gods, makes the world of the tragic poets seem less secure than the world of the Homeric poems. It would be wrong to make this difference seem greater than it was; in the Homeric poems heroes face many dangers and death is the ultimate end of even the greatest hero. Still, the hero could, while alive, trust in his own talents in facing danger, and, though the gods might intervene in human action, they did not do so out of envy toward mere mortals.

In the world of the tragedians, even the most innocent person had to fear the gods, and one could never tell when or whom they might strike.

In such a world, what role could virtue play? In the Homeric poems, the virtues were characteristics and skills that enabled the possessor to survive danger and attain glory; how could they aid the tragic hero, facing the forces of fate? In particular, what was the value of wisdom in a world of tragic dilemmas, where there was often no good choice for the hero to make? These were problems that much concerned the tragic poets. For the remainder of this chapter, I shall consider the answers suggested by two of the greatest ancient tragedies, the *Antigone* and *Oedipus the King* of Sophocles.

Though Aeschylus and Euripides have much to say about these questions as well, I shall consider Sophocles for several reasons. First, he is the tragedian who brought classical tragedy to its greatest perfection of form, as Aristotle (whose model tragedy was the *Oedipus*) recognized in the *Poetics*. Second, these Sophoclean plays give us individual heroes who are direct successors of the Homeric hero, whereas Aeschylus' plays and the *Oresteia* in particular focus on the fate of whole families or nations rather than individual heroes, and Euripides' heroes are self-conscious departures from the classical norm. Third, the world portrayed in these Sophoclean plays better represents what I take to be the "classical" view of the human condition than either the Aeschylean world, with its progressive revelation of divine justice or the Euripidean world of willful, irrational divine forces. Finally and most importantly, Sophocles has the most to tell us about wisdom, and he tells us about it primarily in these plays.

Sophocles and fifth-century Athens

Sophocles' life nearly spans the fifth century: he was born in 497 or 496 BC and died in 406. This period coincides with the rise and fall of his native Athens. Sophocles was active in public affairs and, though we cannot know this for certain, it seems likely that the course of Athenian history influenced his outlook on life. Therefore, we need to examine Sophocles' life and work in relation to the history of this period.

During the fifth century Athens became the center of Greek

23

civilization. Before this period the main cultural centers of Greece were not found in Greece itself, but in Greek cities which had grown up on the coast of Asia Minor (in what is now Turkey) and in Sicily and Italy. Athens' rise to political and cultural supremacy was sparked by a series of events at the beginning of the fifth century. The leading political power in the region at this time was the empire of Persia. The Greek city-states on the coast of Asia Minor were under Persian control. When they revolted, the Athenians sent them aid. The Persian King Darius crushed the revolt, and decided to punish Athens as well for her impertinence.

Darius sent out a great army to invade Greece. The Athenians, greatly outnumbered, faced the Persians virtually alone and, in one of the miracles of military history, defeated them decisively at the Battle of Marathon in 490 BC. A decade later the Persians again invaded Greece, and again the Athenians, in alliance with Sparta, defeated them in battles on land and sea. The Persians did capture Athens and destroy its acropolis (the high ground around which the city was built) but this proved to be a blessing in disguise. It led the Athenians to rebuild the acropolis, and the result of this reconstruction project was the magnificent Parthenon and other temples still visible today. As Herodotus, the "father of history," tells the story of the Persian Wars in the latter books of his *History*, it takes on the character of an Athenian national epic.

Athens emerged from the Persian Wars as the savior of Greece and its chief political and military power. Her actions during these wars were the most glorious episodes in her history, and later generations of Athenians recalled them with pride and wonder. Her subsequent actions were not as noble, however. She collected a great number of smaller city-states into an alliance which she eventually turned into an empire of her own.

Her only serious rival for supremacy in Greece was Sparta. The Spartans, who were acknowledged to be the supreme military power in Greece as Athens was the supreme naval power, became alarmed at the growth of the Athenian empire, and war between the two states became inevitable. The war, called the Peloponnesian War after the peninsula in Greece where Sparta was located, began in 431 BC and continued, with intermittent periods of truce, until 404. The war resulted in the defeat of Athens and the eclipse of her military power. If Herodotus' account of the Persian Wars resembles Homeric epic, the *History of the*

Peloponnesian War, by the great historian Thucydides, likewise describes a national tragedy.

Sophocles lived through, and participated in, Athens' rise and fall. As a youth he was selected to lead the chorus in the celebration of the Athenian naval victory over Persia at Salamis. As an adult, he served in 443—2 as a treasurer of the league of Greek states that became the Athenian empire. He was elected general in 441—40 and was thus, with the Athenian political leader Pericles, one of the directors of a war Athens fought with the island of Samos, a rebellious member of the empire. When, in 420, the Athenians received the cult of Asclepius into their city as a protection against the plague (from which the city had suffered greatly in the early years of the war), Sophocles received the god, in the form of a snake, into his home, a service for which he himself was venerated, after death, as the hero Dexion ("receiver"). After the devastating Athenian defeat in Sicily in 413 Sophocles was chosen as a *proboulos*, a counselor or city manager, of Athens. When he died, in 406, Athens was on the brink of defeat. Sophocles thus saw Athens in her greatest glory, and himself participated in her government during her decline from greatness. He knew both the possibilities and the dangers of civic life, and these became themes of his tragedies.

Antigone

Sophocles began his career as a tragedian in 468; he is said to have won first prize in the tragic competition with his initial entry. When the *Antigone* was produced (probably in 443 or 441), Sophocles was a veteran of a quarter century of theatrical experience and a master of his art. The *Antigone* concerns a conflict between two people: Antigone, the daughter of Oedipus, and Creon, the ruler of Thebes. It is also about the conflict of ideas. Antigone defends the institution of the family and ancient religious traditions concerning burial of the dead; Creon defends the *polis*, the city-state. Few plays deal so overtly with topics of philosophical interest as does the *Antigone*.

When the play begins, Antigone and her sister Ismene are all that remains of the family of Oedipus. Not only are Oedipus and Jocasta his wife dead, but Oedipus' two sons, Eteocles and Polynices, have just killed each other in a war for the throne of

Thebes. Thebes has repelled the invading army of Polynices, and Creon, Antigone's uncle and Eteocles' successor as ruler of Thebes, has decreed that, while Eteocles is to be buried with full military honors for his service to Thebes, Polynices is to be left unburied for his treasonable invasion of his homeland. The penalty for disobedience to this decree is death by stoning.

Antigone, like many a tragic hero, faces a dilemma: is she to bury her disgraced brother and incur the enmity of the state, and in particular of its new head, or is she to obey the decree and prove disloyal to a beloved member of her family? For Antigone, the choice is clear: she is determined to bury her brother. Creon's decree has no force with her: "It's not for him," she says, "to keep me from my own" (l. 48; Wyckoff's translation). She asks Ismene for assistance, but Ismene counsels obedience

> We'll perish terribly if we force law
> and try to cross the royal vote and power.
> We must remember that we two are women
> so not to fight with men.
> And that since we are subject to strong power
> we must hear these orders, or any that may be worse
>
> (*Antigone*, 59—64)

To a modern audience, this advice might seem cowardly and unduly submissive, but to the fifth-century Athenian audience it must have seemed simply prudent and sensible. Antigone, however, dismisses her sister and her cautions with contempt as cowardly, and resolves to perform the burial alone. As Ismene is a well-meaning and loving sister who merely lacks Antigone's courage, this response seems over harsh, and its result is to portray Antigone in an unsympathetic light, as a fanatic — "senseless indeed" her sister calls her (99).

Creon, on the other hand, initially seems the embodiment of sweet reasonableness. No one, he says, should place a personal friend above the good of the city (182—3); accordingly, though Polynices is a relative, he will punish him like any other enemy of the state. As he tells the chorus

> Nor could I count the enemy of the land
> friend to myself, not I who know so well

that it is she who saves us, sailing straight,
and only so can we have friends at all.
With such good rules shall I enlarge our state.

(Antigone, 187—91)

Every Athenian would have approved of these sentiments: having survived two Persian attempts at conquest, the Athenians knew that their individual fortunes depended on those of their city.

It does not follow, however, that all Athenians would have approved of Creon's plan to leave Polynices unburied. Early in the play the chorus gives indications that they find this course of action problematic. When Creon announces his plan, the chorus says

This resolution, Creon, is your own,
in the matter of the traitor and the true.
For you can make such rulings as you will
about the living and about the dead.

(Antigone, 211—14)

This is hardly a ringing endorsement. When a guard arrives with the message that the body has been given a ritual burial, the response of the chorus is, "Isn't this action possibly a god's?" (279). Finally, when the chorus sings its great ode on human ingenuity, it ends with these words

Clever beyond all dreams
the inventive craft that he has
which may drive him one time or another to well or ill.
When he honors the laws of the land and the gods' sworn right
high indeed is his city; but stateless the man
who dares to dwell with dishonor. Not by my fire,
never to share my thoughts, who does these things.

(Antigone, 362—72)

The fear of the chorus, hinted at in these lines, is that Creon's policy, though it has upheld the city, has ignored the just claims of the gods of the underworld. When Antigone is captured and brought before Creon as the violator of his decree, she appeals to the gods in her defense

For me it was not Zeus who made that order.
Nor did that Justice who lives with the gods below
mark out such laws to hold among mankind.
Nor did I think your orders were so strong
that you, a mortal man, could over-run
the gods' unwritten and unfailing laws.
Not now, nor yesterday's, they always live,
and no one knows their origin in time.

(Antigone, 450—7)

With this defense we begin to understand the nature of the
dispute between Creon and Antigone. Antigone has failed to
acknowledge the authority of the city, and in this she is wrong.
Creon, however, has committed a more serious error, for he has
failed to acknowledge the authority of the gods. He has exalted a
limited, temporal power over the unlimited, absolute power of
divine authority. With Antigone's defense, the recognition begins
to grow that Creon is in the wrong, and sympathy for the girl grows
correspondingly.

As the tide of public opinion swings in Antigone's favor, Creon
becomes more and more a tyrant in the modern sense. Already, in
an encounter with the guard, he has shown himself to be an unwise
ruler. He had accused the guard of burying the body himself, of
having sold out Thebes for money. "How terrible to guess," the
guard had replied, "and guess at lies! (323). Now, his son Haemon
arrives with news of how

the whole town is grieving for this girl,
unjustly doomed, if ever woman was,
to die in shame for glorious action done. . . .
Isn't her real desert a golden prize?

(Antigone, 693—5, 699)

In spite of the fact that he is engaged to marry Antigone, Haemon
professes loyalty to his father, and such were the relations between
fathers and sons in classical Greece that his profession is plausible.
He urges his father to relent, for his own sake, and the chorus
approves of his advice. Creon, however, proves intransigent. He
calls his son a "woman's slave" (756) and threatens to kill the girl
before his eyes. (From the start Creon has been obsessed with the

fact that his authority has been challenged by a woman; cf. 484—5.) Haemon leaves with the words, "you will not/ ever lay eyes upon my face again" (761—2).

Creon sentences Antigone to be walled up in a cave and she is led off after a heartrending lament. Only with the arrival of the prophet Tiresias does it come home to Creon that he has acted unwisely. The fire has refused to burn on his altar, and Tiresias lays the blame at Creon's doorstep. He, like Haemon, counsels change

> Think of these things, my son. All men may err
> but error once committed, he's no fool
> nor yet unfortunate, who gives up his stiffness
> and cures the trouble he has fallen in.
> Stubbornness and stupidity are twins.
> Yield to the dead.
>
> (*Antigone*, 1023—8)

Even at this point, Creon refuses to listen. He accuses Tiresias of having betrayed Thebes for money; only when the prophet predicts the death of Haemon does he relent.

Shaken by the prophecy of death within his own family, Creon, on the advice of the chorus, resolves to free Antigone

> Now my decision has been overturned
> shall I, who bound her, set her free myself.
> I've come to fear it's best to hold the laws
> of old tradition to the end of life.
>
> (*Antigone*, 1111—14)

But Creon's change of heart has come too late: Antigone has hanged herself in her cave. Creon's wife and son commit suicide as well. The once-proud ruler has been reduced by a series of hammer-blows, caused by his own stubborn intransigence, to "a breathing corpse" (1167). The chorus ends the play with this comment

> Our happiness depends
> on wisdom all the way.
> The gods must have their due.
> Great words by men of pride

29

bring greater blows upon them.
So wisdom comes to the old.

(*Antigone*, 1347—52)

The wisdom of which the chorus speaks is synonymous with reverence toward the gods. Antigone possesses it; Creon lacks it, and comes to have it only after the most grievous suffering. When we dealt with Achilles and Odysseus, we were able to distinguish two aspects or sorts of wisdom: the correct perspective on human good and evil and the ability to discern the right thing to do in a concrete situation. In the *Antigone*, these two aspects are fused. Antigone knows that the burial of her brother is the right thing to do *because* she has the proper perspective on what is good, it is because Creon lacks this perspective that he acts wrongly (as he puts it at 1342, "My life is warped past cure"). This close connection between knowledge of good and evil and the ability to choose correctly will be a prominent feature of Socrates' philosophy.

The closing lines of the chorus indicate that the tragic conflict between Antigone and Creon, between the claims of the gods and the claims of the state, is not inevitable, but can be resolved through wisdom. What wisdom dictates in this case is that the gods be given superior allegiance, that the laws of the state be made with divine commandments in mind. When the chorus utters its praise of wisdom, it is at least implicitly criticizing Creon's lack of it. As a messenger says late in the play, announcing the deaths of Haemon and Antigone, "he has made it very clear to men/ that to reject good counsel is a crime" (1242—3). It is he, not Antigone, who is the cause of the tragedy. It is only if Creon is intransigent that the tragedy must unfold; but, given this, an otherwise avoidable tragedy *becomes* inevitable. In the face of Creon's stubborn error, the wisdom of Antigone and the good advice of Haemon are unavailing. Their wisdom ennobles their character but does not save them from destruction. The gods whom Antigone serves destroy Creon, but they do not save her. Wisdom thus appears to be a necessary, but not a sufficient condition for human flourishing.

Antigone, it is true, lacks the sort of skills that enabled Odysseus to win his homecoming, perhaps *he* could have persuaded Creon to change his mind. In fact, Antigone has much more in common with Achilles than with Odysseus. Like Achilles, she is faced with a dilemma that has no good outcome; like him, she resolutely chooses the course that will lead to her death. Throughout her final appearance on stage the chorus regards her action, like that of Achilles in opposing Agamemnon, as excessive: "You went to the furthest verge/ of daring," they tell her, "but there you found/ the high foundation of justice, and fell." (852—4) Her courage contrasts with the prudence of Ismene, and like Achilles she shows a harsh contempt for those who lack her resolution.

She also is like Achilles in her alienation from the society in which she lives. Because of the tragic fate of others in her family, she has given up on any hope of a good life: "if I die/ before my time," she tells Creon, "I say it is a gain" (461—2). Later, she says to Ismene, "My life died long ago./ And that has made me fit to help the dead" (559—60). In her final lament, she has come to fear that even the dead may not welcome her service

> I go to the fresh-made prison-tomb.
> Alive to the place of corpses, an alien still,
> never at home with the living nor with the dead.
>
> (*Antigone*, 849—51)

Antigone differs from Achilles, however, in three important respects. First, she does not act out of excessive anger, but out of love for her dead brother: "I cannot share in hatred, but in love," she tells Creon (523). True, she has little love for Ismene — she seems to find it easier to love the dead than the living — but her motive for acting on behalf of Polynices is noble. Second, she lacks Achilles' physical strength and skill as a warrior: Ismene's evaluation of the futility of opposing Creon is correct. This makes her opposition hopeless from the outset, but all the more heroic for that. Third, whereas Achilles sometimes acts wrongly because of his excessive anger, the poet makes it clear that Antigone's actions are right. Antigone is not perfect, but she does not deserve her fate. It is a feature of this world, Sophocles seems to be telling us, that those preeminent in virtue sometimes cannot find a place in it, that their very virtue can lead them to destruction.

Oedipus

The action in *Oedipus the King* takes place before that of *Antigone*, though the play was written later, probably during the early years of the Peloponnesian War. This play has been widely regarded as the greatest of Greek tragedies at least since the time of Aristotle; it is somewhat surprising, therefore, that Sophocles finished second in the tragic competition in the year it was entered.

At the start of the play we see Oedipus at the height of his fame, as King of Thebes. Years before he had arrived in Thebes as a stranger and solved the riddle of the Sphinx, a creature that had been terrorizing the city. By freeing Thebes from the monster's wrath he had earned the gratitude of the Thebans and a reputation for quick wit. He ascended the throne of the city and married Jocasta, former wife of King Laius (who had just been killed while on a journey).

Thebes has been afflicted with a plague and the people ask Oedipus to save them from it, as he had saved them from the Sphinx. A priest, speaking for the populace, says to Oedipus

> We have not come as suppliants to this altar
> because we thought of you as a God,
> but rather judging you the first of men . . .
> (for I have seen that for the skilled of practice
> the outcome of their counsels live the most).
>   (*Oedipus the King*, 30—31, 44—5, Grene's translation)

Oedipus, however, has already acted; he has sent his wife's brother Creon (the same person who becomes king in the *Antigone*, but portrayed in this play as a very different character) to the oracle of Apollo at Delphi to ask for aid. Creon returns with the word that the god requires the Thebans to expel the murderer of Laius. The identity of the killer is not known; the story in Thebes is that he was killed by thieves. Oedipus, however, undertakes to solve the mystery:

> I will bring this to light again. . . .
> And justly you will see in me an ally,
> a champion of my country and the God. . . .
> I will not serve a distant friend's advantage,

but act in my own interest. Whoever
he was that killed the king may readily
wish to dispatch me with his murderous hand;
so helping the dead king I help myself.

(*Oedipus the King*, 133, 135—6, 137—41)

Oedipus announces a decree of banishment for the killer and
summons the prophet Tiresias to aid in his identification. Tiresias
is at first reluctant to speak, then, angered by Oedipus' doubts
about his loyalty to Thebes, announces that Oedipus himself is the
killer, and that he is guilty of even fouler crimes. Oedipus, enraged,
accuses Tiresias of plotting with Creon to seize the throne; Creon
is saved from execution only by the intervention of Jocasta, his
sister and Oedipus' wife. Jocasta tells Oedipus not to worry about
the sayings of prophets: an oracle had predicted that Laius would
be killed by his own son, yet the boy had been exposed at birth, left
to die on a mountainside, and Laius was killed by robbers. As she
relates the details of Laius' murder, however, Oedipus begins to
suspect that he was himself the murderer; on his way to Thebes he
had killed a man of Laius' description at a crossroads similar to
that where Laius had died. He sends for a servant, the only
surviving eyewitness to the attack on Laius, to reconfirm the story
that Laius was killed by several robbers, not a single man.

At this point in the play, though Oedipus suspects that he may
be the killer of Laius, and that he may thus have pronounced the
sentence of banishment on himself, he does not suspect that he
may be Laius' son. "Polybus was my father, king of Corinth,/ and
Merope, the Dorian, my mother," he states (774—5). He had been
spurred by a drunk's charge that Polybus was not his father to
inquire of his parentage at Delphi and there he had learned only
that he was fated to kill his father, marry his mother, and bring
forth children who would be his own brothers and sisters. He had
thus resolved not to return to Corinth, "When I heard this I fled,"
he says (794). The man he had run straight into, he now fears, was
Laius.

A messenger arrives from Corinth with the news that Polybus
is dead and that the people wish to make Oedipus their king.
Jocasta regards this as further proof that oracles are unreliable, but
Oedipus still fears to return to Corinth because of Apollo's
prophecy that he would marry his mother. There is nothing to

worry about, says the messenger: Polybus and Merope were not Oedipus' real parents. He had himself received Oedipus as a baby from a shepherd on Mount Cithaeron, a servant of Laius, and given him to the king and queen, who raised him as their own.

Jocasta now knows the truth, and begs Oedipus not to inquire further into his origins. Just as he had earlier mistaken the motives of Tiresias and Creon, however, he now mistakes his wife's fear: he thinks she is afraid that he will discover that he is the son of some palace servant. "I at least shall be/ willing to see my ancestry, though humble," he declares (1076—7). At this point the servant who had witnessed the attack on Laius arrives; the messenger identifies him as the shepherd who gave him the baby. The shepherd is forced to reveal that the baby was Laius' own son, and Oedipus at last understands that he has in fact fulfilled the prophecy. Not only is he the murderer of Laius, but Laius was his father and Jocasta his mother

> O, O, O, they will all come,
> all come out clearly! Light of the sun, let me
> look upon you no more after today!
> I who first say the light bred of a match
> accursed, and accursed in my living
> with them I lived with, cursed in my killing.
>
> (*Oedipus the King*, 1182—5)

Jocasta, unable to live with the truth, hangs herself and Oedipus puts out his own eyes. He embraces Antigone and Ismene in sorrow and shame; as the play ends, he begs Creon, now the ruler of Thebes, to banish him.

Oedipus throughout the play displays two chief characteristics. The first is a hot temper, which he vents on Tiresias, Creon, and others; the second, and for our purposes more important, is an acute intelligence, which he uses as a king should, to benefit his people. The beginning of the play makes known his reputation for wisdom; and, though his wisdom seems to forsake him on occasion (for instance when he fails to discern the real reason for Jocasta's request that he not inquire into his origins), he in general acts intelligently. In pursuing the murderer of Laius, even after he suspects himself, he shows his dedication to the welfare of Thebes; in seeking the truth about his birth he displays a desire for knowledge that outweighs all other considerations, including his own well-being. When the shepherd says that the truth he must tell is horrible, Oedipus replies, "And I of frightful hearing. But I must hear" (1170).

Interpreters of this play who have thought it necessary to find in the tragic hero some "flaw" that is responsible for his fate have seen in Oedipus' anger and pride the source of his punishment. This will not do, for two reasons. First, Oedipus' anger at Tiresias and Creon has in fact no bad consequences: it injures no one. It does not merit, therefore, such extreme punishment. Second and more important, however, Oedipus is not punished as a result of something he has done in his life; he is cursed, and was so before he was born. His murder of Laius, his marriage to Jocasta and their ultimate revelation, are not a divine punishment but the working out of Oedipus' preordained fate.

Yet Oedipus co-operates with the gods to bring his fate to accomplishment. He says to the chorus about his own mutilation

> It was Apollo, friends, Apollo,
> that brought this bitter bitterness, my sorrows to completion.
> But the hand that struck me
> was none but my own.
>
> (*Oedipus the King*, 1329—32)

This statement could be extended to all Oedipus does. Though the gods have ordained that he would kill his father and marry his mother, the irony of the play lies in the fact that Oedipus' own intelligence leads him to fulfill the prophecy by inquiring into his origins and fleeing his supposed home when he learns of Apollo's prediction. Further, it is his own intelligence that sets him on the trail of the killer of Laius, and keeps him on the trail even when it leads to himself.

It is this intelligence, coupled with the good intentions of others, that dooms Oedipus to his ordained fate. The general absence of human malice and ill-will in the play is remarkable. Apart from Oedipus' anger toward Tiresias and Creon, no character displays base motives in the play. Rather, the characters, both noble and humble, act out of compassion for Oedipus and concern for his well-being: as the shepherd says when Oedipus asks him why he gave him away, as a baby, to the messenger

> O master,
> I pitied it, and thought that I could send it
> off to another country and this man
> was from another country. But he saved it
> for the most terrible troubles. If you are
> the man he says you are, you're bred to misery.
>
> (*Oedipus the King*, 1177—81)

This human good will makes the divine malice toward Oedipus all the more striking.

It could be argued that Oedipus' wisdom is limited, flawed, that a truly wise person would not try to outwit the gods and flout their oracle. Yet it is hard to see what Oedipus could do when faced with the prophecy; how could anyone passively acquiesce in such a fate? Moreover, Oedipus nowhere in the play shows the confidence that Jocasta does that the oracle had been disproved. Rather, it seems clear that Sophocles does regard Oedipus as wise, and that he sees wisdom as a virtue. After all, by outwitting the Sphinx Oedipus saved Thebes, and Jocasta's policy of willful ignorance of her own past actions produces no better results than Oedipus' relentless pursuit of truth.

The "lesson" of the play, if it is fair to talk about it in those terms, is that even wisdom, celebrated in the *Antigone*, is no guarantee of happiness. The wisest of men may suffer the greatest of sorrows. Happiness is transient, and fate is fickle; as the chorus says of Oedipus and Jocasta

> The fortune of the days gone by was true
> good fortune — but today groans and destruction
> and death and shame — of all ills can be named
> not one is missing. (1283—6)

Conclusion

In this chapter we have looked at several portraits of virtue in ancient Greek literature. Beginning with Homer, we saw that wisdom was one of several virtues, and not the most important in Homeric society. In the *Iliad* it took a back seat to the military virtues of courage, loyalty and physical strength, which were the primary means by which the hero attained the glory that was the goal of life. The Homeric poems themselves, however, could be said to argue for a more central place for wisdom. Achilles, who possesses one form of wisdom (a penetrating insight into the limits of the Homeric scheme of values), suffers a tragic fate because he lacks the other form, the practical ability to control his passions and determine the proper course of action. Odysseus, on the other hand, survives ten years of trials at sea and achieves a successful homecoming because he possesses this practical form of wisdom. His vision of the good life is more domestic than that of the typical Homeric hero; his wisdom enables him to achieve it.

In Sophoclean tragedy, wisdom has become the virtue of central importance. Yet the Sophoclean world is more uncertain than the Homeric; whereas in Homer the possession of virtues is likely to lead to success and glory, at least in the short run, in Sophocles virtue ennobles its possessor but often does not lead to success. Both Antigone and Oedipus possess wisdom of a sort: Antigone knows that the gods demand burial of her brother, and Oedipus is characterized by a general desire to know. Antigone suffers a tragic death not because she lacks wisdom, but because her uncle Creon, ruler of Thebes, lacks it; Oedipus suffers not from an absence of wisdom, but as a result of his own relentless curiosity.

If it is fair to summarize these four portraits in a general conclusion, the conclusion is this: there are several virtues, of which wisdom is perhaps the most important. The absence of wisdom can lead to disaster, the presence of wisdom helps greatly in the pursuit of happiness. But even wisdom cannot guarantee happiness; the wisest, most virtuous hero may be doomed to a life of misery by fate.

This traditional Greek vision of the relations between virtue, wisdom and the good life thus attains its quintessential expression in the works of Sophocles and Homer. Greek philosophers, beginning with Socrates, rejected this vision, though to different degrees. They could not accept a picture of life in which virtue was connected with success so problematically, they therefore sought to make the connections between the virtues and the good life tighter, as we shall see in the chapters ahead.

2

THE SOPHISTS AND SOCRATES

In Chapter 1 we looked at the portrayal of virtue and knowledge in Greek literature; in this chapter we turn to philosophy. Ethics becomes philosophical in ancient Greece in the fifth century BC. The people primarily responsible for this development are a diverse group of thinkers, called collectively the Sophists, and that remarkable individual, Socrates. Before the Sophists and Socrates, the Greek philosophers had concerned themselves primarily with questions about the nature of the cosmos and reality. Socrates and the Sophists made ethics one of the main areas of philosophical reflection, a status it has retained ever after.

The crisis in values: the Sophists

The Sophistic movement grew up in Greece in the fifth century BC, during the "Golden Age" of Greek literature discussed in Chapter 1. At the very time when the traditional culture of Greece was getting its noblest expression in the works of the great Athenian tragic poets and in the history of Herodotus, the events of the Peloponnesian War cast doubt on the values of that culture and helped to bring on a crisis in values. The prosecution of the war had a hardening effect on the Athenians: it made them cynical and amoral, whereas they had previously taken pride in their noble idealism. The difference between Athenian attitudes at the beginning of the war and later can be seen by contrasting the funeral oration of the Athenian statesman Pericles (Thucydides, Book I) with the Melian Dialogue, Thucydides' account of the debate between Athenian ambassadors and the political leaders of Melos, a city-state the Athenians besieged and eventually destroyed (Book V). Many Athenians thought the Sophists contributed to this moral degeneration.

Today when we describe someone as a sophist we mean that he uses faulty reasoning, invalid argument, to make his case. "Sophist" is for us a term of abuse. The word itself, however, literally means "wise man", and Protagoras, the greatest of this group, was not ashamed to call himself a Sophist. The Sophists were a diverse group of people, and it is dangerous to make sweeping generalizations about their views. They traveled from city to city in Greece, offering instruction for a fee. What they taught varied; some offered instruction in mathematics and astronomy, whereas others taught courses on the meaning of words. They were best known, however, for teaching rhetoric, the art of public speaking, and the related art of political leadership. In most Greek cities at the time, and particularly in democracies such as Athens, human excellence (virtue) was closely associated with political leadership. To be a political leader one had to be good at public speaking, in order to persuade the citizenry that one's political views and policies were correct. Thus, many people desired what the Sophists sold.

Because the Sophists made their living by traveling from city to city, they had to deal with the fact that the laws in Athens, say, were different from those in Corinth. An Athenian or Corinthian citizen would naturally look to the laws of his city as the source of justice, but the Sophists could not present their views on justice in Athens by appealing to the laws or customs of the Corinthians. The question arose for the Sophists whether justice was entirely based on *nomos*, convention or local custom, or whether there was some additional basis in nature (*physis*). Many of the doctrines we associate with the Sophists arose from their attempts to solve this problem.

The traditional answer to the problem was that justice was divinely sanctioned: the gods, and Zeus in particular, ensured that justice was honored and injustice punished. This answer dates at least as far back as Homer's *Odyssey*. The citizens of the various Greek cities saw their particular laws as specifications of divine justice, and as undergirded by the support of the gods. In the *Eumenides*, the third play of his *Oresteia* trilogy, the tragedian Aeschylus portrays the establishment of the Athenian *areopagus*, a court for the trial of homicide, as the work of the goddess Athena. The ordinary Greek citizen, then, saw the laws of his nation as part of a general system of universal, divine justice.

The Sophists, however, generally abandoned this traditional view of justice. Protagoras was openly dubious about the existence of the gods:

> Concerning the gods I cannot say either that they exist or that they do not, or what they are like in form; for there are many hindrances to knowledge: the obscurity of the subject and the brevity of human life. (Fragment 4; Guthrie, translator)

Perhaps his agnosticism was the result of his having visited many Greek cities and seen the gods invoked to justify different, even contradictory laws. Perhaps it resulted from the speculations of the Pre-Socratic philosophers, who proposed many alternatives to the traditional gods of Homer in their inquiries concerning nature. Perhaps belief in the Olympian gods simply seemed quaint and naive to Protagoras, something that needed to be replaced by a more "modern" view. Certainly, his dismissal of the question of the existence of the gods is itself a very modern, indeed a radical move; one can hardly imagine the typical Athenian leaving a performance of *Oedipus the King* expressing such a sentiment.

In any case, once Protagoras had removed the divine underpinnings from legal institutions, he had to find another support for them; his students would naturally have asked him what justice was based on, if not divine will. Protagoras looked to human nature to provide the answer: "Man," he said, "is the measure of all things, of those that are that they are, and of those that are not that they are not" (Fragment 1). This fragmentary remark, the most famous single sentence we have from the Sophists, is susceptible to different interpretations. Perhaps all Protagoras meant by it is that it is up to us, as citizens of a state, to determine for ourselves what is just or unjust, and that we should not look to external standards such as the gods to validate our choices. On this interpretation, it is people collectively who decide what justice is and, despite the fact that the statement refers to "all things," Protagoras may not have thought of applying it beyond the political arena (after all, it was political excellence he claimed to teach). As Plato interpreted the statement in the *Theaetetus*, however, it meant the *individual* was the ultimate judge of the truth of *any* statement, and that a statement was true for any individual who believed it. In other words, Plato saw Protagoras as a *subjective relativist*, one who regards the truth of a statement as relative to the perceptions of a single individual.

Whatever Protagoras may have meant by his celebrated remark, he was certainly a relativist of some sort: he could find no higher standard of truth than the agreement of human beings. If the Athenians and the Corinthians disagreed about the law, then what the Athenians decided was just for them, and what the Corinthians decided was equally just for them. This view made it easy for Protagoras to teach in different cities without offending the local authorities, for he could with a clear conscience advocate that his students obey the laws of their various home states. The laws of a given state were based not on *physis* or nature, but on *nomos* or custom, but that did not weaken their claim to authority, at least in the eyes of Protagoras.

Not all the Sophists agreed with Protagoras on this point; not all were relativists of his sort. The Athenian Antiphon argued that there is a natural law which differs from the conventional civic law. Civic law, which is based on *nomos*, requires people to do many things which run contrary to nature, natural law, on the other hand, commands that people act in their own interest. For instance, it may be to my advantage to injure my enemies, but civic law forbids me to do so except in self-defense. When *nomos* and *physis* thus conflict, the wise thing to do is to adhere to the conventions of one's state when one is under observation in public, but to follow nature in private, when one is sure he will not be found out. A theory such as this requires some account of what one's "real" or natural interests are, but this the Sophists did not provide. Antiphon seems to assume that people are by nature selfish pleasure-seekers; an extreme version of this picture of human nature is presented by the Sophist Thrasymachus in Plato's *Republic* (see below, Chapter 3). Clearly, if this were the true nature of human beings, the good life and the virtues would be different from what the Greeks had traditionally supposed.

The Sophists did not succeed in replacing the traditional view of human nature, justice, virtue and law with a new view of their own. In part this failure was due to disagreements among themselves about the content of such a new view, an example of which is the disagreement between Protagoras and Antiphon mentioned above. The Sophists may have agreed with the Protagorean critique of the divine basis of the law, but they did not agree with him or with each other on what should replace it. In part their failure was due to the radical nature of their proposals. Their views differed so greatly from the tradition in which the citizens of Greece had been raised that they could not get a sympathetic hearing among the general populace. Finally, they failed in part because the new theories they advocated did not aid them in their practical task of making excellent political leaders. Protagorean relativism offered no way to resolve a disagreement which might arise within a state between leaders of opposed factions. When faced with a dispute over the course of action a state should follow, the citizen would naturally look toward objective standards of justice or advantage to determine which course of action was in fact better. Protagoras' view, however, had no room for such standards; one could only determine what action was right *after* it had been enacted into law!

Though the Sophists did not succeed in replacing the tradition with their own views, they did weaken public confidence in that tradition. When they taught their students that the laws of their native city were based on custom rather than divine sanction, this inevitably weakened the students' respect for those laws; for it is hard to see why one should regard decisions made by people of a previous generation as sacrosanct. It is not clear how many Greeks of the fifth century abandoned traditional morality and embraced the views of the Sophists. Probably it was only a small minority who did so; but this minority doubtless included many of the brightest members of the younger generation of Greeks, who were the prime source of pupils for the Sophists. Regardless of their success in winning converts, the Sophists were perceived to be a significant cultural phenomenon. This is shown by the fact that their views and the views of some of the Pre-Socratic philosophers are brilliantly parodied by the great comic poet Aristophanes in his play, the *Clouds* (about which more below). The Sophists would not have received Aristophanes' attention if he had not thought them important.

The net effect of the Sophists, then, was to undermine public confidence in the traditional view of morality, without substituting a satisfactory new account for the tradition. In the absence of such an alternative, one might think that moral distinctions had *no* foundation at all, in other words, one might well become a *moral skeptic*. For a moral skeptic, all moral judgments become problematic, doubtful; worse still, the very enterprise of trying to determine the right course of action seems hopeless. The Sophists were not skeptics themselves, for they were confident in the superiority of their own accounts of the basis of moral judgment to that provided by the tradition; but skepticism was a legacy of their failure to supplant the tradition with their own views.

Many traditional Greeks, seeing the skeptical outcome of the Sophistic movement, reacted angrily to the views of the Sophists. The Sophists produced, in other words, a conservative backlash. In Athens this backlash was heightened by the belief that Sophistic teachings had produced bad political leadership, and that this leadership had lost the Peloponnesian War. Yet many opponents of the Sophists were in an awkward position. They rejected the consequences of Sophistic teaching but, not being philosophers themselves, they were unable to show where the arguments of the Sophists went wrong. It is extremely frustrating to be in such a position and this helps to explain the anger of the opponents of the Sophists. It is one of the ironies of the history of philosophy that the chief victim of this backlash was Socrates, a man who rejected the teachings of the Sophists and was in fact their major intellectual opponent.

The life of Socrates

The influence of the Sophists was not entirely negative. They succeeded in raising explicitly many of the key philosophical questions about ethics for the first time, and their practice implicitly raised others. Though their own answers to these questions were unsatisfactory, they must be given credit for raising them. Their concern with the basis of justice led naturally to questions about all the virtues: what are they? on what are they based? The claim of Protagoras and others to teach virtue for a fee raised the question of whether virtue could be taught, or, if not, how it could be acquired. And their portrayal of the life of natural justice raised the question of the nature of the good life: did it consist in pleasure, in political success, or what? These questions became the focus for Socrates and his successors.

Socrates was born in 469 BC, about a quarter of a century after Sophocles. That is, he was born after the Athenian victories over the Persians discussed in Chapter 1, but almost four decades before the start of the Peloponnesian War. Thus, the first half of his life coincided with the years of Athens' greatest political and cultural glory. The last three decades of his life, in contrast, spanned the period in which Athens fought and was eventually defeated by Sparta. After the defeat of Athens in 404 BC the city entered a period of political bitterness and recrimination in which Socrates himself was caught up. When he was born the "Golden Age" of Athenian literature was just beginning; when he died, in 399 BC, it was virtually over.

Socrates thus witnessed the zenith of Athenian civilization as well as its decline and fall. He was not merely a spectator to these events, however; he was a prominent figure in the landscape of fifth-century Athenian intellectual life. In fact, he was a public figure of such fame that when Aristophanes satirized the philosophical theories of the Sophists and the Pre-Socratics in the *Clouds*, he gave the name Socrates to the leading character in his play, into whose mouth he put those theories.

Socrates' reputation is inexplicable if we consider only the external circumstances of his life. He was an Athenian citizen, the son of a sculptor named Sophroniscus, a person of no great renown. He may have been a stone-cutter himself, though we have little evidence that Socrates ever engaged in any gainful employment. In Plato's *Theaetetus* he describes his mother, Phaenarete, as a midwife and claims to practice an art of intellectual midwifery similar to hers. This, of course, is the art of philosophical inquiry which made him so famous; but in the *Apology* he explicitly says he never practiced this art for money.

He lived all his life in Athens, leaving the city only when serving in the army. Though Plato mentions his courage in combat in several places, most notably in the *Symposium*, he apparently never rose in rank to a position of leadership. Unlike Sophocles, he was not honored with political office. He describes his few brushes with Athenian politics in the *Apology*; they were not, from a popular standpoint, happy encounters. He was married to a woman named Xanthippe and had three children, all boys. The marriage does not seem to have been particularly blissful; Xanthippe has acquired in biographies of Socrates the reputation of a shrew. This may be unfair: surely living with a man who cared for nothing but philosophy would tax the patience of anyone.

Socrates was physically unattractive, almost comical in

appearance, with a snub nose and bulging eyes. In speech also he was anything but elegant: one of his partners in conversation laments that he never stops talking about "cobblers and fullers and cooks and doctors" (*Gorgias* 491a: page references are to the standard Stephanus edition of Plato's dialogues). In short, he lacked every feature that the Greeks recognized as noble: distinguished ancestors, wealth, political or military office, good looks and rhetorical skill. He did have a legendary capacity to drink without becoming drunk, but though these features may add up to a portrait of a charming eccentric, they do nothing to explain his lasting fame.

Despite all this Socrates was able to converse with the greatest political figures in Athenian life; he moved without difficulty in the highest circles of Athenian society. When famous intellectuals such as Protagoras or the philosopher Parmenides came to Athens, one could expect to find them sooner or later in conversation with Socrates. Socrates' friends and companions praised him as few men in history have been praised. At the end of the *Phaedo*, the work in which Plato describes Socrates' death, he is called "the bravest and also the wisest and upright man" of his times. The Sophist Protagoras, after losing an argument with the young Socrates, says to him, "I admire you most especially among the people I have met, and in particular among those your age; and I say that I would not wonder if you were to become one of the men most renowned for wisdom" (*Protagoras* 361e).

Alcibiades, one of Athens' brightest young men and Socrates' lover, describes Socrates' impact on him thus

> when we listen to someone else speaking on other topics, even a very good orator, it makes no difference to anyone, so to speak. But when someone hears you, or another person saying what you have said, even if the speaker is quite poor, whether the hearer is a woman or a man or a youth, we are astonished and gripped ... Whenever I hear him ... my heart leaps and my tears flow at his words, and I see a great many others in the same state. When I heard Pericles and other good orators I thought they spoke well, but I never experienced anything of this sort; my soul was not thrown into turmoil, or annoyed at its slavish condition. But on many occasions I have been put into such a state by this Marsyas [a flautist of legendary,

45

hypnotic power, rather like the Pied Piper of Hamelin], that I thought that life wasn't worth living for me in my present condition (*Symposium* 215d—216a).

Not everyone responded to Socrates so positively. The Sophist Thrasymachus accuses Socrates of talking nonsense and of needing a nurse to wipe his nose for him in the first book of the *Republic* (336b—d, 343a). Callicles in the *Gorgias* likens him to a mob orator, accuses him of unfair argument, and says that his pursuit of philosophical wisdom is unworthy of a grown man (482c—486d). Throughout Plato's dialogues, people who have been reduced to utter perplexity by Socrates' relentless questioning express their anger toward him.

The explanation for both responses to Socrates is the same. The devotion of his friends, the admiration of his contemporaries in philosophy, and the antagonism of his enemies are not due to any of the external factors mentioned above. They are due rather to his single-minded pursuit of philosophy and his unsurpassed philosophical gifts. For Socrates, as perhaps for no other philosopher in history, the meaning of life was to be found in the search for wisdom; it is no exaggeration to say of him that philosophy was his life. It is because of his extraordinary dedication to and skill in philosophical inquiry that Socrates was able to transcend the limitations of his birth, poverty and lack of elegance and take a central place in the intellectual life of fifth-century Athens; and it is for these reasons we know of him today.

Even more than the Sophists, Socrates is responsible for making ethics a philosophical subject. It was Socrates who formulated the moral questions that subsequent philosophers have tried to answer, and Socrates' own answers to these questions are of interest even today. In the history of ethics, Socrates is the first figure of truly major importance; he is the first great moral philosopher.

Socrates and Plato

Socrates' lasting fame is made all the more remarkable by the fact that he himself wrote nothing. Other philosophers of the past live today through their own written works; Socrates lives for us through the writings of his follower, Plato. Several of Socrates' companions have left us written portraits of him, but Plato's dialogues are by far the most vivid of these, and the most philosophically acute as well. It is largely thanks to Plato's works that Socrates has received his proper place in the pantheon of great philosophers.

Plato was born in 427 BC, when Socrates was 42 years old. He came from an aristocratic family and possessed the outward trappings of nobility that Socrates so conspicuously lacked. Legend has it that when he met Socrates he was considering becoming a tragic poet, but that the influence of Socrates caused him to abandon that career and devote himself to philosophy. Whether or not the legend is correct, it reflects three important truths about Plato which we can discern from his works. The first is that he was a superb writer, probably the greatest writer of Greek prose and the finest stylist among the philosophers of the Western intellectual tradition. The second is that he became, thanks in part to the influence of Socrates, a true philosopher; indeed he is recognized along with Socrates as one of the greatest philosophers who ever lived. The third is that he began his philosophical career as Socrates' loyal disciple.

Socrates was no doubt extremely fortunate in attracting as a disciple someone with the right combination of philosophical and literary abilities to ensure his place in history; it is a measure of Socrates' own genius, though, that he could attract such a gifted follower. Plato doubtless began to associate with Socrates only in the last decade or so of Socrates' life. He does not portray himself in his dialogues as the closest of Socrates' disciples; in fact, he mentions himself only in the *Apology* and *Phaedo*, and in the latter case notes his absence on the day of Socrates' death. Nonetheless, it is clear that Socrates made a profound impression on Plato, one that never entirely faded as he grew older and developed his own answers to the questions Socrates had raised.

Aside from some letters which may or may not be genuine, Plato's writings consist entirely of dialogues: philosophical conversations between two or more persons. Scholars customarily classify the dialogues as early, middle or late based on similarities and differences in style and content. In the early dialogues, Socrates is invariably the central figure; and Plato's portrait of him in these works is so detailed and lifelike that few people doubt its faithfulness to the historical Socrates. In the middle dialogues,

Socrates remains the central character; but he begins to propound views not found in the earlier works. Most scholars believe that at this point Plato began to use Socrates as a spokesman for his own philosophical views. In the late dialogues Socrates recedes into the background, as the discussion moves ever farther from his own concerns; in Plato's final work, the *Laws*, he disappears entirely.

It seems reasonable, therefore, to look for the views of the historical Socrates in Plato's early works; and that is what I shall be doing in the rest of this chapter. First, however, a caution is in order. I have noted above that Plato began his career as a disciple of Socrates, and that his early dialogues give us our best picture of Socrates and his philosophy. I should emphasize, however, that even these dialogues are not accurate records of conversations that actually took place. Some dialogues recount conversations that would have occurred, if they actually took place, before Plato was born. Only in the *Apology* is Plato referred to as present. We should not, therefore, regard these works as history; they are, rather, philosophical literature. Plato's literary aim was to capture the spirit of Socrates and the give-and-take of Socratic conversation. One of his philosophical aims was, no doubt, to present Socrates' philosophy to the reader of the dialogue; but another was to explore the issues raised by Socrates. We must never forget, in reading the early dialogues, that Plato is both a literary artist and a philosopher, but not a recording secretary.

The early dialogues show us Socrates in a variety of situations. The *Apology* is not strictly speaking a dialogue at all; it is Socrates' speech in his own defense at his trial, and as such contains very little conversation. The other early dialogues show Socrates in conversation either with ordinary Athenian citizens or with one or another of the Sophists and their disciples. No matter whom he is speaking with, however, Socrates is concerned with questions about ethics, "What is courage?" he asks; "What is justice?" Sometimes, as in the *Meno*, his concern is not with some particular virtue, but with virtue itself, and with the question whether it can be taught. These were the questions that dominated Socrates' philosophical life. To understand that life and the philosophical concerns that motivated it, we must turn to an examination of the dialogues themselves, beginning with those that portray the trial of Socrates and its aftermath.

Socrates on trial

When the Spartans finally defeated Athens in 404 BC, bringing an end to the Peloponnesian War, they imposed on the Athenians a puppet government composed of conservative Athenians sympathetic to Sparta. This government was referred to as the government of "the Thirty Tyrants," or simply "the Thirty." It was apparently a most repressive regime; Plato, no friend of democracy, says that "these men in a short time made the previous constitution look golden" (the *Seventh Letter*, 324d). This oligarchy was overthrown in 403 BC and the democracy restored. Four years later, in 399 BC, Socrates was brought to trial. He was indicted by three men, Meletus, Anytus and Lycon; the charges against him, as stated in the *Apology*, read, "Socrates does wrong in corrupting the youth and in not believing in the gods which the city honors, but in other strange spiritual matters" (*Apology* 24b).

Why was Socrates put on trial? There are several reasons, not all of which have much to do with the official charges. First, Socrates was the most famous intellectual in Athens; and, as we have seen, many Athenians blamed the intellectuals of the fifth century for the decline of their culture and the loss of the Peloponnesian War. It is unlikely that people knew enough of Socrates' views to distinguish them from those of the Sophists or the Pre-Socratic philosophers; he would have been seen by most as "part of a bad lot."

Unless they had encountered Socrates personally (not a particularly unlikely occurrence, since he made a point of conducting his philosophical inquiry through conversations held in public places), people would have based their beliefs about Socrates on his general reputation. This was no doubt shaped in part by Aristophanes' portrait of "Socrates" in the *Clouds*. This play was first performed in 423 BC and later revised; the revised version is the one we possess today. In the play Strepsiades, in debt because of the riding expenses of his son Pheidippides, becomes a student in the *phrontisterion* ("think-tank") of Socrates to find a way to avoid paying his debts. Socrates offers to teach him the secrets of natural philosophy: he denies the existence of Zeus and tells Strepsiades that "the Whirlwind," or vortex, a principle used by several Pre-Socratic philosophers to explain the cosmos, is the ruler of the universe.

When Strepsiades proves an inept pupil, he persuades his son to study in his place. In the climactic scene of the play, Socrates introduces Pheidippides to two characters who personify "just" and "unjust" argument. These characters actually represent the attitudes of the older and younger generation of Athenians, the heroic generation of Marathon and the generation of the Peloponnesian War. They debate, and just argument, which defends tradition, truth, justice, discipline, modesty and duty, is defeated by unjust argument, which denies that truth and justice exist, and defends self-indulgence, shamelessness and self-interest. Pheidippides learns how to use the "worse logic" to defeat the "better"; but instead of using his skill to get his father off, he uses it to justify beating him. Strepsiades, realizing the immorality of using fallacious argument to avoid paying his debts, burns down the *phrontisterion*, saying that Socrates and his students "have blasphemed the gods."

The *Clouds* was not well received when it was first performed; it finished third in its competition. Nonetheless it must have been a powerful source of prejudice against Socrates. We cannot know whether it was Aristophanes' own idea to put the views of the Pre-Socratic philosophers and the Sophists into the mouth of Socrates, or whether he merely developed a view of Socrates already existing among the general public; however that may be, Aristophanes was certainly partially responsible for the bad reputation of Socrates, as Plato brings out in the *Apology*. Is there any truth in Aristophanes' portrait? We cannot answer this fully until we contrast it with Plato's own portrayal of Socrates. On the one hand, Aristophanes certainly knew Socrates personally; Plato shows them at the same party in his *Symposium*. On the other, accuracy in depiction was even less of a priority for Aristophanes than it was for Plato; a comic poet would necessarily prefer humorous caricature to serious truth.

In addition to the general distrust of intellectuals and the portrait of Socrates in the *Clouds*, there were two other facts that would have accounted for public hostility toward Socrates. The first he mentions himself in the *Apology*: when he set out to discover who, in Athens, was wiser than himself, he examined many people of high reputation, including the poets, the craftsmen and the political leaders of the city. The result of his examination of these influential men was always the same: none of them turned out to know the great and important things they and their followers thought they did. Rather, Socrates' refutation of their views held them up to public scorn and ridicule. One can easily imagine the resulting anger toward Socrates, especially among the politicians.

The second fact also involves the political leaders of Athens; but unlike the first, Socrates does not mention it in the *Apology*, perhaps because it is the most dangerous piece of evidence against him. Socrates did not make enemies of all the political figures of his time; three men were particularly close to him. Two of these are Charmides and Critias; the third is Alcibiades. The former were relatives of Plato, and were members of the Thirty Tyrants mentioned above. Though Plato, in his dialogue the *Charmides*, depicts Socrates as exposing them to the same relentless examination he inflicted on democratic politicians, the mere fact of Socrates' association with these two members of the hated oligarchy would have aroused suspicion of him among the populace. This suspicion would only have been heightened by the fact that Socrates was known to be critical of democratic government; Charmides and Critias may have drawn intellectual support for their policies from Socrates' anti-democratic ideas.

Socrates was even closer to Alcibiades than to Charmides and Critias. He describes himself as Alcibiades' lover and, though Plato insists in the *Symposium* that their relationship was not physical, homosexual relations between older men and youths were fairly common in ancient Athens. Alcibiades was the most infamous political leader Athens produced during the Peloponnesian War; it could be argued that he was directly responsible for her defeat. Brilliant but undisciplined, Alcibiades was known for his passions for horse-racing (Pheidippides in the *Clouds* may be modeled on him), sex and political power. He argued the Athenians into undertaking a massive invasion of Sicily in 415 BC. He was to have been one of the three commanders of the expedition, but was summoned back to Athens shortly after its departure on suspicion of having defaced some religious statuary. He instead fled to avoid prosecution, eventually going over to the Spartan side. He provided the Spartans with advice which led to the defeat of the Athenian expedition, their most serious setback of the war. Though he later betrayed the Spartans and returned to the Athenian side, it can hardly have been a point in Socrates' favor that he was regarded as the mentor of such an unprincipled opportunist.

The *Apology* describes in detail the trial of Socrates. It purports to be Socrates' own defense at his trial. It is impossible to determine how faithful the dialogue is to Socrates' actual remarks. On the one hand, the trial of Socrates was a public event, and Plato was among those present in the audience (*Apology* 33d—34a), so he would have known what Socrates said, as would many other Athenian citizens. On the other hand, I noted above that we cannot expect historical accuracy from Plato's dialogues: his aims were philosophical and literary rather than historical. Xenophon, like Plato a follower of Socrates, wrote his own account of Socrates' defense, which differs greatly from Plato's. It is possible that the *Apology* gives us an account of what Socrates actually said at his trial, but perhaps it is Plato's attempt to answer on Socrates' behalf the charges raised against him, and to explain to the Athenians what manner of man they had put to death.

Socrates' answers to his accusers

In the first part of the *Apology* Socrates responds specifically to the charges against him. Socrates explicitly recognizes some of the prejudice against him mentioned above; he attributes it to a largely anonymous group he calls his "first accusers." The charges of these accusers, he thinks, are more dangerous than the charges of the official indictment submitted by Anytus, Meletus and Lycon. Socrates describes the slanders of the first accusers as follows:

> there is a certain Socrates, a wise man, a theorist about the heavens and an investigator of all the things under the earth, and one who makes the worse argument the better.
>
> (*Apology* 18b)

A little later (19b—c) he adds to this imaginary indictment another charge: that he teaches these things to others.

These are stock accusations which are made against philosophers in general (26d); they tell us nothing about the nature or content of Socrates' philosophy. In saying that Socrates has theories about the heavens and things under the earth they link Socrates with the Pre-Socratic philosophers, who put forth accounts of the nature of the cosmos. In saying that Socrates makes the weaker argument appear the stronger they classify him as a Sophist, for some of the Sophists had promised to do this by teaching rhetoric.

These accusations are, however, related to the official indictment. The charge of being an investigator of nature bears on the issue of Socrates' impiety because, as Socrates says, "those who hear them believe that investigators of these things do not believe in the gods" (18c). The charge of making the weaker argument the stronger leads to the charge of corrupting the youth, for it suggests that Socrates, like the Sophists, weakened the respect of the younger citizens for the traditions of Athenian society, and that he did so by rhetorical tricks.

Socrates lays these accusations in part at the feet of Aristophanes

> you have seen these things yourselves in the comedy of Aristophanes: a certain "Socrates" being swung about there, saying he walks on air and spewing forth a lot of other nonsense about things of which I understand nothing, not in the slightest. (19c)

As we have seen there is material in the *Clouds* to support both the "unofficial" charges of natural speculation and Sophistry and the official charges of impiety and corrupting the youth.

Socrates' response to the charge that he is a natural philosopher is quite straightforward and effective: Aristophanes' portrait of him is in fact completely inaccurate

> I am not expressing contempt for knowledge of this sort, if there is anyone who has it — I hope I never have to defend myself against Meletus on *those* charges — but these matters, my fellow Athenians, are no concern of mine. And I offer the majority of you as witnesses, and charge you to inform one another, those of you who have ever heard me in discussion — and many of you have — tell one another if you have *ever* heard me talking about such things, even a little; and from this you will understand that the other things which the majority say about me are likewise false. (19c—d)

Socrates' reply to this charge of his first accusers is convincing, especially because it contains an appeal to the jury as witnesses. His response to the other charges is not so successful. Socrates construes the charge that he teaches others as an attempt to link him with the Sophists. He responds, "if you have heard from anyone that I try to teach people and charge money for it, that is not true either" (19d—e). Later he adds

> even my accusers here, though they have shamelessly accused me of everything else, were not shameless enough to offer evidence that I ever charged or demanded money from anyone. But I can provide adequate evidence that I speak the truth: my poverty. (31b—c)

Socrates thus acquits himself of the charge of teaching for pay, in the manner of the Sophists. Yet, as he himself says, his more recent accusers have never charged him with *that*. They are not concerned with whether he got money for teaching, but rather with whether he taught at all. Socrates admits that

> I have never have never been the teacher of anyone; but if someone should desire to listen to me speaking and pursuing my own activities, whether he is young or old, I have never refused him; nor do I engage in discussion only when I receive money and not otherwise. Rather, I offer myself to be questioned by rich and poor alike, and to answer if anyone is willing to hear what I have to say. (33a—b)

Socrates does not consider this teaching, and if teaching means the imparting of doctrines from teacher to disciple, it is not. It does seem to be teaching by example, however; and if, like Socrates' accusers, one thought the example a bad one, it could easily lead to the charge of corrupting the youth.

What about the charge of making the worse argument appear the better? Though the debate between just and unjust argument in the *Clouds* must surely have been one source for this charge, Socrates does not here mention Aristophanes. Instead, he explains that this charge arose from his conversations with some of the leading citizens of Athens. As I have noted, Socrates examined the politicians, the poets and the craftsmen. His aim was to find someone wiser than himself, or, failing that, to show that these people did not have the wisdom they thought they had. Instead of being convinced of this fact, his interlocutors and their followers assumed that they had been defeated by verbal tricks, that they really did know what they thought they did, but Socrates made them look bad through a kind of linguistic sorcery. That is, they thought that Socrates could "make the worse argument the better." Yet to say this is only to explain the origin of the charge; it is not to refute it. Plato and Socrates no doubt believed the charge to be false, but nowhere in the *Apology* do they effectively answer it.

Leaving this charge unanswered, Socrates turns from his first accusers to his current ones. The current charges against him are two: impiety and corrupting the youth. In this part of the dialogue we have an opportunity to see the kind of Socratic examination that got Socrates into trouble in the first place; for Socrates answers the charges by cross-examining one of his accusers, Meletus.

Socrates focuses first on the charge of corrupting the youth. He gets Meletus to state that virtually everyone in Athens except Socrates improves the youth, that only Socrates makes them worse. Socrates then asks whether it is true of horses and other animals that almost everyone improves them; isn't it rather that only trainers (a small group of people with special knowledge) improve them, whereas most people do them harm?

This kind of argument is one Socrates frequently uses; it is an argument by analogy from one case to another. The inference he wants to draw is that, just as only the rare individual with knowledge of horses benefits them, so only the rare individual with knowledge of human nature benefits young people. Socrates frequently disclaims having such knowledge in the *Apology*, but it is hard to avoid the suspicion that Plato thought Socrates to be just that sort of rare person. The weakness of the argument is that one can escape its conclusion simply by denying the analogy. If Meletus were clever (as he certainly is not), he could simply say that the education of humans differs from that of horses in this respect. In the *Protagoras*, Plato shows Protagoras making just such a move against Socrates, claiming that the teaching of virtue is not like training in a craft but like the teaching of Greek, something everyone does (327e–328a).

Socrates' next argument trades on a characteristic Socratic

claim: that no one does wrong willingly. It is better, he says, to live in a good community than in a bad one. A bad community is one in which one is surrounded by bad people. Bad associates harm one, and no one prefers to be harmed rather than benefited. No one, then, would willingly make his associates bad people; either Socrates does not corrupt the youth at all, or he does so unintentionally. If Meletus believes that Socrates corrupts the youth unintentionally, he should have taken him aside and privately shown him the error of his ways, not dragged him into court.

Socrates probably believed that no one willingly does wrong, that all wrongdoing is the result of ignorance, and that virtuous action is the result of knowledge. We shall discuss these claims (known as the "Socratic paradoxes") below. For now we need only note that they *are* paradoxes, that they run counter to common opinion. If Socrates is correct in claiming that all wrongdoing is involuntary and that the courts only exist to punish voluntary wrongdoing, then it would follow that there is *no* legitimate function of the courts in the punishment of criminals. Socrates' reply to Meletus is thus unconvincing, for it relies on assumptions that no Athenian juror would accept. Doubtless arguments such as these were partially responsible for Socrates' bad reputation in Athens.

Socrates has, however, another answer to the charge of corrupting the youth, and he makes it later in his defense

> If I corrupt some of the youth and have corrupted others, it is necessary, I suppose, either that some of them, having grown older, will have recognized that I at one time advised them badly, and they now will come forward to accuse me and seek retribution; or, if they themselves are not willing, some members of their family, fathers and brothers and other relatives, if ever one of their own family ever suffered some evil at my hands, would now remember that and seek retribution.
> (33c—d)

He then names several of his associates and their relatives present in the audience and invites Meletus to call them as witnesses. In fact, he claims, they are all ready to come to his defense, and "can there be any other reason for the willingness of the uncorrupted, older men, the relatives of these, to help me than the true and right one, that they know Meletus is lying, and that I am telling the truth?" (34b).

Socrates now turns to the other charge of his current accusers: impiety. Socrates links this charge with the charge of corrupting the youth

> tell us, how do I corrupt the youth, Meletus? Or isn't it clear that, according to the indictment which you wrote, it is by teaching them not to believe in the gods which the city accepts, but other strange spiritual matters? (26b)

Meletus agrees, and goes on to claim that Socrates is a complete atheist. Rather than believing that the sun and moon are gods, says Meletus, "he says the sun is a stone and the moon earth." (26d) Socrates' response is immediate

> Do you think you are accusing Anaxagoras, my dear Meletus? And do you have so little respect for these men and think them so uneducated that they do not know that the works of Anaxagoras teem with such claims? And would the youth learn these things from me, since it is possible for them to buy them on occasion in the market-place for no more than a drachma and laugh in derision at Socrates if he pretended they were his own, especially given their uniqueness. (26d—e)

Socrates at once rejects the charge of Meletus and strengthens the supposition that he is being condemned for views he never held.

At this point in his defense Socrates makes a serious mistake: he becomes too clever for his own good. The most effective response to the charge of atheism would have been a simple denial. Socrates could have affirmed his belief in the gods of the state, mentioned his observance of the civic religious festivals, and called his friends to testify on his behalf. Instead, he traps Meletus in an inconsistency. Meletus had accused Socrates of introducing new gods, then called him an atheist. Yet he can't be both: if he believes in gods other than those of the state he is not an atheist, and if he is an atheist he would not be guilty of introducing new gods. The argument makes Meletus look foolish, but it does not answer the charge. The jury would be left wondering whether Socrates was an atheist or a religious innovator, but in either case he would be guilty of not honoring the gods of the state (i.e. of impiety).

With this unfortunate response to the charge of impiety Socrates completes his response to the charges brought against him by both his older and his more recent accusers. How well has he defended himself? His appeal to the jury to testify to his lack of interest in the investigation of natural phenomena was doubtless an effective answer to the charge of being a philosopher of the Pre-Socratic type. Likewise, his challenge to Meletus to call as witnesses the people he has allegedly corrupted or their relatives was a powerful refutation of the charge of corrupting the young. In general, Socrates has gone far in showing that the portrayal of him by his accusers is inaccurate, and is based more on the stereotype of the philosopher than on his own views.

On the other hand, Socrates has not disproved the charges that he makes the worse argument appear the better and that he teaches others (though he has shown that he did not profit monetarily by his teaching, as the Sophists did). Most importantly, Socrates has not disproved the charge of impiety; for all he has said, an Athenian juror attempting to reach a fair verdict might well wonder what religious convictions, if any, Socrates had. We have in the *Apology* only Socrates' reply to the charges against him; we do not know whether the accusers argued effectively for his guilt on the charge of impiety (though given Meletus' bungling in response to Socrates' questions this seems unlikely). Nonetheless, it seems clear that Socrates' defense is at best incomplete.

The *Apology* contains more than Socrates' answer to his accusers, however; it is not merely a legal document. A large part of it is devoted to giving us a portrait of Socrates' life; a self-portrait, if the dialogue contains a historically accurate reproduction of the actual defense, but a portrait by one of his disciples in any case. As the suspicion arises naturally that Socrates may be on trial, not for a set of specific actions but because of the kind of person he is, this information is relevant to his defense. In any case, Socrates the man is inseparable from Socrates the philosopher; if we want to understand his philosophy we must understand his life. The *Apology* gives us information about that life that is unsurpassed in other sources. Let us therefore turn to an examination of it.

Socrates' defense of his life

Socrates' opening remarks tell us a good deal about him. Unlike his accusers, he says, he will speak the truth. Though they have warned the jury that he is a "clever speaker," Socrates claims that his only cleverness is his truthfulness. Because this is his first appearance in a court of law, Socrates claims to be unfamiliar with its language. Therefore, he says, he will defend himself in the same language he uses in speaking to others in the marketplace.

These remarks, like many Socrates makes, are tinged with irony. We have no reason to doubt that this is his first court appearance, and no reason to distrust his promise to speak the truth. Still, Socrates must know that his reputation as a speaker is not based on his truthfulness. Rather, it is based on his legendary ability to tie his interlocutors in knots, as he does in this dialogue with Meletus. Moreover, Socrates is widely suspected of not revealing his own honest opinion about the things he discusses with others. It is a common charge made against him that he refutes others but never says what he himself thinks, and he acknowledges this in the *Apology*: "those present on each occasion think that I must know the answers to the questions I raise for others" (23a). In addition, Socrates' profession of ignorance of what goes on in the law courts is disingenuous; later in his speech he shows that he knows a good deal about standard Athenian legal practice (see, for instance, 34b ff.).

Socrates has promised to tell the truth about himself, but what is that truth? In the course of explaining the hostility that has arisen against him, he gives a remarkable explanation of his devotion to philosophy. He examines others, he says, in obedience to a divine command (22a; cf. 23b, 30a). His friend Chaerephon had asked the oracle at Delphi whether anyone was wiser than Socrates, and the priestess of the oracle had answered, "no one." Now the oracle at Delphi was perhaps the most sacred spot in all of Greece; the Greeks believed that it revealed the words of the god Apollo, and they took these revelations most seriously. Thus, for Socrates to support his philosophical activity with the backing of the oracle was to appeal to the highest religious authority.

Socrates' response to the oracle is completely in character. Any other Greek philosopher or Sophist would simply have added the endorsement of the oracle to his advertisements for himself and used it to attract more customers: "study with X, declared by Apollo himself to be the wisest man in all Greece!" Socrates, in contrast, finds the response of the oracle deeply puzzling. He *knows* that he is not wise; on the other hand, the god would not lie, for "that wouldn't be right for him" (21b). So Socrates decides to test the truth of the oracle

> I went to one of those with a reputation for wisdom, in order to put the statement to the test and show the oracle that, at least in this case, "Here is someone wiser than I, but you said I was wisest." (21b—c)

The result of this interview is one of the best-known parts of the dialogue

> I reasoned to myself as I went away that I was wiser than this man; it is likely that neither of us knows anything wonderful, but he thinks that he knows something when he does not, and I do not think that I know what I do not know. It seems then that I am wiser than he by this little bit, that I don't think that I know things I don't know. (21d)

As noted above, Socrates repeated the process many times, with politicians, poets and craftsmen; the result was always the same. Socrates claims, with a good deal of plausibility, that public hostility towards him is the product of his examination of others.

Despite this hostility, however, Socrates won't cease to examine others. As noted above, he regards his efforts in this regard as obedience to a divine command: "I must describe my wandering journey to you as a series of labors undertaken to prove to myself that the oracle was irrefutable" (22a). The true message of the oracle is that "in all likelihood that the god is wise, and this is the meaning of the oracle, that human wisdom is worth little or nothing" (23a). Socrates thinks he is supporting that view whenever he unmasks another pretender to wisdom.

What are we to make of Socrates' appeal to the oracle as justification of his life? It would seem to be a most effective refutation of the charge of impiety: what greater proof of one's piety can one give than to show that one has devoted one's life to the service of the god? Modern readers tend to distrust this appeal: they assume that Socrates is using this public endorsement of his wisdom as an excuse to do what he would have done anyway, and that his real reason for philosophizing lies elsewhere.

Yet Socrates' explanation is not so easily dismissed. In the rest of the *Apology* he is relentlessly honest: he says what he thinks to the jury, even when it hurts his case. It is hard to believe that his appeal to the god is insincere, especially since Socrates later (37e) acknowledges that many in the jury will not believe he is serious. In other words, Socrates brings up his obedience to the god, though he knows it will not persuade people; what other reason could there be for doing so than that he thinks it is the truth? In addition, Plato in other dialogues portrays Socrates as a pious man who does believe in the gods of Greek religion, though not in all the stories told about them (cf. *Euthyphro* 6a—c).

We must admit that Socrates' piety is of a peculiarly philosophical kind: when the oracle states that no one is wiser than he is, he decides to "serve" the god by showing him that he is mistaken. Only after he has examined those who pretend to be wise does he come to the conclusion that the god is correct, and undertakes to defend his oracle by continued refutation of others. Only a philosopher, moreover, could take a brief statement by the priestess of the oracle and transform it into a command to philosophize.

The oracle of Apollo was not Socrates' only justification for engaging in philosophical activity: at 38a he says that philosophical examination "seems to me to be the greatest good that can befall a human being . . . and that the unexamined life is not worth living for a human being." It does, however, seem to be one he believed in. Indeed, in the course of his defense Socrates turns the oracle's negative declaration not only into a divine command to philosophize but into a mission, and declares himself the god's gift to Athens

> I am far from making a defense on my own behalf, as someone might think, but on yours, lest you do wrong concerning the gift of the god to you in condemning me. For if you kill me, you will not easily find another like me; for, even if it is somewhat humorous to say it, I seem simply to have been attached to the city by the god as if to a large and noble horse, which by virtue of its size was somewhat sluggish and needed

to be roused to action by a gadfly; so the god has bestowed me on the city, so that I might ceaselessly rouse and persuade and reproach each one of you, alighting on you everywhere the whole day long. (30d—31a)

Naturally, Socrates thinks of his mission as a great benefit to the Athenians; so much so, in fact, that when he is asked to state some alternative to the death penalty he suggests that he be rewarded for his public service like an Olympic victor, by being given free meals at public expense. He is so dedicated to his mission that he tells the jury he would not accept acquittal on condition that he cease to examine others

if you were willing to let me off on these conditions, I would say to you, "I am very fond of you, my fellow Athenians, and I love you, but I shall obey the god rather than you, and as long as I draw breath I shall not cease philosophizing and exhorting you and arguing with any one of you I happen to meet on any occasion. (29d)

Socrates is well aware that remarks such as these are certain to arouse the envy and anger of the jury, and contribute to his conviction and death sentence. Throughout the *Apology*, however, he shows a disdain for preserving his life at the expense of his convictions. The following remarks illustrate his attitude

Perhaps, though, someone might say, "Aren't you ashamed, Socrates, to have pursued a career which has brought you now in danger of death?" I would rightly respond to him, "You do not speak well, fellow, if you think that a man who is in the least worthy ought to take into account the risk of life or death, and not consider this alone whenever he acts, whether he acts rightly or wrongly, and whether his deeds are those of a good person or of a bad. (28b)

Socrates does not fear death, he says, because he does not know it to be evil

to fear death, gentlemen, is nothing else but to think oneself wise when one is not; it is to think that one knows what one does not. For no one knows whether death might not be the greatest of goods for a human being, but people fear it as if they knew it was the greatest of evils. (29a)

This explanation is a classic example of Socratic intellectualism (about which more below): he treats the emotion of fear as a cognitive state, either knowledge or ignorance; and he ignores the fact that what people fear about death is precisely that it is unknown. Later he augments this argument with another:

Death is one of two things: either it is ceasing to exist, and the person who has died has no experience of anything; or, as it is said, it is a certain transformation and a migration of the soul from this place to another. And if there is no experience, but it is like a sleep without dreams, death would be a wonderful benefit. (40c—d)

If, on the other hand, life continues in the underworld, Socrates says he looks forward to being judged there by "genuine jurors," not like his present jurors, and to conversing with and examining the heroes of past ages. At least in Hades, Socrates remarks ruefully, people are not put to death for philosophizing (41c).

Socrates' fearlessness is buttressed by two more facts. The first is the silence of his *daimon*, a voice which comes to him from time to time and warns him against certain conduct (31d, 40a—b). This voice, which we would call the voice of conscience but which Socrates thinks of as a divine sign, has not opposed his present defense. This indicates, says Socrates, that death (which he must have been aware was the likely outcome of the trial) is a blessing rather than evil.

The second is Socrates' conviction that a good person (in this case himself) cannot be harmed by a worse one (in this case his accusers). Socrates explains this paradoxical view by claiming that neither death nor exile harm someone, but that falsely procuring the death of an innocent person does (30d). Clearly, Socrates means something unusual by "harm." In fact he thinks that the only good one can do for oneself or another is to improve the moral quality of one's soul, and the only harm is to make the soul worse. In that sense, but only in that sense, is it true that killing an innocent person does not harm the person killed but the person doing the killing.

Throughout the trial Socrates acts on the basis of his convictions that he has a divine obligation to philosophize and that one should fear immoral conduct but not death. He also behaved in this manner when on military service (28d—29a). This indifference to death shows Socrates to be a man of great courage. He does say that he avoided political involvement because no one who opposes the popular will in a democracy can avoid being put to death (31e—32a). His concern seems to be not with prolonging his life, however, but with pursuing his mission: "if I had tried a long time ago to engage in political matters," he remarks, "I would have perished a long time ago and not have benefited either yourselves or myself at all." (31d—e)

His own description of his two unhappy encounters with public life illustrate this claim and in addition confirm his courage. When Socrates was serving as one of the presidents of the Council (an organ of the executive branch of Athenian government), the public demanded a group trial of ten naval commanders who had won a victory in the battle of Arginusae but who had failed to rescue many of their own sailors. A group trial was strictly illegal, and Socrates alone opposed the prosecutors, though they threatened to have him stand trial with the ten. Similarly, when the Thirty asked him and some other Athenians to bring in one Leon of Salamis for execution, Socrates alone refused to co-operate, an act which he says would likely have led to his own death if the government hadn't fallen soon after. (32b—d)

The picture of Socrates that emerges from the *Apology* is thus that of a courageous person of absolute integrity. He shows humility in his profession of ignorance, but he also he shows a high sense of self-worth in his description of himself as a divine gift to the city. Many members of the jury doubtless took offense at this; they must have perceived his description of his divine mission as haughty arrogance, and must have been annoyed by his refusal to plead for mercy (34b—35d). It is easy to see how a man like Socrates could win the devoted discipleship of many Athenians and the hatred of others, and this gives us reason to think that Plato's portrait of Socrates is to be preferred to that of Aristophanes. Though both give us a person the Athenians might easily have condemned to death, only Plato's shows us a man who could inspire the devotion of serious minds such as his own.

The verdict

As the *Apology* indicates, Socrates was convicted of the charges brought against him. When he offered as a substitute for the death penalty the reward of free meals at public expense, which he changed only because of the pleas of his friends to a small fine, the jury, angered at such a display of arrogance, condemned him to death. It is easy to understand why the Athenians reached the verdict they did: as I noted above, there was great hostility toward Socrates because of his political associates, his cross-examination of famous politicians, and his general reputation as an intellectual. In addition, Socrates' conduct at the trial doubtless made him new enemies among the jurors.

It is not so easy to justify the verdict, however, as it is to explain it. Several features of Athenian law made it easier for Socrates' opponents to obtain his conviction than it would be in a modern democracy. In the first place, impiety was regarded as a crime against the state and not a matter of private conscience, because observance of the state religion was a requirement of citizenship. Second, the charge could be brought by any citizen against another; there was no public prosecutor to interpret the law in an expert manner and determine whether or not Socrates should have been brought to trial. The third feature is that a unanimous vote for conviction was not necessary. Athenian juries were quite large: this consisted of 500 or 501 members. The size of the jury was a way to ensure impartiality and prevent the bribing of individual jurors, but it made unanimous verdicts virtually impossible. Instead, cases were decided on the basis of a majority vote. The actual vote that convicted Socrates was very close; as he notes, "if only thirty of the votes had been changed I would have been acquitted" (*Apology* 36a).

Finally, the trial had to be completed in a single day. When the *Apology* begins, Socrates' accusers have already made their case to the jury. Socrates has only a limited time in which to clear himself of the charges. At one point in the dialogue he remarks that he would be surprised if he could remove all the prejudice against him in so short a time (24a; cf. 37a—b). It may seem to us that a single day, part of which is taken up by the charges of the prosecution, is too little time to devote to such a serious matter as the life or death of a person, especially when we contrast Athenian policy in this regard with our own elaborate legal protections.

Athenian legal procedures, then, raise doubts about the fairness of Socrates' trial. Certainly the death penalty is harsher than anyone would receive in a modern democracy for the expression of unpopular views. Athens, lacking our elaborate prison system, did not typically imprison criminals; exile, fine, or confiscation of the criminal's property were more common punishments. Probably even Socrates' accusers did not want to see him put to death: they wanted to frighten him into silence. When it became clear that Socrates would not be intimidated, however, Athenian law allowed him to be put to death. Again, one must wonder about the justice of such a law.

Aside from these procedural and legal questions, there remains the substantive question of Socrates' guilt or innocence. The Athenians may have convicted him because of his political associates or because they did not like his attitude, but would a fair and impartial jury have found Socrates guilty of the official charges of impiety and corrupting the youth? The prosecutors may not have succeeded in proving their case against Socrates, if we can judge from Meletus' bungling during Socrates' examination of him; but is there a case to be made out against him?

Though Socrates was not an atheist, he did doubt the traditional stories about the gods. He was, moreover, willing to subject these stories to rational criticism, a process they were unlikely to survive. The effect of such criticism would have been the weakening of traditional beliefs among Socrates' followers. In this, the influence of Socrates would have been like that of the Sophists. As in the case of the Sophists, the weakening of traditional religious beliefs was connected with the weakening of faith in established governments; in addition, however Socrates was willing to subject the principles of Athenian democracy to the same rational criticism he applied to traditional religion, and, indeed, to all facets of human existence.

Plato speaks in the *Republic* (Book X, 607b) of an old "quarrel between philosophy and poetry." There is a similar quarrel between philosophy and traditional religion and practical politics. Philosophy requires that every assumption be subjected to rational criticism; religion, on the other hand, requires that some claims be accepted as matters of faith, and practical politics requires that certain principles be accepted as the basis for the functioning of government. Though Socrates was hardly guilty of corrupting the youth in any ordinary sense of that phrase, he certainly did lead some young men to take a critical stance toward religion and politics. To that extent he was a genuine threat to the Athenian state.

Were the Athenians justified, then, in executing him? Certainly they were not. First of all, the kind of threat any philosopher poses to the state is limited by the fact that few people are likely to be seriously influenced in their thinking by philosophy. Second and more important, no state is justified in doing whatever it needs to do in order to ensure its survival. Sometimes philosophers say things that politicians need to listen to; Socrates was not wrong, though he was certainly injudicious, in describing himself as "God's gift to Athens." If the state silences its philosophers it deprives itself of their benefits as well as their threats. Third and finally, in convicting Socrates the Athenians failed to live up to their proud and noble tradition. We remember Athens not because it produced a form of government remarkable for its concord and efficiency (it did not), but because it produced a form of government in which individuals like Sophocles, Pericles, and Socrates could flourish. The verdict was not merely unjust; it was petty and small-minded.

The moral philosophy of Socrates: the *Crito*

The portrait of Socrates Plato gives us in the *Apology* resembles in many ways the heroes of Greek literature discussed in Chapter 1. Socrates calls our attention to this fact when he compares his conduct with that of the heroes of the Trojan War, and particularly Achilles, who chose death rather than dishonor (*Apology* 28b—d), and when he cites Palamedes and Ajax as heroes who died after an unfair trial like his own (41a—b). The closest parallel, however, is one he does not mention: that with Sophocles' Antigone. Like Socrates, Antigone suffered an unjust death because of her service to the gods; both went to their deaths because of their high principles and sense of duty. The *Crito* and *Phaedo* show that the friends of Socrates felt a great sense of loss at his death; together the dialogues contain ample material for a Greek tragedy.

Given the closeness of the two cases and the obviously tragic aspects of Socrates' death, why did Plato not make a tragedy out of the trial and death of Socrates? It is not because this event was recent, while tragedies dealt with the ancient past; Aeschylus in his *Persians* had written about the Persian Wars and other tragedians had dealt with contemporary themes. The reason is rather that Socrates himself does not see his death as tragic; he refuses to cast himself as a tragic hero. We saw why above: he does not fear death because he does not know it to be evil (29a). He fears not death, but wrongdoing (28b); he regards death as either a state like a dreamless sleep or as the continuance of existence in the underworld (40c—d). His *daimon* has not warned him that he is acting wrongly (40a—b), and he thinks that a good man cannot be harmed by worse (30c—d; cf. 41d). Socrates is able to face death without Antigone's lamentations because he does not share her conviction that death is evil.

Socrates behaves as he does at his trial because of his beliefs. In this he is not unique; all the great heroes of Greek literature, including Achilles and Antigone, act with integrity and on the basis of their convictions. What sets Socrates apart from these heroes is the content of his beliefs. I have noted that Socrates the man and Socrates the philosopher are inseparable; therefore, to understand the man we must investigate his moral philosophy. Some of this is laid out in the *Apology* and more is presented in the *Crito*. In the *Apology* Socrates had said that the highest human task is the care of one's soul. The *Crito* shows the connection between this claim and the statements above that wrongdoing, not death, is to be feared, and that a bad man cannot harm a good one. In so doing it presents an account of the good life, one which stands in contrast with those we saw in Chapter 1.

The *Crito* takes place in prison, on the day before Socrates' execution. The normal practice of the Athenians was to execute convicted criminals immediately following their trial; but unusual circumstances (described at the start of the *Phaedo*) prevented this from occurring. The day before the trial the Athenians had sent their annual mission ship to Delos, to celebrate the victory of Theseus over the Minotaur; civic law forbade executions to occur until the ship returned, in order to keep the city ritually pure. Thus, Socrates was imprisoned until the ship returned.

These circumstances allowed Socrates to continue to converse with his friends; it also allowed his friends the opportunity to plan a jailbreak. In this dialogue, Socrates' old friend Crito has come to him with just such a plan, and a list of reasons why Socrates should escape. If Socrates refuses to escape, Crito says, he will lose an irreplaceable friend and those who do not know Socrates will think his companions were too cheap to put up the money needed to bribe the officials to let Socrates out (such "escapes" were apparently not uncommon). In addition, Socrates would be abandoning his parental responsibilities to his children, which is immoral.

Socrates addresses Crito's concerns only briefly. At the end of the dialogue, he points out that his friends will care for his children and that they would lose the privileges of Athenian citizenship if they went into exile with him. Socrates imagines that the laws of Athens, personified, are speaking to him; they urge him to "treat neither your children nor your life nor anything else as more important than justice" (54b). His response to Crito's concern about "what people will think" is similar. We should not care what the majority think, but only about the views of reasonable people. These are the wise, the people who have expert knowledge about justice and injustice

> We ought not to take so seriously, my good friend, what the many will say about us, but the one individual who professes to have knowledge concerning justice and injustice, and the truth itself. (48a)

In fact, Socrates says, the only question that should be considered is whether escape would be just or unjust

> we, since the argument compels us, ought to consider nothing other than what I just said, whether we would act justly in giving money and favors to those who would lead me out of here, and in escaping ourselves and being led out, or whether in truth we would do wrong in doing all these things. (48c—d)

What is the argument that leads to the conclusion that only right and wrong should be considered? At 44d Socrates rejects the view that ordinary people have the power to harm or benefit others, on the grounds that "they are unable to make one wise or unwise." Why should wisdom (*phronesis*), the expert knowledge of right and wrong, be equated with good, and its opposite with evil? Socrates draws an analogy with physical training

> If we should destroy the part of us [i.e. the body] that is improved by health and injured by disease by following the opinion of those who do not have knowledge, will life be worth living when this part has been destroyed? (47d—e)

Just as life is not worth living if the body is ruined, it is not worth living if "the part of us that is maimed by injustice and benefited by justice" (i.e. the soul; 47e) is ruined. The soul is more precious than the body, the health of the soul is thus even more important than physical health. Only the wise person knows which actions can improve or ruin the soul, thus, only the wise person can tell what is good for the individual.

"We ought to make not living, but living well the most important thing," says Socrates (48b). Living well is the same thing as living nobly (*kalos*, a word with connotations of beauty, elegance and grace) and justly (*dikaios*, 48b8). Thus, the good life is the virtuous life and though Socrates mentions here only one of the virtues, justice, the Greek word for "justice," *dikaiosune*, is often used as a synonym for "righteousness" or "rightness" in general. Socrates, as we shall later see, believes that whoever possesses one of the virtues must possess them all, so he would certainly not object to the addition of "temperately, courageously and piously" to his description of the good life.

This argument is of the utmost importance for our understanding of Socrates' moral philosophy. What it does is to establish the closest relations among the key concepts of our inquiry: virtue, knowledge or wisdom, and happiness or the good life. Socrates claims that the good life is *the same as* the virtuous or just life: virtue and happiness are identical. Furthermore, only wisdom can make life worth living, thus, wisdom is a necessary condition for happiness. Though he does not explicitly say so here, the argument suggests (and Socrates will claim elsewhere) that wisdom is both necessary and sufficient for the good life: for if the only thing that matters for living well is right action and wisdom tells us which actions are right, then wisdom will be the only thing that matters for living well. Thus, if the good life and the virtuous life are one and the same, and wisdom is both necessary and sufficient for living the good life, then wisdom, virtue and happiness will be inseparable.

The factor that unifies all three of these concepts is the soul. As Socrates had claimed in the *Apology*, the highest human task is the care of one's soul. In light of the argument above, we can see why Socrates said that. To care for one's soul is to maintain its health. Right actions benefit the soul, improve its health while wrong actions mutilate or damage the soul, destroy its health. The ultimate question one must consider in determining whether to perform some action or not is, "Will this action benefit or damage my soul?" Ethical justification is, for Socrates, *egoistic*: an action is right if and only if it benefits the agent who performs it. Ordinarily, we associate egoism with selfishness, but Socrates' version of egoism is decidedly *not* selfish. Consider his view of his own conviction (*Apology* 30c—d). Socrates tells his accusers and the jury that if they convict him, they will harm themselves and not him. This is because the only harm Socrates will countenance is harm to one's soul, and the only way to harm one's soul is to perform unjust or otherwise immoral actions. Convicting Socrates unjustly will thus not harm him, but it will harm those who convict him. Socratic egoism, therefore, requires that I act justly in my dealings with you, but that I do so for my sake, not for yours!

By basing ethics on the care of one's soul, Socrates provides the strongest motive for moral action; he makes right conduct a matter of the greatest importance for each individual, not a matter of conformity to social convention or acting in the interests of others, as the Sophists had thought. His limitation of harm to harm to one's own soul explains his indifference to death and his belief that wrongdoing, not death, is to be feared (*Apology* 28b—29b). His conviction that only wrong action harms one's soul explains his insistence in the *Crito* that the question of his escape should be confined to the issue of its rightness. His identification of the good life with the life of the healthy soul, and of this life with that of moral knowledge and virtue is the source of the famous "Socratic paradoxes," which we shall encounter when we discuss the *Meno*: that virtue is knowledge, that wrongdoing is based on ignorance, and that no one does wrong voluntarily. For if wisdom, moral knowledge, is the sole cause of virtue, then it is practically equivalent to virtue; and if wrongdoing harmed the most precious part of oneself, no one would willingly do wrong; only ignorance of the morally relevant facts could explain apparently intentional wrongdoing.

Of course, Socrates' view about the relations between virtue, wisdom and the good life are themselves paradoxical; the paradox is not lessened by showing that all of the paradoxes in his moral philosophy are connected. In the *Gorgias*, after Socrates has expressed views similar to those just discussed, one of his interlocutors, Callicles, remarks, "if you are serious and the things you say are true, then doesn't this turn the life of humans upside down?" (481b—c). One need not side with the view Callicles develops in that dialogue to agree with this observation. Certainly Socrates' view about the relation between virtue and happiness is different from the one we found in Greek literature in Chapter 1: there happiness appeared to be an end distinct from virtue, but which one hoped to gain by virtuous acts, but Socrates has identified virtue and happiness. Moreover, wisdom seemed to be one virtue among many; but, on Socrates' view, it is the sole cause of all virtue and happiness.

One might disagree with Socrates on any of several points: that the greatest good is a healthy soul, that wrongdoing and only wrongdoing damages the soul, that life with a damaged soul is not worth living, that wisdom is necessary and sufficient for right action, that wisdom is restricted to moral experts, or that the effect of an action on the agent's soul is the sole determinant of moral action. Much subsequent Greek philosophy, and later moral philosophy in general, is devoted to a discussion of these debatable points. Plato shows Socrates defending them against the objections of others, both Sophists and ordinary Athenians, in other early dialogues including the *Protagoras* and *Gorgias*; he adopts some of them and rejects others in the *Republic*. Aristotle, the Stoics and the Epicureans also discuss these claims, the Stoics defending a view much like Socrates'. It is not the least benefit of Socrates' unorthodox beliefs that they generated so much later reflection.

In this dialogue, however, Crito agrees with Socrates that the good life, the virtuous life and the life of practical wisdom are one. Given this agreement, Socrates is able to show that it would be wrong for him to escape. He first claims that one must never do wrong, even in retaliation for a wrong done to oneself (49b—c). To wrong another is to injure him, therefore, one must not injure another, even in response to an injury one has received. Further, one ought to fulfill all of one's just agreements (49e). Next, he argues that his escape would violate all of these principles: it would wrong, and thus injure the state, as well as violating a just agreement he had made.

To convince Crito of these points, Socrates adopts the brilliant rhetorical stratagem of imagining that "the laws and constitution of Athens were to come and oppose us" (50a). Socrates' disobedience to the law threatens the destruction of the state, they urge, for the state cannot survive if its legal judgments are disobeyed. The laws made it possible for his father to marry his mother, and saw to his upbringing and education; therefore they ought to be honored even more highly than his parents, and Socrates ought to obey them (50d—51c). Moreover, Socrates had agreed to abide by the judgments of the state: he had entered into a social contract with the laws of Athens. The laws allow anyone who is dissatisfied with them to emigrate with all his property on reaching manhood

> But whoever of you remains, seeing the way we judge cases and in other matters order the city, we say has already agreed by deed to do for us whatever we command. (51e)

Socrates has accepted this agreement more clearly than most Athenians; he has never left Athens except on military service. Finally, Athenians have the option of persuading their fellows that particular laws are wrong and ought to be changed but Socrates has not done this. He could have accepted exile at the time of his trial, and left without damaging the laws, but chose not to do so. To accept exile now, by escaping, would be an unjust attack on them.

Socrates' conclusion is that he must, in obedience to the laws, await his execution rather than escape. Crito, unable to rebut the argument, is forced to agree. Socrates' argument is a powerful one, and disturbing to modern readers. It seems, on the surface at least, to rule out the possibility of civil disobedience to unjust laws and its assertion of the priority of the state over the individual is in conflict with modern democratic thought. Yet it is not easy to find a glaring flaw in the argument. There is, in addition, an apparent contradiction between what Socrates says here and what he said to the jury in the *Apology*. In the *Crito*, as we have seen, the laws say that, by staying in Athens, Socrates has agreed to do "whatever we command." In the *Apology*, on the other hand, Socrates says that, if the jury were to offer to acquit him on the condition that he cease to practice philosophy (that is, examine others), he would refuse to obey (see *Apology* 29d; quoted above, p. 62).

Even if Socrates' words are inconsistent here, it would be easy enough to modify them into a consistent position, simply by limiting disobedience to the case of cases where the "higher laws" of God are at issue. This issue aside, the *Apology* and *Crito* show us a Socrates who is remarkably consistent in word and deed. His identification of the virtuous life and the good life, his rejection of the views of the majority in favor of that of the moral expert, his claim that only wrongdoing, not death ought to be feared, and his view that a worse man cannot harm a better — these philosophical positions are not merely consistent with Socrates' conduct at his trial and his refusal to escape, they explain that conduct by showing its rational basis. The *Crito*, like the *Apology*, reveals a Socrates who has the courage of his convictions, in addition, it tells us considerably more about those convictions and the rationale behind them than did the *Apology*. Much of the devotion philosophers have felt toward Socrates from Plato on is due to the fact that he both expressed such noble views and was willing to live by them.

The Socratic quest: method and paradox

The *Crito* explains much about Socrates' moral philosophy, but it does not explain everything. In particular, it does not explain why Socrates engaged in the philosophical examination of others. In the *Apology* he had claimed that he examined others in obedience to the god's command, and we found that this justification could not be rejected out of hand. The *Crito* suggests another answer, more closely connected with Socrates' philosophical principles. We need not accept this second explanation instead of the first, Socrates perhaps believed both.

The *Crito* tells us that we ought to listen to the moral expert, but it does not tell us who that expert is. The reader's natural assumption is that Socrates saw himself as such an expert; but Socrates repeatedly claims not to have this kind of knowledge. This expert will have knowledge of the actions that benefit and harm the soul of the agent, that make life worth living or not, that is, since the good life is the life of virtue, and the bad life that of vice, he will know which actions are virtuous and which vicious. In order to know this, Socrates thinks, he will have to know the nature of virtue and vice themselves. Thus, in order to find someone with the moral expertise necessary for living the good life, Socrates must look for someone who knows what virtue is.

In fact, most of the early dialogues involve a search for a moral expert of just this sort. At the same time, they involve a search for the definition of various virtues: courage in the *Laches*, temperance in the *Charmides*, piety in the *Euthyphro*, justice in the first book of the *Republic* (which may have been written separately as an early dialogue). Since the moral expert is the person who knows what virtue is, the two searches are in fact one and the same. The general Nicias puts the matter well in the *Laches* when he tells Lysimachus that

> whoever is closest to Socrates and engages in conversation with him, even if he begins at first to talk about something else, cannot stop being led about by him in argument until he falls into giving an account of himself, how he now lives and how he has lived previously; and when he falls into this, Socrates will not let him off before he weighs all these things sufficiently and well. (187e—188a)

Socrates finds no shortage of people who are willing to tell him what piety, justice, temperance, courage or virtue in general are; they include both ordinary people, such as young Charmides, and alleged experts, such as the general Laches, the prophet Euthyphro and the Sophist Protagoras. The question for Socrates is to determine which of them, if any, really knows what he is talking about. Socrates' method for doing this is called the *elenchus*.

The method of elenchus

Elenchus is a Greek word meaning "examination," "test" or "trial" but because the results of the examination Socrates undertakes in the early dialogues are always negative, the word comes to mean "refutation." Socratic *elenchus* is thus the examination of a claim made by an interlocutor, aimed at refutation. Though the immediate aims of the *elenchus* are negative, its ultimate aim may be said to be positive, for if a definition and its proponent survive

Socrates' most strenuous attempts to refute them, there is reason to think that the definition may be correct and the proponent a genuine moral expert. Surviving the Socratic *elenchus*, however, is no easy task, as the early dialogues show.

Socrates, protected by his denial of moral expertise, never puts forward a definition himself. His dialectical opponents, often suspecting that Socrates' denial is ironic, frequently object to this procedure; nonetheless, Socrates always cajoles a definition from his quarry. Once this has been accomplished, Socrates then elicits from his interlocutor a number of other admissions, which usually are matters of common sense. Then he shows that these other admissions contradict the original definition. One of the two must be abandoned and, since the other claims made by the interlocutor are so uncontroversial, it is always the proposed definition that is rejected. At this point Socrates gets his interlocutor to propose another definition and matters proceed in this way until the interlocutor is at a loss. Most of the early Socratic dialogues end at this juncture, with everyone in a state of perplexity.

The *Euthyphro* provides a text-book example of the method of *elenchus* in operation. Socrates encounters Euthyphro, a religious prophet, at the court of the King Archon. Socrates is there to face the indictment of Meletus and the other accusers; Euthyphro is prosecuting his own father on a charge of murder. Socrates is astonished to learn this, but Euthyphro defends his act as a matter of piety or religious obligation, a field in which he claims to be an expert (4e—5a). Socrates, offering to become his pupil and thus escape the attack of Meletus, asks Euthyphro for a definition of piety: "What sort of thing do you say the pious and the impious are, both as concerns murder and in all other cases" (5c—d).

Euthyphro, like many interlocutors in the early dialogues, responds with a definition based on an example: he says that

> the holy is what I am doing now, prosecuting the wrongdoer, whether he has committed murder or temple robbery or anything else of the sort, and whether it happens to be one's father, or mother, or whoever it may be. (5d—e)

Socrates is quick to point out that this is not what he had in mind

> Remember, then, that this is not what I asked of you, to teach

76

me one or two of the many holy things, but that form (*eidos*) itself, by which all the holy things are holy. . . . Teach me what this form (*idea*), in order that, looking to it and using it as a standard, I may say that whatever you or anyone else does that resembles it is holy, and that what does not resemble it is not holy. (6d—e)

Euthyphro responds with the claim that piety is what is pleasing to the gods (6e—7a). Socrates confronts Euthyphro with the problem that the gods (at least in Euthyphro's view, if not in Socrates') might disagree about what is pleasing, he then prompts Euthyphro to modify his definition to state that what pleases *all* the gods is holy, and what displeases them all is unholy (9d). This definition, however, proves no more satisfactory than the previous one; for Socrates shows through an intricate argument that "being loved by all the gods" names at most an attribute of holiness, but does not state its essential nature (10e—11b).

At this point in the dialogue, Euthyphro is perplexed

Socrates, I don't know how to tell you what I think. Whatever we put forth always goes around us in circles somehow and isn't willing to stay where we put it. (11b)

Rather than let the conversation end there, Socrates (after a comparison of himself to the legendary sculptor Daedalus, whose statues were so lifelike they ran off) offers Euthyphro some genuine help. Piety, he suggests, is a part of justice (12d); Euthyphro says it is that part which has to do with service to the gods (12e). Socrates approves of Euthyphro's suggestion, but asks him to explain what "service" is. Euthyphro makes several attempts to define service, all of which fail and in his last effort, he reverts to the earlier, discredited view that piety is what pleases all the gods. When Socrates points out to him that he has once again gone around in a circle, Euthyphro makes his escape, saying "On another occasion, then, Socrates, for I am in a hurry, and it is time for me to leave" (15e). The *Euthyphro*, like other early dialogues, ends in failure.

The quest of the dialogue fails because Euthyphro is unable to provide a definition of the sort Socrates is looking for. What sort of definition is it Socrates seeks? A passage from another early dialogue, the *Meno*, may help to make this clear. When Meno fails to define virtue, in a way similar to Euthyphro's failure to define piety, Socrates says

> If I were to ask you what was the nature of the bee, and you said that there were many different kinds of bee, what would you say if I asked, "Is it in virtue of being bees that you say they are many and various and different from one another? Don't they differ not in this respect, but in beauty or size or something of the sort?" ... Then do likewise concerning the virtues; even if they are many and various, all of them have one and the same form (*eidos*) because of which they are all virtues. (72b—c)

Socrates is looking for the essential nature of virtue, the character which all virtuous actions have in common. As Meno has difficulty understanding Socrates' request, Socrates goes on to give the further examples of health, size and strength. A strong child would be unable to do many of the feats of strength of a strong adult, nonetheless, there is a definition common to both cases of strength. The nature of strength is the same in both.

According to Aristotle (*Metaphysics* I.6, 987b1—4), Socrates was the first person to seek definitions of this sort. The nature of his inquiry explains his profession of ignorance. When Socrates claims not to know what virtue is, or what some particular virtue, such as piety or justice is, his interlocutors are often surprised or incredulous. This is because they assume that what Socrates is looking for is a set of examples: a list of virtuous actions and character traits. Socrates, however, is as familiar as the next person with common examples of the virtues; what he lacks is a definition of virtue, or of the particular virtue in question, that fits every instance and explains its essential nature.

Why does Socrates seek such a definition? Why isn't he happy with examples? One reason is that these examples are drawn from Greek common opinion. They may include actions which are not really virtuous. For instance, in the *Republic* Polemarchus claims that justice is the ability to help one's friends and harm one's enemies. This is certainly a widely accepted Greek view but Socrates argues that it is not the function of a virtuous person to harm anyone at all. The argument shows the failings of the traditional view but without an account of the nature of virtue, how can anyone know for certain whether a particular action is virtuous or not?

What Socrates is searching for, as he says in the *Euthyphro* (6e), is something he can use as a standard against which alleged instances of the concept in question can be measured, to determine whether they are really cases of it or not. This standard he calls an *eidos* (*Euthyphro* 6d, cf. *Meno* 72c) and an *idea* (*Euthyphro* 6e), a "form." Scholars have debated whether these early uses of these terms show that Socrates originated the famous "theory of forms," which Plato develops in the middle dialogues, and which we shall consider when we come to the *Republic* in Chapter 3 but these texts make it clear that Socrates is seeking the essential nature of piety. He is not necessarily looking for a dictionary definition, which explains the meaning of the term or the ordinary Greek usage of it. Rather, he is looking for something comparable to the chemical formula for water, H_2O. When chemists discovered that water was composed of two molecules of hydrogen and one of oxygen, they did not discover the *meaning* of "water", instead, they discovered the *nature* of water. Socrates is searching for something similar in the case of piety and the other virtues.

Socrates wants to discover the essential nature of virtue so that he may be able to identify correctly alleged cases of it, and so that he may be able to know what additional properties a virtuous action or person may have. He wants a definition that will give him *episteme*, or scientific knowledge, of virtue.

Plato, reflecting on the nature of the knowledge that Socrates sought and the method of *elenchus* by which he sought it, saw a parallel with mathematics. He develops this parallel in the *Meno* and in several dialogues of his middle and late periods, including the *Republic*. Mathematics, and in particular geometry, was for the ancient Greeks the paradigm case of a science. Geometry begins with certain statements which are taken to be true: definitions, axioms and postulates. From these it constructs theorems. Socrates, thought Plato, hoped to find definitions of ethical terms that enable him to construct theorems in moral philosophy parallel to those in geometry; that is why he insisted on beginning with definitions. The assertions elicited from his interlocutors in the *elenchus* function as do the axioms and postulates of geometry. Unfortunately, when combined with the proposed definitions, they do not produce theorems, but inconsistencies. Still, Socrates had every right to hope that, if the correct definition were found, theorems would result.

Given the parallel between geometry and the method of the *elenchus*, the failure of this method to produce results comparable to those of mathematics must have been troubling to Plato. In the *Republic*, as we shall see in the next chapter, he largely abandons the method of *elenchus* after Book I. In the *Meno*, however, he attempts to construct a defense of the method that is based in part on the parallel with mathematics. This defense involves doctrines, such as the theory of recollection, that go beyond anything found in the earlier Socratic dialogues. Most scholars attribute these doctrines, and the positive view of the *elenchus* that they support, to Plato rather than to the historical Socrates. Though we cannot know for certain, as I said earlier, where Socrates ends and Plato begins, I think this scholarly consensus is likely to be right. Socrates described his mission in the *Apology* in negative terms, as revealing the ignorance of everyone, and he employed the method of *elenchus* to that end. This negative aim is most safely associated with the historical Socrates, whereas the more positive view of the *elenchus* described in the *Meno* is likely to be Plato's.

The new view of the *elenchus* begins to emerge at the point in the dialogue where Meno is reduced to perplexity. As Euthyphro had complained that Socrates had made his thoughts go around in circles, Meno complains that Socrates has numbed him in the manner of a sting ray; he likens Socrates to a magician or wizard, and advises him against traveling abroad (79e—80b). Socrates responds that he is "numb" himself, and that he infects others with his own perplexity, but offers to continue the investigation with Meno nonetheless. Meno then asks

> And how will you search, Socrates, for this when you don't know at all what it is? How will you set up as the object of your search something you don't know? Even if you happen to encounter it, how will you know that it is this thing that you do not know? (80d)

The question seems a fair one for a procedure such as the *elenchus*, which only provides a method for showing that a proposed definition is wrong, not that it is correct, Socrates, however, calls the question an "eristic argument," that is an argument used by someone who is only interested in winning a debate, not in discovering knowledge.

Socrates responds to Meno's challenge with the theory of recollection. He claims to have heard it from "men and women who understand the truths of religion ... priests and priestesses of the sort who make it their business to be able to account for the function they perform." (81a—b) It is likely that this is a veiled reference to members of the so-called "Pythagorean Brotherhood," disciples of the philosopher-guru Pythagoras. The doctrine of recollection contains Pythagorean teachings, and Plato encountered some members of this religious association when traveling in Sicily in 388 BC, shortly before the composition of the *Meno*.

These priests and priestesses say that

> since the soul is deathless and has been born many times, and has seen both the things here and all the things in Hades, there is nothing it has not learned. Thus it is no wonder if it is able to recollect, both in the case of virtue and in other matters, what it knew before. Since all nature is akin, and the soul has learned all things, nothing prevents it, when it has recollected even a single thing — what people call learning — from discovering everything else, if it is brave and doesn't grow weary of searching; for seeking and learning are in general recollection. (81c—d)

To illustrate this theory, Socrates examines one of Meno's slaves on a question of geometry: how to construct a square double the size of an original square. The slave-boy is initially confident, but after two failures is reduced to a state of perplexity like that of his master. Socrates uses the slave's state to show Meno that his own perplexity is not harmful

> SOCRATES: Do you recognize, then, Meno, where he is going in the process of recollecting? At the start he did not know what the line is that makes a side of an eight-foot square, nor does he know it yet, but he thought then that he knew, and answered bravely as if he knew, and didn't believe he was puzzled. But now he knows he is puzzled; and, as he doesn't

know, he doesn't think he knows.

MENO: True.

SOCRATES: Isn't he in a better state concerning the matter he doesn't know?

MENO: It seems so to me.

SOCRATES: Then in making him puzzled and in numbing him like the sting ray, have we harmed him at all?

MENO: It does not seem so to me.

SOCRATES: In fact we have done something helpful for his discovery of the truth. For now he will be happy to search for it, since he doesn't know it. (84a—b)

The Socrates of the *Apology* had recognized the negative effect of the *elenchus* on people, and had accepted it as a necessary side-effect of making them aware of their ignorance. This was apparently not good enough for Plato, he wanted to show that the *elenchus* was a necessary stage on the path to knowledge, so that anger directed at Socrates for leading people into it was misplaced.

Once the slave has been reduced to perplexity, Socrates guides him by a series of questions to the correct solution to the problem. At the end of the examination of the slave-boy, Socrates remarks to Meno that

Now these opinions are only recently stirred up in him, like a dream; but if someone should question him many times and in many ways about the same thing, you can be sure that finally he will know them as clearly as anyone. (85c—d)

The doctrine of recollection is supposed to explain how it is possible to come to know something: coming to know is bringing to consciousness knowledge which is already latent in the soul. There are many problems with the theory. Many readers object that Socrates' questions to the slave boy are so leading that they virtually provide him with the answer. It is not clear how the experience of the slave in reaching the right answer is psychologically different from his experience in reaching the wrong ones: if he recollected the former, did he recollect the latter as well? Furthermore, the doctrine of recollection may seem to be a rather extravagant theory. After all, it answers the question how one can acquire knowledge by building into the human mind before birth all the knowledge that might later be acquired. It seems to assume that the acquisition of new knowledge really is impossible, so it makes such acquisition unnecessary.

This is not the place to deal with these difficulties. At present, I want only to note that the theory provides a positive as well as a negative role for the Socratic *elenchus*. The slave, like the rest of us, has both true and false beliefs in his mind. The doctrine of recollection cannot tell us how to distinguish them, but this is precisely where the *elenchus* shows its value. The *elenchus* shows the false beliefs to be false, and Socrates suggests that it can turn the true beliefs into knowledge. He later says to Meno that the "true opinions" that exist in the soul "when aroused by questioning, become knowledge" (86a).

The doctrine of recollection suggests that the method of *elenchus*, like related methods in mathematics, can yield scientific knowledge. In the *Meno* Plato adds an explicit tool of mathematical reasoning to his arsenal: the method of hypothesis. When Meno insists that the question whether virtue can be taught be answered instead of the question what virtue is, Socrates says he can to so if allowed the use of an hypothesis. He explains that geometers, when asked about certain problems to which they do not have an answer, invoke a hypothesis which will enable them to solve the problem. That is, they assume the truth of some higher proposition, and show what the answer to the problem will be if this hypothesis is correct.

The hypothesis Socrates demands of Meno is that virtue is knowledge. Nothing except knowledge can be taught, according to Socrates' rather restrictive notion of teaching; so virtue will be teachable if and only if virtue is knowledge. When Meno accepts, Socrates announces that "next after this, as it seems, we must investigate whether virtue is knowledge or something other than knowledge" (87c). This shows Socrates' understanding of the device of hypothesis, for a hypothesis must be "discharged" — shown to be true — before the proof that follows from it can be known to be correct. It is also a deft move in the context of the dialogue, for it returns Meno to the question Socrates regards as primary, "What is virtue?", and slips in unobtrusively Socrates' own preferred answer. By showing that the question whether virtue can be taught can only be answered by a hypothesis about what virtue is, Socrates illustrates his point that we must determine the nature

83

of a thing before discussing its properties.

Socrates' use of the method of hypothesis is more than a dialectical trick, however, it is a valuable methodological tool, as the discussion shows. The *elenchus*, as we have seen, relies on the ability of Socrates' interlocutor to provide definitions. What happens when, as in this dialogue, the interlocutor runs out of definitions? In the typical early dialogue, the discussion ends. With the addition of the method of hypothesis to Socrates' dialectical arsenal, however, the dialogue can continue, even though neither Socrates nor the interlocutor knows the correct definition. For by raising the discussion to a higher level, one may be able to discover a plausible definition; or one can use as a hypothesis a possible definition in which one has no confidence, and simply explore the consequences of accepting it. Hypothesis gradually ceases to be an adjunct to the method of *elenchus*, and becomes itself the dominant method of the middle Platonic dialogues, including the *Republic*.

The "Socratic method," then, changes gradually in the course of the early dialogues. Though the search for definitions remains constant, the *elenchus* ceases to be merely a destructive tool and, backed by the theory of recollection and supplemented by the method of hypothesis, becomes a device for positive inquiry. Though the method of *elenchus* itself is eclipsed in the middle dialogues, the doctrine of recollection and the method of hypothesis remain important parts of Plato's philosophy.

The Socratic paradoxes

The claim that virtue is knowledge is one of a set of "paradoxes" for which Socrates is famous. Other statements in the set are: all of the virtues are one (so that, if a person has one virtue, he or she has them all); wrongdoing is (the result of) ignorance; and no one does wrong willingly. Because in the early dialogues Socrates never proposes his own solution to the questions he raises about virtue, he only brings up the paradoxes when examining the views of others. This is true also of the *Meno*, though here, perhaps because the dialogue is transitional between the early and middle dialogues, between Socrates' views and Plato's, two of the paradoxes come in for fairly detailed discussion. None the less, most scholars would identify these paradoxical statements as Socrates' own.

A "paradox" is literally a statement that runs counter to (*para*) common opinion (*doxa*) and these Socratic propositions are all paradoxes in the literal sense. They are also, as we should expect from Socrates, closely related to one another and to the other views we have attributed to him. Consider the claim that all of the virtues are one, and that possession of one guarantees possession of all. This claim is the focus of the *Protagoras*. In that dialogue, Protagoras defends the common-sense belief that one may be virtuous in one respect, and vicious in another: brave, for instance, but unjust or intemperate. Socrates argues for the unity of the virtues, which is not surprising if he believes that virtue is knowledge. For the kind of knowledge that is required for the possession of virtue, as Socrates argues in the *Laches* (198b ff.) is knowledge of good and evil; and if one knows what good and evil are in those situations that call forth courage, it is natural to think that one could transfer that knowledge to cases that demand justice or piety.

If the thesis of the unity of virtue is connected to the definition of virtue as knowledge, so is the thesis that wrongdoing is ignorance connected to the claim that no one does wrong willingly. Both claims are paradoxical, for common sense says that many people know what is right and do what is wrong. Socrates, however, would criticize the common view. He would say that those people who know merely that some action is wrong in a conventional sense (who know for instance that "stealing is wrong") but who are tempted to do the action because they think it may be to their advantage do not really know that the action is wrong. Socrates, it will be recalled, is an ethical egoist: he believes that wrong actions harm the soul of the agent. Thus, to know that an action is wrong in Socrates' sense of the term is to know that performing the action will damage one's soul. Since no one wishes to harm his or her soul, Socrates thinks that no one would willingly do something that had that effect. Thus, no one would willingly do wrong. Those people who do wrong, therefore, must be unaware of the harmful effects of their actions on themselves; they must be ignorant. Even the most vicious criminal, therefore, is seen by Socrates as a candidate for education and it should come as no surprise that Socrates thought the aim of punishment was the reform or improvement of the wrongdoer.

Socrates argues in the first part of the *Meno* (77b—78b) that no one desires evil. The argument closely resembles that I have just given: to desire evil is to desire to possess evil for oneself, with full awareness that it will make the possessor miserable and unhappy and since no one desires to be unhappy, no one desires evil. In the *Protagoras*, Socrates considers the objection that one may know what is about to do is evil and yet be led to do it by irrational desire: one may, to use the example most familiar to us, know that smoking cigarettes is bad for one's health and yet continue to smoke. He treats this as another case of ignorance: the person led on by pleasure in fact miscalculates the balance of pleasure and pain involved in doing wrong. If he were to calculate correctly, he would choose the right (that is the most pleasant) act. Thus moral weakness, knowing the better course and choosing the worse, is impossible.

Socrates' treatment of wrongdoing as ignorance, his denial of moral weakness, and his equation of virtue and knowledge are part and parcel of his intellectualistic approach to morality, which I have already mentioned. The key proposition in the set of Socratic paradoxes, the one from which the rest follow, is the definition of virtue as knowledge. Interestingly enough, Socrates rarely discusses this claim; this is at least in part because his method is to criticize other views, and not to put forward his own. I have noted above one place in the *Meno* (87c ff.) where Socrates puts forward the claim as a hypothesis. To establish the hypothesis, he presents the following argument: virtue is good. If there is some good other than knowledge, virtue may not be knowledge; but if knowledge "embraces" every good, virtue must be knowledge (87d). All goods, including virtue, are advantageous. Among the things which are advantageous are physical goods such as health, strength, good looks and wealth; and spiritual goods, such as "temperance, justice, courage, ease of learning, memory, nobility of character, and others" (88a). Both sets of goods, however, are sometimes disadvantageous, harmful; what makes them advantageous is right use. Right use is the result of the guidance of wisdom, which leads to happiness. Socrates concludes

> If then virtue is one of the things in the soul and if it is necessary for it to be beneficial, it must be wisdom, since all the things in the soul in themselves are neither beneficial nor harmful, but become beneficial or harmful with the addition of

wisdom or folly. By this argument if virtue is beneficial it must be a kind of wisdom. (88c—d)

Though this argument shows that knowledge is the only human attribute that is *always* advantageous, and thus that it is a necessary condition for virtue, it does not show that knowledge is sufficient for making one virtuous. In fact, the argument itself indicates that knowledge or wisdom is the right use of *other* attributes, such as temperance, justice and courage. It turns these attributes into genuine virtues by being "present with" them. Thus, the argument shows only part of what Socrates needs to establish to prove that virtue and knowledge are identical. Socrates, however, overlooks this flaw in the argument and he presents it again in very similar terms in the *Euthydemus* (278e—282a). In the *Protagoras* Socrates attempts to show that the other virtues are in fact identical to knowledge, and not just made good by knowledge but these arguments prove in the end unsuccessful.

Why does Socrates defend the view that virtue is knowledge? Part of the reason, at least, is that he has a peculiar picture of the soul. I use the word "picture" because I do not want to suggest that Socrates has an explicit "theory" of the nature of the soul. Rather, I think that his views about the soul are implicit in his thought, and that Socrates may not have been consciously aware of them. In practice, however, Socrates treats the soul as if it were equivalent to reason; every psychological trait he discusses he treats as a cognitive state. We saw above in our discussion of the *Apology* that Socrates analysed fear of death as a belief that death is evil. In the *Laches* also, at 198b ff., he treats fear in general as the expectation of future evil and courage as the knowledge of what is really fearful. We also saw above that in the *Protagoras* he describes the phenomenon of moral weakness as a case of miscalculation. The conflict between reason and desire, which Plato will come to see in the *Republic* as a dispute between rational and irrational parts of the soul, Socrates sees as a conflict within reason itself, a conflict among various cognitive states, such as knowledge and belief. If the contents of the soul are limited to such states as knowledge and belief, it is natural to identify virtue, the best moral quality in the soul, with knowledge, the best cognitive state. (Before Plato developed the tripartite view of the soul in the *Republic* he portrayed the conflict between reason and appetite at *Phaedo*

64c ff. as a conflict between soul and body. This view represents, I think, an intermediate position between the Socratic view that appetites and emotions are really cognitive states and the view of the *Republic*, but note in any case that it identifies the soul with reason.)

Whatever the reasoning or intuition behind Socrates' identification of virtue with knowledge, Plato apparently came to have doubts about it. These doubts emerge at the end of the *Meno*, immediately after the argument discussed above in favor of the claim that virtue is knowledge. If virtue is knowledge, Socrates says, there must be teachers of it (89d). He then goes on to consider the claims of several groups who claim to be able to teach virtue. With Anytus, a friend of Meno and one of Socrates' accusers, he discusses the claims of the Sophists to teach virtue. Anytus rejects the Sophists with horror, but says (as did Meletus in the *Apology*) that the good citizens of Athens can teach virtue (92e). Socrates points out in reply that the leading Athenian statesmen, such as Themistocles, Aristides, Pericles and Thucydides (not the historian) failed to transmit their own virtue to their children. Anytus, misunderstanding Socrates' point as a criticism of these political leaders, leaves with a warning to Socrates that he had better be careful about what he says (94e).

Socrates' point, however, is not that these Athenian leaders were bad men, but that they seemed unable to teach others to be virtuous. Meno subsequently comes to agree with Socrates that there are no teachers of virtue, and goes on to state, "I wonder, in fact, Socrates, whether there are any good men at all, or what the process of generation is of those who do come to be" (96d). It is easy to underestimate the seriousness of this problem. After all, we know today of many areas of knowledge that had no teachers in Socrates' time, such as calculus and nuclear physics. What does the absence of teachers show? In fact, though, the two situations are not parallel. In ancient Athens there were no professors of calculus, but there were also no people who were proficient in the subject. There were, however, generally accepted examples of virtue. How could this be, if virtue were knowledge?

The argument that virtue cannot be knowledge because there are no teachers of it is thus a serious criticism of the Socratic claim that virtue is knowledge. Moreover, the problem Socrates raises in the *Meno* for his own view must have been a real difficulty for Plato himself. Throughout the dialogues, after all, Plato holds Socrates up as an outstanding example of virtue, but Socrates disclaimed all knowledge of these matters. How could Socrates be virtuous if virtue were knowledge and Socrates were ignorant?

The solution that Socrates proposes at the end of the *Meno* is actually, I think, Plato's response to this Socratic paradox. As he had done with the doctrine of recollection, Plato here attempts to go beyond a limitation in the Socratic view and, in fact, the two doctrines are related. Plato has Socrates introduce a state intermediate between knowledge and ignorance: the state of opinion (*doxa*). Opinion, when it is correct, is as good a guide to conduct as knowledge (97b—c); the only problem with it is that it will not remain with the individual unless it is "tied down" or converted to knowledge, by "reasoning out the explanation" (98a), which is accomplished by recollection. Those people, such as Themistocles, Pericles, and, perhaps, Socrates himself, who were virtuous without knowledge owe their right opinion to a kind of divine inspiration

> If we throughout this conversation have searched and spoken well, virtue will be neither natural nor taught, but it comes by divine providence without thought to whomever it comes, unless someone should be the sort of statesman who can make another statesman. If there were someone of this sort, someone might say of him that he was among the living just about what Homer said Teiresias was among the dead, saying of him that he alone among those in Hades was wise, but the rest were flitting shades. Such a person would be here, with respect to virtue, the same: a real thing among shadows.
> (99e—100a)

The statesman who could produce another like himself is, of course, the philosopher-king of the *Republic*, and it is fitting that the *Meno* should conclude with an anticipation of that dialogue, to which we shall turn in the next chapter. Though the ostensible conclusion of the *Meno*, the positive result I hinted at when discussing the slave-boy episode, is that virtue is right opinion, the reference to the statesman with knowledge leaves open the possibility of a partial vindication of the Socratic paradox. The *Republic* exploits the distinction between opinion and knowledge, and the corresponding distinction between ordinary and philosophical virtue, suggested by this passage.

In this chapter we have described the life and views of Socrates, as Plato represented them in several early dialogues. In the *Apology* we saw a Socrates of absolute integrity and courage, willing to face death before giving up his philosophical vocation. In the *Crito* we discerned some of the philosophical principles that lay behind this Socratic determination, including his identification of the good life with the life of virtue. In the *Euthyphro*, *Meno* and other dialogues, we saw the Socratic method of *elenchus* put to work on the question of the nature of virtue, and augmented by the doctrine of recollection. We saw some indication of how Socrates himself would have answered the question, "What is virtue?" and, finally, we saw Plato's modification of the Socratic paradox that virtue is knowledge. Socrates, in his philosophical principles and in his personal conduct, constituted a stark challenge to the adequacy of the traditional views about the virtues and the good life we discussed in Chapter 1. It was Plato's task in the *Republic* to complete the discussion of that Socratic challenge and to formulate his own response to the tradition.

3

PLATO'S MORAL PHILOSOPHY: THE *REPUBLIC*

Plato's moral philosophy developed out of, and in response to, that of Socrates. Socrates had raised the central issues in Greek ethics by his investigation of the concept of virtue; he had developed the method of *elenchus* to aid him in his investigations; and he had formulated his own views about the questions his investigations raised. Socrates had held that the good life was the life of virtue, that virtue was knowledge of what was good for the moral agent, and that wrongdoing was caused by ignorance of the agent's own good. He had denied the possibility of moral weakness, asserting that anyone who knew what was good would surely do it. These Socratic views were paradoxical but Plato was greatly influenced by them. He saw that Socrates' moral philosophy was an extension of his character and, as he admired Socrates' character, he was attracted to his philosophy.

Gradually, however, Plato developed his own views on the topics Socrates had discussed. In the preceding chapter I suggested that the doctrine of recollection and the view that virtue could be right opinion as well as knowledge were Platonic answers to difficulties in Socrates' philosophy. It is, of course, impossible to determine precisely where Socrates leaves off and Plato begins in the dialogues but most scholars would agree that the Socrates of the *Republic* is the spokesman for Plato's ethics rather than his own. Plato probably thought it fair to put his own views in the mouth of Socrates because those views were heavily indebted to those of his master but the Socrates of the *Republic* does not express the same views as the Socrates of the early dialogues.

The *Republic* is one of the greatest works of philosophy ever written. Though it does not contain Plato's last word on many topics, it is the one dialogue where he brings together his views on ethics, politics, metaphysics, epistemology, psychology and aesthetics. Just to synthesize views on so many topics is an accomplishment few philosophers have been able to achieve and Plato's views in each of these areas are, in addition, of great intrinsic interest. Further, the philosophy is set forth in the *Republic* with great artistic mastery: Plato adds literary genius to the philosophical power of his ideas, with the result that the work makes a vivid, and sometimes overwhelming, impression on the reader. This impression is often produced despite the reader's strong aversion to many of Plato's ideas; for Plato's philosophy is in many ways as radical as Socrates', and features such unpalatable proposals as genetic engineering, censorship and the elimination of the family and private property, at least among the ruling class of his ideal state.

Of Plato's dialogues only the *Laws*, his final work, is longer than the *Republic*. The *Republic* was divided into ten books. In general, the divisions do not mark changes in philosophical form or content but many scholars believe that Book I was originally written as a separate, early dialogue, to which the body of the work was later grafted. Certainly Book I shows us the Socrates of the early dialogues: critical, questioning, with no theory of his own to put forth but interested in the pursuit of one virtue, justice. Book I functions in the complete work as a prelude (as Socrates calls it at 357a), the main argument takes place in the later books.

Book I: what is justice?

The *Republic* is set in the Piraeus, the port city of Athens, where Socrates has gone to see a festival. He is gently coerced by Polemarchus into coming to the house of his father, Cephalus, where he turns the holiday gathering into an arena for philosophical discussion. He begins by asking Cephalus what it is like to be old, and what is the greatest value of wealth (virtually the only topics on which Socrates could have expected to learn much from him). When Cephalus claims that the value of wealth is that it relieves one's anxiety about whether one has made the proper sacrifices or unintentionally cheated someone, Socrates reformulates his remarks as a definition of justice: justice consists in telling the truth and paying one's debts. Socrates then rejects this definition on the grounds that it does not hold in all cases: it would be wrong to pay one's debt to a madman who asked for the return of dangerous weapons.

Socrates' critique of Cephalus is unfair in two ways. Cephalus had proposed no definition of justice, and Socrates had not asked him for one; it was Socrates who shifted the discussion from the value of wealth to the nature of justice. Second, it is not obvious that a definition of justice has to be the absolutely exceptionless rule that Socrates demands. Cephalus's remark may state a useful rule of thumb about just action, or it could form part of a general theory into which exceptions of the sort Socrates mentions are built in. There might be a hierarchy of principles of justice, of which Cephalus has mentioned only one. There is, however, a serious objection to trying to define justice by a list of just actions: the list would not explain what all just actions had in common; it would not explain the nature or essence of justice, which (as we saw in Chapter 2) is what Socrates wants.

At this point Cephalus leaves to attend to some sacrifices, bequeathing his place in the argument to Polemarchus, his son and "heir." Polemarchus quotes the poet Simonides, who says that justice consists in "giving to each what is due" (331e). As Polemarchus interprets this remark, this means helping one's friends and harming one's enemies. Socrates demolishes this claim with a series of arguments. First, he asks what sort of an art (*techne*) justice is, and when it is useful. The doctor is best able to help friends and harm enemies in illness, the navigator at sea, and the expert in general in all cases involving expert knowledge. The just person turns out according to Polemarchus to be expert only at keeping money safe when it is not in use, and, since Socrates argues that the person best able to do something is also most gifted at doing its opposite, the just person turns out to be a kind of thief (334a—b). Second, Socrates notes that one may be mistaken about who one's friends are and, when Polemarchus revises his account so that justice is helping our friends who are good people and harming our enemies who are bad, Socrates argues that it is not the function of justice to harm anyone at all. Justice improves people; injustice makes them worse (335).

These arguments differ in quality. The first argument seems to show only that it is wrong to treat justice as a *techne* at all since it is not on a par with medicine or navigation (though Socrates does not draw this inference). The second is a good argument against Polemarchus, but yields no new knowledge of justice. The third, however, indicates clearly the degree to which the Socratic conception of justice departs from that common among the Greeks (Meno expressed a similar view of justice in his first definition of virtue). Socrates' claim does not imply that one should never punish another, or even put another to death, for Socrates distinguished between being put to death and being harmed in the *Apology*. It does require, however, that the just person never acts so as to make another a worse person and by advocating this position, Socrates takes justice out of the familiar sphere of Greek partisan politics, the realm of "us" versus "them," and gives it a more universal scope.

None of the arguments, interestingly enough, attacks the statement of Simonides, though Socrates acts as if they did (335e): they attack Polemarchus' interpretation of that statement. The claim that justice is giving each person his due is a counterpart of the definition of justice Plato reaches in Book IV, that justice is each person's doing his proper task. It encapsulates an important feature of justice, that justice involves fairness in the distribution of goods, just as Plato's definition stresses fairness in the division of labor.

With the defeat of Polemarchus, Thrasymachus bursts into the conversation. The historical Thrasymachus was a Sophist. As Plato portrays him, he lacks the urbanity and grace of such leaders of the Sophistic movement as Protagoras and Gorgias, and his view of justice is a cynical, selfish one. He begins by castigating Socrates for refusing to give his own answer to the question, thus showing awareness of and contempt for Socrates' method of argument throughout Book I. Socrates says he has no account of justice to offer, especially since Thrasymachus has forbidden him to say that justice is "the obligatory or the beneficial or the useful or the profitable or the advantageous" (336c—d). Thrasymachus treats Socrates' refusal as a dialectical trick, but is none the less cajoled into giving his own account of justice. Justice, says Thrasymachus, is "the advantage of the stronger" (338c). As he goes on to explain

Each form of government establishes laws with a view toward its own advantage: democracy, democratic laws, tyranny, tyrannical laws, and the others likewise; and when the laws have been established it declares that what is advantageous for the rulers is "just" for the ruled; and they punish one who violates this law as a transgressor and unjust. It is this, then, my friend, that I say is just, the same in all cities, the advantage of the established government; and this is strong, I suppose, so that it follows logically that justice is everywhere the same, the advantage of the stronger. (338e—339a)

Thrasymachus' definition of justice cuts it off altogether from the moral traditions of Greek civilization and identifies it entirely with actual legislation, relativizing it thereby to the government of particular states. (This is the sort of thing that gave the Sophists a bad name.) When Socrates objects that rulers make mistakes and enact laws that are not to their advantage, Thrasymachus responds that the ruler in the precise sense of the term is infallible. Socrates then argues that the other arts look out for the advantage of their subject, not of the artist: the doctor cares for the patient, the horse-trainer, the horse. So the ruling art also must look after its subject, not after the welfare of the ruler.

At this point (343a) Thrasymachus takes a new tack. Socrates doesn't realize, he says, that shepherds care for their sheep in order to profit from their slaughter. He redefines justice as the advantage of another, and injustice as one's own advantage. Injustice, he argues, is always more profitable than justice; the unjust individual always gets the better of the just, and this is especially clear in the case of the tyrant, who can commit crimes with impunity. Thrasymachus' new account is literally inconsistent with his earlier one. Previously he had defined justice as the advantage of the rulers, now, in claiming that injustice is superior to justice, he is thinking of injustice as action in one's own interest. Yet, according to his first definition, when rulers act in their own interest their acts are just, so even the crimes of the tyrant should be just acts on Thrasymachus' first definition. We can harmonize the two accounts by saying that justice is the self-interest of the rulers and injustice the self-interest of the ruled but Thrasymachus is not clear enough about his own thought to do that.

Like his first definition, Thrasymachus' new theory would have profoundly disturbed a traditional Greek audience, for it rejects moral restrictions wholesale in favor of naked advantage. By using the analogy of a shepherd and his sheep, which had since Homeric times been used to describe the relation between a king and his people, Thrasymachus suggests that all government is immoral. His position also disturbs Socrates, for whom virtue and true self-interest must coincide. Again, he directs several arguments against Thrasymachus' position. First, he argues that the shepherd's art, like that of the doctor or the sea-captain, must be distinguished from the art of money-making. Not as a shepherd, but only as a businessman, does the keeper of sheep seek to earn a profit. Likewise with government: good people do not wish to rule, for governing requires looking after the interests of others rather than their own, which is why they demand compensation.

Next, Socrates argues that the just person is wise, and the unjust person ignorant. The wise practitioner of any art tries to outdo the ignorant person, but not to do better than another person with knowledge. So the just person tries to outdo the unjust, but not another just individual. The unjust person, however, like one ignorant of an art, tries to outdo everyone. Third, Socrates argues that justice, not injustice, is a source of strength: injustice produces hatred and division among people and makes them incapable of acting together. There must be honor even among thieves if they are to succeed at their enterprise.

Finally, Socrates argues that the human soul has a function, just as do horses, eyes and pruning knives. With every function there is a corresponding excellence or virtue, which enables it to perform its function well. The function of the soul is to live and the virtue of the soul, which enables it to live well, is justice. Therefore the just soul lives well, prosperously and happily; the unjust soul, badly and miserably. So, Socrates concludes (354a), injustice does not pay better than justice.

There has been much disagreement over the quality of these arguments. The last argument is an anticipation of an important argument in Aristotle's *Nicomachean Ethics* I.7, which we shall examine in the next chapter: as it stands, however, it is too terse to be convincing. In any case, the arguments Socrates propounds satisfy none of the interlocutors. Thrasymachus states that he is unconvinced at 350d—e, and after this participates only in a perfunctory way in the conversation. Glaucon suggests at the beginning of Book II (357a—b) that Socrates has produced only apparent and not real conviction. Even Socrates is dissatisfied: as he states at the end of Book I

before we found what we were looking for at the start, what

justice is, we left that question and set off eagerly on the inquiry into whether it is evil and ignorance or wisdom and virtue, and when we encountered the statement that injustice is more profitable than justice, we did not refrain from moving from that question to this, so that for me no knowledge has come from the discussion. For since I do not know what justice is, I can scarcely know whether it happens to be virtue or not, and whether the person who has it is either happy or not. (354b)

Clearly, a new beginning is required, and that is provided by two other interlocutors in the dialogue, Glaucon and Adeimantus, who have so far been nearly silent.

The challenge of Glaucon and Adeimantus

Plato was apparently as dissatisfied as Socrates with the outcome of the first book of the *Republic*. In Books II–X the format of the dialogue changes radically, as does the nature of Socrates' participation. Whereas the first book had been a dialogue of refutation, in which Socrates attacked the views of others but put forth no position of his own (as Thrasymachus had predicted he would at 337a), Books II–X are constructive rather than elenctic: they articulate and defend an elaborate theory of justice and the related virtues in the state and in the individual. Moreover, Plato puts this theory into the mouth of Socrates; though few people think the theory is anything other than Plato's own, Plato casts Socrates as its expositor. Thus, the Socrates of *Republic* II–X is considerably different from the Socrates of Book I. As Socrates changes, so does the mode of argumentation. The format of question and answer, which was a mark of the *elenchus*, is retained, but now it is primarily Socrates' interlocutors who raise questions for Socrates' view and these questions do not lead to the refutation of this view, but enable Socrates to expound and clarify it further. It is likely that these changes reflect Plato's dissatisfaction with the limitations of the *elenchus* as a vehicle for constructive thought but they also reflect the fact that Plato has developed an answer to the question of justice that he wants to put forward.

Glaucon and Adeimantus, who reopen the discussion by reformulating Thrasymachus' view of justice, are Plato's half-brothers. Glaucon begins his challenge by asking Socrates whether he wants his listeners to be really or only apparently convinced by his argument. Socrates, of course, wants to produce genuine conviction but it is an oft-mentioned fault of his method of *elenchus* that it fails to do this. Glaucon divides "goods" into three types: those we desire for themselves (harmless pleasures such as reading an entertaining novel), those we desire for their consequences (such as visits to the dentist), and those we desire both for themselves and for their consequences (among which he lists wisdom, sight and health). In which class does justice belong? Socrates says in the best class, that of things desirable in themselves and for their consequences. Justice, according to him, is like health (a comparison he makes more of in Book IV). Glaucon replies that the normal view is that justice is "in the painful class, which ought to be pursued for the sake of rewards and reputation, but which in itself ought to be fled from as difficult" (358a).

The common view of the origin of justice, according to Glaucon, is that it is agreed to as a compromise between the greatest natural good, which is to inflict injustice on others, and the greatest natural evil, which is to suffer injustice oneself. As the disadvantages of suffering at the hands of others are greater than the advantages of inflicting suffering on them, people "agree with one another neither to do nor suffer wrong. And thence they begin to establish laws and agreements among themselves, and they call the injunction of the law lawful and just" (359a). Despite this agreement, anyone would commit injustice if he could do so with impunity: Glaucon illustrates this point by the story of the ring of Gyges (359d—360b). Discovering a ring that made him invisible, Gyges used it to seduce the queen and kill the king of Lydia, and to seize the throne himself. So would anyone else, Glaucon urges.

Glaucon completes his case against justice by comparing two hypothetical people: a just man with a reputation for injustice, and an unjust man with a reputation for justice. The unjust man acquires all the social goods that accrue to one with a reputation for justice: wealth, power and status. The just man, because of his reputation for injustice

> will be whipped, racked and bound; his eyes will be burned out, and finally, when he has suffered every evil, he will be crucified, and will recognize that one ought to wish not to be but to seem just. (361e—362a)

Glaucon's challenge to Socrates is to show that this man is happier than his unjust rival.

Glaucon's challenge to Socrates is a philosophical one: it contains a theoretical account of the nature of justice and uses both a concrete example and abstract types to make a general point about justice and injustice. The theory of justice is rooted in the views of the Sophists, discussed in Chapter 2, so also is the question whether the just or unjust individual is happier. Adeimantus adds to this a challenge based on Greek literature. Quoting Homer, Hesiod and other Greek poets, he claims that justice is always praised for its consequences, not for itself; that virtue is difficult, whereas vice is easy, and that the gods can be bribed to overlook past wrongs. The consequence of this is that one should attempt to acquire the reputation of being just while being secretly unjust, and then propitiate the gods with sacrifices to avoid punishment. Thus, both traditional literature and current philosophical theory agree about the nature and value of justice; the Platonic Socrates is at odds with both.

Plato has Socrates respond to this challenge in two ways. First, he presents an alternative account to the theory of justice contained in Glaucon's attack. This account takes up the bulk of Books II—IX, and exhibits the nature of justice and injustice, as Plato understands them, in the state and in the individual. Second, he offers a critique of traditional Greek education and the poets who were largely responsible for it, and proposes what he takes to be a superior educational system to replace it. This critique occurs in Books II—III, but Plato returns to the question of poetry again in Book X. Though the critique of poetry and traditional education occurs in the midst of Plato's positive account of justice, I shall deal with the two separately. I shall begin with Plato's theory of justice.

The just state

Neither Glaucon nor Adeimantus believe in the truth of the theory of justice they have put forth as a challenge to Socrates; as Adeimantus says at 367a—b, they have presented the theory because they want Socrates to refute it. It is perhaps no surprise, then, that the two interlocutors do not attempt to defend their account of justice in opposition to Socrates' view. In fact, the two become very retiring after their brief appearance at center stage; they only raise occasional questions in the course of Socrates' exposition of his own (actually Plato's) view. Plato retains the dialogue form in what follows, but the remainder of the *Republic* is in fact more of a systematic exposition of Platonic philosophy than an instance of intellectual give-and-take.

Socrates proposes to discover the nature of justice by describing the origins of a *polis*, a city-state. He claims that it will be easier to discern justice in a large institution like a city than in an individual (368e—369a), but this seems to be merely a pretext to enable Socrates to discuss both personal and civil justice, which would in any case be necessary for any complete account of the virtue. Though Socrates will eventually (IV, 443c—d) claim that justice is really something internal to the individual rather than social, both common sense and the theory of Glaucon and Adeimantus assume that justice is primarily a civil concern, so it is appropriate for Socrates to begin with the *polis*.

Socrates begins his account of justice by explaining the origin of the city

> "The city comes to be, then," said I, "as I think, since each of us happens to be not self-sufficient, but in need of many things; or do you think the founding of the city has any other origin?"
> (369b)

Adeimantus says he does not: apparently he has forgotten Glaucon's rival account of the origin of justice. According to Glaucon, justice was a convention established by people to avoid being victims of harm and it would certainly be possible to argue that society originates in the same way (indeed, later social theorists derived justice from such a "social contract"). The two accounts are quite different: on Socrates' view civil society is based on human nature, for our basic needs and our lack of self-sufficiency are aspects of our natural condition and, as we shall see, the resulting concept of justice is tied to nature in the same way; however on the "social contract" account society and justice are artificial, conventional. Socrates' shifting of the context of discussion from the conventional theory of Glaucon to an account based on human nature is a move of the utmost importance for the ensuing discussion as it makes it much easier for Socrates to answer Glaucon's challenge.

The basic human needs are for food, clothing and shelter; people form communities to satisfy these needs better than they could individually. Thus, the *polis* in its earliest stage of development requires a farmer, a builder, a weaver, a shoemaker and one or two other craftsmen (369d). Because people differ in their natural aptitudes, they will be suited for different jobs and efficiency is increased if each person does the job he is best suited for, rather than shifting from job to job. This principle of the division of labor seems innocuous when first introduced (370c), but it soon will have the most far-reaching effects on the constitution of the state. Plato has Socrates add a number of other occupations, such as smiths, merchants and manual laborers, to the city, but at that point he says the state is complete (371e). When Socrates asks where justice and injustice are to be found in the state, Adeimantus suggests that it is in the mutual dependence of the citizens on each other. (372a) As Socrates will eventually define justice in terms of each person's doing his or her own job, this is a shrewd guess on Adeimantus' part.

Socrates describes the life of the inhabitants of this state in idyllic terms (372a–c), but Glaucon objects that the vegetarian fare on which they live is fit for a "city of pigs!" (372d). He demands modern comforts, and Socrates suggests that it is here that we may locate the origin of justice and injustice

"Well, then," I said, "I understand. We must examine, it seems, not just how a city comes into being, but also how a luxurious city does. Perhaps that is not a bad plan, for in examining such a city perhaps we shall discover how justice and injustice grow up in cities. The true city seems to me to be the one we have described: it is like a healthy man. But, if you wish, we shall also investigate an inflamed city; nothing prevents us. These arrangements and this lifestyle won't satisfy some people, it seems: but couches and tables will have to be added, and other equipment, and rich food and perfumes and incense and courtesans and cakes, and each of these in great variety. And we must no longer include just the necessities we spoke of at first, houses and cloaks and sandals, but painting and embroidery must be introduced, and gold and ivory and everything of that sort must be obtained." (372e—373a)

The distinction between the first state and this new one is based on the distinction between necessary and unnecessary goods. Socrates describes the first city as "the true city . . . like a healthy man," because its citizens are content with a fair exchange of necessities. Such a standard of living could not fail to disappoint a young man like Glaucon, raised among the luxuries of Athens. What Socrates sees as healthy, Glaucon sees as subhuman, an existence suited to pigs. The disagreement between them indicates a good deal about Plato's attitude toward the luxuries Glaucon demands. Plato's disapproval of these luxuries marks him as an ascetic, a trait we shall see emerge again in later portions of the *Republic*. Despite his asceticism, however, Plato seems to be aware that such cravings for luxury will inevitably arise at some point in the development of the city, and that the original state he has described has no resources for containing them. As we shall see, his own strategy is to introduce these goods into the state and then to create a ruling class to curtail the appetite of the citizenry for them: a class of "physicians" (as he refers to them more than once) for souls diseased by the love of luxury.

The evils produced by the love of luxury are quickly made manifest: there will be new occupations, including herdsmen to care for livestock if meat is to be eaten (373c). This creates a need for more land, and that leads to war (373e). Because military service is a profession, and because the principle of the division of labor introduced above requires that each person work at only one profession, the necessity of fighting wars requires the establishment of a class of professional soldiers. Members of this class are chosen on the basis of certain characteristics: they must be physically swift and strong, high-spirited and courageous, friendly to their fellow citizens but hostile to the city's enemies. Socrates compares them rather unflatteringly with watchdogs, and labels them "guardians" (375). At this point in the dialogue a digression on the early education of the guardians takes place (376c—412a, discussed below). At the end of this digression Socrates divides his guardian class into two classes: the eldest and best, those who care most for the city and identify their own interest with the city's, are to be the rulers (412c—e) while the rest are to be called "auxiliaries."

With this division of the guardian class the city assumes its final form. It is made up of three classes

1 the ruling class of "guardians"
2 the military class of "auxiliaries," and
3 the economic class (the farmers and craftsmen who had composed all of the first stage in the city's development)

Plato has Socrates express their relationship in a famous "myth" to be taught to the members of the community: their memories of their upbringing are only a dream and in reality they were fashioned in the depths of the earth, so they must think of the land they inhabit as their mother. He offers this story to the citizens of the state

"All of you in the city are brothers," we shall say to them in this myth; "but when the god made you he mixed gold in those of you who are capable of ruling, who are therefore the most highly honored; in the auxiliaries he mixed silver, and in the farmers and other craftsmen iron and bronze." (415a)

The greatest danger to the state is the mixture of these "metals," and specifically the ascent to the ruling class of someone fitted by nature to be only an auxiliary or a member of the economic class; this is what the guardians are primarily to guard against.

Though this myth is literally false, it does contain a symbolic representation of the basic feature's of Plato's ideal city: a class system based on differences in native ability, a common fellowship that unites all the classes despite the distinction among classes, and a charge to the rulers to preserve both the class system and the unity that underlies it. Plato has often been criticized for the class structure of his society, which is certainly anti-democratic, but it is necessary for the critic to remember that he insists both on the class system *and* the unity of the classes into a single city. Class systems in which the rulers exploit the lower classes (systems of the sort Thrasymachus extolled in Book I) fail to meet Plato's unity requirement, and criticism of them (which Plato would agree with) does not entail criticism of Plato's city.

The function of the guardians, as Plato describes it, is to see that citizens of the state will be friends and unwilling to harm the state, and that external enemies will be unable to (414b). To do this they must preserve both the class system, by regulating reproduction and education, and the unity of the state. The great threat to unity that Plato sees is that the auxiliary class will turn on the economic class, that they will become "like wolves instead of dogs." (416a) He believes that the education they receive will be the primary deterrent to this, but he also attempts to prevent the guardians from exploiting the economic class by preventing the guardians from owning private property

> First, none of them shall possess any private property that is not absolutely necessary. Next, no one may have a dwelling or storehouse of the sort that anyone who wishes may not enter. . . . They shall live in common, going to meals together as if on campaign. We shall tell them that they always have divine gold and silver in their souls, a gift of the gods, and they do not need the human kind in addition. (416d—e)

When Adeimantus objects that the guardians will not be happy under these conditions, Socrates replies that, though it would not be surprising if they *were* happy, his objective was to make the state as a whole happy, not one class within it, and that these measures are necessary for the welfare of the entire state (420b—421c).

After making some final provisions to secure the unity of the state, Socrates asks where justice is to be found in it. In addition to justice, the state should possess the virtues of wisdom, courage and temperance. The state turns out to be wise because of the wisdom of the guardian class, the smallest element in the state (428c—429a). It is brave because the auxiliaries have been trained to preserve, in the face of both fear and desire, true beliefs about what is dangerous (429b—430b). It is temperate because "the desires of the inferior majority are controlled by the desires and wisdom of the superior few" (431c—d), and because the three classes in the state are in harmonious agreement about which class is to rule (431e—432a). Temperance, unlike wisdom and courage, resides in the whole city and not just in a single class. The same is true of justice, which is "discovered" after an elaborate bit of comedy in which Socrates pretends to "beat the bushes" after an elusive quarry, only to discover that it was right before them all the time (432d). Justice, says Socrates, consists in "tending to one's own affairs and not those of others" (433a); that is, it results from the principle of division of labor introduced above, according to which each person is to do the one job he or she is most suited for. Because the greatest evil that can befall the state occurs when members of the lower classes attempt to rule, the interlocutors agree that this interference with another's job is injustice (434a—c).

At this point the first stage of Socrates' reply to Glaucon is complete: he has offered a theory of justice in the state. Before he can claim to have given a full answer to Glaucon, however, he must provide a similar account of justice in the individual, and an account of injustice. Our next task is to examine those accounts. I shall defer till later a critical examination of Plato's claim to have discovered the nature of justice in the principle of division of labor, but one point about the construction of the just city needs to be noted now. Plato, as we have seen, has attempted to find a natural basis for justice to replace Glaucon's conventional one. In the course of doing so, he has introduced the love of luxury into the city, and established a warrior class to serve that love. Yet this class is never allowed to undertake the wars of conquest envisioned at 373c. No sooner is it introduced than Plato begins the task of transforming it from a class of conquering warriors to a class of protectors of internal order. The guardians, if they do their job, must eliminate as far as possible the unlimited material desires that gave rise their existence in the first place. This is a curious bit of sleight of hand on Plato's part, accomplished so smoothly that the reader is apt to overlook it, yet it is one of the ironies of the work that the guardian class, product of unrestrained desires, functions to eliminate or restrain those desires rather than to satisfy them.

Justice in the individual

Socrates now turns from the state to the individual. If the analogy between the individual and the state is sound, then the individual will be just in the way the state is. This means that there must be three elements in the soul of each person, corresponding to the three classes distinguished in the state (435b—c), but are there? Do we, he asks learn with one of the parts within us, and feel angry with another and desire the pleasures of nourishment and generation and whatever is akin to these with a third, or whenever we initiate action do we do each of these things with the whole soul? (436a—b)

Plato attempts to establish that there are three parts in the soul by exhibiting different forms of psychological conflict. "The same thing," Socrates states, "cannot do or undergo opposite things in the same respect and in relation to the same thing and at the same time" (436b). This is the first formulation of the logical law of non-contradiction, which says that a proposition p and its contradictory, not-p, cannot be both be true. Plato's version is formulated in terms of things rather than propositions, but the net result is the same. If, then, someone claims that I am both healthy and unhealthy, this must mean either that I am healthy at one time and unhealthy at another, or that part of me is healthy and part not, or that I am healthy in relation to one person (someone with a terminal illness, let us say) and unhealthy in relation to another; without these qualifications, the claim would be self-contradictory.

With the law of non-contradiction established, Plato shows that there are cases where we want to say of someone that his or her soul is affected in two opposite ways. A person may be thirsty, have a desire to drink, and at the same time resist this desire (perhaps because of knowledge that the only drink available is poisoned): the same person may fairly be said to have an impulse toward and an aversion from the particular drink in question. In order for this description to be consistent with the principle of non-contradiction, the desire and the aversion must be lodged in different parts of the soul, which Socrates labels respectively the appetitive and the rational (439d). Again, someone might feel a desire and at the same time recognize that desire as shameful, a point Plato illustrates with the story of Leontion, who both wanted to view some corpses and was disgusted with himself for doing so. This leads to a distinction between the appetitive part of the soul and what Plato calls the *thumos*, the spirited part, the seat of the noble emotions, such as indignation and pride. Finally, Plato distinguishes *thumos* from reason: we exhibit spirit from birth, but develop our ability to reason only as we mature, if at all; and, in a rare passage where he quotes Homer with approval, Plato notes that Odysseus "struck himself on the chest and spoke to his heart and scolded it" (441b; cf. *Odyssey* 20, 17), using reason to quell his indignation.

With three parts of the soul distinguished, Plato proceeds to describe the virtues of the individual on the analogy with the previous description of the virtues in the state. Reason in the individual corresponds to the guardian class in the *polis*, and wisdom therefore resides there (441c). The spirited part of the soul corresponds to the auxiliary class in the *polis*, and is the seat of courage (441d). Temperance in the individual is also similar to temperance in the city

> Isn't one called temperate by virtue of the friendship and harmony of these parts of the soul, when the ruling element and the ruled agree that it is necessary for reason to rule and do not rebel against it? (442c—d)

Justice is that very order in the soul that the parts of a temperate person harmoniously agree to: "it is fitting for reason to rule, being wise and having forethought for all of the soul; and it is fitting for the spirited part to be its obedient ally," says Socrates (441e) and

> When these two have been brought up thus, and have been taught and have learned their own true tasks, they should be put in charge of the appetitive part, which is the largest part of the soul in each person and by nature the most insatiable for material things. It must be guarded so that it does not become filled with the so-called pleasures of the body and, having become large and strong, no longer do its own job but try to enslave and rule those parts which it is not naturally suited to rule and overturn the whole life of everyone. (442a—b)

The person who is just in the Platonic sense will not commit acts generally regarded as unjust, such as embezzlement, theft, treason, breach of promise, adultery, and the like (442e—443a); presumably this is because such acts are the products of a disordered soul, not a properly ordered one. As Socrates concludes

> The truth, as it seems, is that justice was something of this sort,

though not concerned with affairs external to oneself, but those within, those that are truly one's own and concern oneself: not allowing each part in one to do the business of another and the parts in the soul to meddle with each other's affairs. Rather, when one has truly put one's house in order, ruled and organized oneself and become a friend to oneself, when one has harmonized the three parts just as if they were three voices, low, middle, high and any other that may be in between, when one has bound these together and made a unity out of many, temperate and harmonious, then whenever the occasion for action arises, in matters concerning the possession of wealth or the care of the body or politics or private contracts, he will believe the act that preserves and augments this disposition is just and fine and will so name it; and [he will call] "wisdom" the knowledge that is in charge of this activity, and "unjust action" whatever destroys it, and "ignorance" the opinion that oversees this action. (443d—444a)

This state of internal order Plato likens to physical health, while injustice, which he describes as a kind of civil war within the soul (444b), he compares to disease. At this point, Glaucon admits, the question that started the discussion, whether the just life was preferable to the unjust, has been answered, or shown to be absurd: just as people think life not worth living without physical health, no one could think it worth living without psychological order (445a—b).

Has Glaucon's challenge been met? Has Plato provided a satisfactory account of justice and of the other virtues, and shown that justice is superior to injustice? As Socrates says in response to Glaucon, we can't give a final answer until we have surveyed the various forms of unjust society and individual (a task completed in Books VIII and IX), still, this is a good place to pause and examine the theory presented so far. Plato's account of the virtues is in many ways different from that suggested by the "Socratic paradoxes" discussed in Chapter 2. In my view, it is a major advance over Socrates' position. The key to Plato's view is unquestionably the theory of the tripartite soul. Socrates, you will recall, had not explicitly proposed an account of the soul, but he had treated psychological states, including emotions such as fear, as intellectual states. Thus we found it reasonable to assume that

Socrates regarded the soul as reason alone, a view developed explicitly by Plato in the *Phaedo*. The new theory of the soul gives non-rational states, such as the appetites and emotions, a legitimate place in the psyche. Since several of the virtues obviously involve such states (temperance being concerned with the appetites, courage with the emotion of fear), Plato's recognition of their role in his new psychological theory gives him the material for a more adequate account than Socrates' of the nature of these virtues.

There is another advantage to the tripartite psychology of the *Republic*. By dividing the soul into three parts, Plato is able to explain the possibility of psychological conflict, and thus of moral weakness. It was one of the Socratic paradoxes that moral weakness was impossible. Though this claim lacked plausibility (for each of us feels familiar with the phenomenon of moral weakness), it flowed naturally from Socrates' treatment of all conflicts as occurring within the rational element and as resolvable by reason. On Socrates' view, once reason had spoken, the matter was settled, but on Plato's view, there were two other parts of the soul to be reckoned with, which might not listen to reason. If these parts were not properly trained, they might win the conflict with reason and lead the individual to act in a manner contrary to what he or she knew to be best. In the story of Leontion we saw how the baser appetites could win out over the nobler emotions and we may assume that Plato thought the same victory could have occurred over reason.

The analysis of the virtues Plato gives shows that he has abandoned the assumptions closest to the heart of Socratic ethics: the view that virtue is knowledge or wisdom and the assumption that the virtues are a unity, so that to have one is to have them all. The ruling guardians, it is true, possess all the virtues, but the auxiliaries are said to be brave, not in virtue of their own wisdom, but because they are able to preserve in their souls opinions about what is fearful inculcated in them by the rulers (429c—d). Thus, the courage of the auxiliaries is a form of right belief, not knowledge, and is produced not by rational discourse but by "nature and nurture" (430a), their innate high-spiritedness and the moral training they receive in youth. (It may well have been the treatment of virtue as right opinion at the end of the *Meno* that enabled Plato to recognize courage of this sort as a virtue.) Not only is this form of courage (which Plato calls "political courage" at 430c, presumably to distinguish it from the philosophical courage of the ruling guardians) defined in terms of opinion rather than knowledge, but it is assigned to a class that by definition does not possess the wisdom of the guardians. Thus, Plato's treatment of courage indicates his abandonment of the views that virtue is knowledge and that all the virtues are one.

This change is indicated also in his treatment of civic temperance and justice. All three classes combine to produce these two virtues in the city: the economic class must do its proper job and must agree that the guardians should rule in order for the city to be just and temperate. Since Plato asserts at 435e that "the same forms and customs that are in the city must be in each of us," it seems to follow that the members of the economic class can be called temperate and just, because they play a necessary role in producing the virtue in the state. If this is correct, then everyone in the city will be temperate and just, but only the guardians and auxiliaries will be brave and only the guardians wise. Once again it is clear that not all the virtues are necessarily found together in the same individual.

Plato's account of the virtues in the individual indicates the same divergence from Socratic doctrine that is shown by his account of virtue in the *polis*. Even in the soul of the ruling guardian, who possesses all the virtues, the virtues are not identical, and they are not all rational states, as Socrates had thought they were. Wisdom is the virtue of the intellectual part of the soul or reason but courage requires the interaction of reason and the spirited part, *thumos*, and temperance and justice involve the appetites as well. So though virtue in the individual always involves the wisdom of the rational soul, it is not *equivalent* to that wisdom. In this respect Plato's account of the virtues resembles Aristotle's (cf. *Nicomachean Ethics* VI.13, 1144b17—25), rather than Socrates'. In abandoning the view that virtue is knowledge and the assumption of unity Plato has constructed an account of virtue with greater psychological plausibility than that of Socrates.

Has Plato discovered the nature of the virtues? Even if it is conceded that his view is an advance over Socrates', is it adequate to explain what the virtues are? One of its problems is its generality: we know that wisdom is the virtue of the rational part of the soul, but we do not yet know what the content of this wisdom is (this is a problem Plato addresses in his account of the philosopher's knowledge of the forms; see below). So also with the other virtues: Plato's account does not tell us what the courageous or temperate person would do in particular circumstances. Aristotle's account of the virtues, to be considered in Chapter 4, is much more detailed and context-sensitive than Plato's, but it might not have been possible without Plato's theory.

The one virtue that Plato does attempt to connect with specific actions is justice. As noted above, he has Socrates state at 442e— 443a that the just person will not break promises, commit adultery, embezzle money and the like. The reason behind this claim is not stated, but it seems obvious that Plato regards these unjust actions as caused by out-of-control appetites. The just individual, by definition, is one whose appetites are under control and such a person will therefore neither commit such acts nor have any desire to do so. It may seem to us that the internal psychological order that causes the just individual to behave well is better described as the *cause* of just behavior, rather than as the virtue of justice itself, but we must remember that Plato has been seeking the underlying cause of just action from the beginning of Book I; when he says that justice is really an internal state and not a matter of external actions (443c—d), he is simply reminding the reader of what he had established in the conversation with Cephalus: that justice is to be defined in terms of an essential attribute, not in terms of a set of actions.

Plato's account of the virtues thus seems to satisfy the requirements he had initially set for it: he has described underlying properties that are essential for the possession of the virtues, rather than simply listing a number of virtuous actions. He has described these states as those natural to a healthy psyche, thus explaining why anyone would prefer them to their unnatural, unhealthy alternatives and why they are valuable for their own sake, and not simply for their consequences. Finally, by defining justice as a property internal to the individual, Plato has answered one of the classic problems of justice: why should one be just? On the normal understanding of justice, it is a virtue that benefits others, not oneself, naturally, one then wants to know why one should do this. By defining justice as the internal order of the soul, Plato makes justice good for the just individual and gives him or her a reason for pursuing it.

Thus, Plato's ethical theory is remarkably successful. The same cannot be said for his political theory. Nearly everyone who reads Plato's description of the best state finds it repugnant. Plato's guardians are supposed to sacrifice all of their personal desires for the sake of the state's well-being; they are to mate sexually but not marry, and are not to know which of the children born within the guardian class are their own. In fact they are to be "bred" eugenically, like prize cattle, and their mating is to be controlled by a deceptive lottery run by the rulers (457c—461e). Though the prohibitions on individual family life and on private property do not extend to the economic class (even Plato realized that they would never agree to this), this class is to be carefully regulated by the guardians with respect to all its economic and personal activities, lest individual members of the class become too rich or to poor to do their jobs well (421d—422a).

Why does Plato propose such unpalatable regulations? The reason is not, as many readers are apt to think, that he has a "totalitarian" or "fascist" mentality, and seeks absolute power for its own sake. As I noted above, Plato's state cannot be criticized by comparing it with modern dictatorships of the right such as Nazi Germany (though it bears some resemblance to dictatorships of the Marxist sort). It will be clear to any reader who studies Plato's account of unjust states and people that he would have regarded Nazi Germany with horror and would have placed both Hitler and Stalin among the worst tyrants. It is rather that he has emphasized one aspect of a good *polis*, its ordered unity, at the expense of another, its provision for individual liberty. Plato's principle of justice is in fact more properly understood as a principle of civic order and surely the state is most united when it is well-ordered. Modern citizens of liberal democracies are apt to under-emphasize this kind of order, perhaps because they take it for granted under most circumstances, but for Plato, who had seen the disorder and civil strife produced by the disunity of factional politics both in Athens and in the rest of Greece during the Peloponnesian War, civic unity and order were highly prized.

What Plato does not seem to prize, or even to recognize, is individual liberty. This may be because he had seen it abused in Athens (in the course of his description of the "defective" regime of democracy in Book VIII, discussed below, he gives a strikingly vivid picture of democratic life that must be drawn from his own evaluation of Athens). It may also be because neither he nor any other Greek political theorist was able to express the idea, commonplace in modern political thought, that liberty is a "right" possessed inalienably by each individual. The language of individual rights was a later invention, so, though Pericles praises the liberty of the Athenian democracy in his "Funeral Oration" (Thucydides, *History of the Peloponnesian War*, II.37), he does not regard it as an absolute claim of the individual against the state. In fact, Pericles does not seem to recognize *any* absolute individual rights against state interference and in this respect the views of the greatest defender of Athenian democracy are at one with those of Socrates (in the *Crito*) and Plato (here), two of Athenian democracy's greatest critics.

Why does not Plato give individual liberty even the place Pericles granted it? Why doesn't he see it, if not as a right, as a clear public good? I suspect that he is misled by his analogy between the individual and the state, though one could argue that the analogy was constructed by Plato precisely to express this misunderstanding (as I see it), and so was the result of it, not its cause. As many critics have noted, the parallel between the three parts of the city and the three parts of the soul is not exact. Reason controls emotion and appetite by exerting its authority over them, by suppressing them when it judges them to be inappropriate and allowing them expression when it thinks this may be fairly granted. The "communication," if it may be called that, among the parts of the soul is immediate and direct; after all, they are all part of the same individual consciousness.

This is not the case with the parts of the city and the individuals within them. When a guardian confronts a shoemaker, he is confronting a person like himself, someone whose soul has three parts just as his does (though, in the case of the shoemaker, the appetitive part must be more developed, and the rational and spirited part less, than in the case of the guardian). The technique of suppression, used by reason against the appetites, is not appropriate for the guardian to use with the shoemaker; the guardian must persuade the shoemaker that his decision or policy is correct. Plato recognizes this in the myth of the metals, when he describes all the citizens of the state as "brothers," in his description of civic temperance as the "agreement" of all classes, and in other passages where he speaks of the guardians persuading their fellow citizens rather than forcing them to do what is right; none the less, the analogy between the city and the individual militates against the recognition that the individual shoemaker, unlike the appetitive part of the soul, is a creature with dignity and intrinsic worth, whose liberty is not lightly to be tampered with.

Whether the analogy between city and individual was the cause of Plato's austere political views or an effect of them, we can say that the difference between the individual and city justifies us in evaluating differently Plato's ethics and politics. His political views are not satisfactory because they do not give sufficient scope to genuine goods such as individual liberty, and because they only deal with one part of justice, the distribution of duties and corollary benefits, and not with other parts, such as the distribution of rights. His ethical views are more satisfactory than his politics because the relation between the parts of an individual soul is not the same as the relation between ruler and ruled in a state: the appetites are not entitled to the same liberties that shoemakers and other people are.

The philosopher-king

I noted above that Plato's account of the virtues is over-general, and in particular that it does not explain what makes the guardians wise. This is a topic that Plato returns to in Books V—VII of the *Republic*, in which the portrait of the ruling guardian is turned from a sketch into a fairly full picture. Though Plato describes this section of the *Republic* as a digression, it is far from an unessential one. One of the basic questions that arises from consideration of the political scheme of the dialogues is, what sort of wisdom must the guardians have in order to justify their political power? If the guardians differed only in degree from the auxiliaries and craftsmen, this would hardly justify placing absolute political control of the city into their hands. Their knowledge must be of a different kind from that possessed by ordinary mortals if it legitimizes absolute power. Is such knowledge possible? How would the guardians come to possess it?

Though these questions are answered in the course of these three books, they do not arise at the outset. Instead, Socrates has been asked to answer certain questions about the social arrangements among the guardians and auxiliaries, in particular the community of women and children (449c—d). This question leads Socrates to argue for equality of opportunity for women (a radical idea in ancient Greece), and to explain the marital and child-rearing policies of the *Republic* as necessary to enable women to perform an equal role in the guardian class. After this rather striking anticipation of modern feminist views, he raises the question of the possibility of such a state's existence. It is not necessary to prove that the state he has described is possible, says Socrates, because "it was for the sake of an ideal standard that we searched for what justice itself is" (472c); just as a painter of an ideal human could not be faulted if a real-life model for the painting could not be found, neither should Socrates be blamed if the state is impossible to achieve. Practice always comes less close to truth than does theory (473a, a claim that jars our modern, empiricist sensibilities, but reveals Plato's own preference for the abstract over the concrete).

Nonetheless, the ideal can be approximated in practice. This can only happen, however, if philosophers become kings

"If the philosophers do not become kings in the cities," I said, "or those who are now called kings and rulers do not philosophize truly and adequately, and if political power and philosophy do not coincide . . . , I think there will be no end of evils for cities, my dear Glaucon, or for the human race. . . . There is no other way for someone to be happy, either in private or in public life." (473d—e)

This shocking admission produces a not-unexpected reply from Glaucon

"Socrates," he said, "you have given forth such a statement and speech that you must expect a great many people of the current generation, and not the worst of them, to take off their cloaks, grab the weapon that happens to be nearest them, and run to attack you, intending to do horrible things to you." (473e—74a)

Because the rule of the philosopher-king is such a well-known feature of the *Republic*, modern readers are not likely to share Glaucon's surprise at Socrates' statement; but our response is apt to be otherwise the same. The rule of the philosopher is no more acceptable in our time than it seems to have been in Glaucon's.

Socrates tries to defuse this explosive reaction by explaining the nature of the philosopher. In the course of so doing he leads the reader into the core of Plato's metaphysics and epistemology. As in my treatment of the doctrine of recollection in Chapter 2, I intend to say only enough about these matters to illuminate Plato's ethics; a full discussion of them would take us far afield. Plato explains who the philosophers are by comparison with another group, the "lovers of sights and sounds." The philosophers love the truth, they recognize the existence of beauty and ugliness, justice and injustice, good and evil, and the like. Each of these things is itself one, but each appears to be many because it appears in many actions and bodies and in a variety of combinations with other things (476a). The lovers of sights and sounds, on the other hand, are devotees of the arts, "they enjoy fine sounds and colors and shapes and all things made from these sorts of things, but their minds are unable to see and enjoy the nature of the beautiful itself" (476b). Instead, the lovers of sights and sounds mistake the instances of beauty they see for beauty itself: they confuse the image for reality, and are thus in a dreamlike state, whereas the philosopher can tell the two apart, and is awake (476c—d).

Over the next few pages Plato distinguishes the philosopher from the lover of sights and sounds by claiming that the philosopher has knowledge (*episteme*), whereas the lover of sights and sounds has only opinion (*doxa*). Knowledge and opinion are different mental faculties: knowledge is the infallible apprehension of what *is*, of reality, and opinion is the fallible apprehension of what *is and is not*, what is between being and not being. Not being, on the other hand, is apprehended by ignorance. Knowledge is the clearest of faculties, and ignorance the darkest; opinion is intermediate between them.

All of this is puzzling. What is this single beauty that lovers of sights and sounds fail to recognize? How can something both be and not be? How can one faculty be clearer than another? Why is Plato describing this distinction, which is clearly of central importance for his philosophy, in such a vague, metaphorical way? Scholars have differed greatly over what Plato's answers to these questions would have been. There is probably no way of explaining his view that is not in some respect misleading. I think the least misleading way to put matters, however, is to say that the distinction Plato is trying to draw between beauty and beautiful things is the distinction between concept and object. Each of the many beautiful things is an individual object and when we group them together under the same description we are in fact applying to each of them a common concept, in this case that of beauty. Normally, when we think of concepts, we think of them as mental entities, things that owe their existence to the workings of our minds. Plato, however, thought that these entities existed independently of our minds, our minds recognize them when we perceive objects, but beauty would exist even if there were no minds to perceive beautiful things. He referred to these things as "ideas" and as "forms." Philosophers call such entities "universals," indicating by this that they are not, like the particular beautiful things, limited to a single place. They can be instantiated in many things, that is, many things can be beautiful, or just, or their opposites.

The view that universal concepts exist independently of the mind is called by philosophers "realism." Plato's version, which makes these universals independent of their instances as well, is called "extreme realism," or "Platonism." It may seem an extravagant view, but it has proved very resilient throughout the history of philosophy. Today many mathematicians consider themselves "Platonists" with respect to mathematical objects: they think that numbers and the relations among them, for instance, are "out there" to be discovered rather than invented. Biologists, too, may think of biological species as "real" in this way, and likewise with other scientists. In any case, the distinction Plato wishes to draw between the philosopher and the lover of sights and sounds is the distinction between a person who thinks about ideas, universals or concepts and a person who thinks about individuals. The lover of sights and sounds enjoys discussing this or that interesting play, or musical performance, or dance recital while the philosopher asks, what makes anything of that sort beautiful? What is beauty itself?

These questions must be approached in different ways. If one wants to appreciate a particular performance of a Shakespeare play or a Beethoven symphony, one must experience that performance: one must use one's eyes and ears. This is what the lover of sights and sounds does, hopping about from one dramatic festival to another (475d). If one wants to understand the nature of beauty, however, reflection is needed (though personal acquaintance with beautiful things is necessary as well). These different pursuits engage different faculties, which Plato refers to as *episteme* and *doxa*. The translation of these simply as "knowledge and opinion," though fairly standard, can be misleading. By *episteme* Plato means the faculty (*dunamis*, 477b) of rational thought and the product that results from its activity; by *doxa* he means the faculty that forms judgments on the basis of observation. We would say that we *know* many things based on observation (that the sky is blue, that rocks are hard, and the like); but Plato would not say that we understood these things or apprehended them through *episteme*. Lovers of sights and sounds, Plato thinks, observe and form opinions, whereas philosophers reason and come to have knowledge. The things we reason about in *episteme* are things philosophers say we know *a priori*, independently of experience. Plato identifies his forms as the objects of *episteme*, and particulars as the objects of *doxa*.

When Plato says that *episteme* is infallible, he does not mean that people make no mistakes when they think abstractly; but he is saying that, insofar as they make these mistakes, they do not have rational knowledge. The English word "knowledge" is like *episteme* in this respect: if one has knowledge, one is thinking what is true. There is no such thing as false knowledge, though there are lots of false opinions and inaccurate observations. *Episteme* is "clearer" than *doxa* in that it always has the truth as its object. Moreover, when one knows the nature of an abstract concept or proposition, such as $2 \times 3 = 6$, there is nothing tentative about that knowledge: it is not subject to disconfirmation on further examination, as most observations are. Again, one can make mistakes, even in simple arithmetic; the point is that one cannot make mistakes here of the sort one can about observational judgments.

When Plato says that the object of *episteme* is "what is," a part of what he means is that one has rational knowledge of the truth whereas, when one forms an opinion about particular things, that opinion may or may not be true. That, however, is only part of the story. Plato believed that the ontological status of the objects of *episteme*, the forms, differed from that of the objects of *doxa*. Particular things exist only for a time, whereas forms, Plato thought, are everlasting. Moreover, particular things change — a beautiful painting may become damaged over time and so cease to be beautiful — but the forms never change. Finally, particular things are what they are relatively, in relation to other things, and may, in different comparisons, be described differently (a person called "tall" in a tribe of pygmies will not be so when compared with people of normal size): thus, they "are and are not." The forms, Plato thought, were what they were not relatively but absolutely: they just "are" (though what precisely he meant by this has been much debated). Forms are more stable than particular things and in this respect also our understanding of them is "clearer" than our opinions about particulars.

What Plato's claim comes to, then, is this: philosophers differ from the lovers of sights and sounds (and in fact from all other folk) in that they have *a priori* knowledge of eternally existing concepts, whereas others have at best observational knowledge of changeable particular things. Only the philosophers know what justice is, so only they have the right to rule. He puts matters in the somewhat vague way he does because the distinctions he draws here — between concept or form and object, between rational knowledge and observational judgment or opinion — are being drawn virtually for the first time. He cannot expect his readers to grasp the distinctions without explanation, and he has no technical terminology with which to explain them. Plato is, if not the discoverer of these distinctions, the first person to base a philosophy on them.

It remains to ask whether Plato is correct to draw these distinctions in the way he does. It must be said that the philosopher and the lover of sights and sounds are pure types: every actual person has some conceptual and some observational knowledge. But is conceptual knowledge superior to observational? If there were a philosopher-king, would he be justified in ruling based on his *episteme*? And are there forms of the sort Plato describes? Are concepts independent of objects? The debate about these matters continues to this day, but it is not unreasonable for Plato to insist that the difference between the philosopher and others resides in the fact that the philosopher is concerned with abstract reasoning about conceptual matters. Even if *episteme* alone is not enough to make one a good ruler, the addition of such knowledge could not help but benefit a ruler already well-equipped with *doxa*. For how could any ruler make decisions in accordance with justice if he or she does not know what justice is?

Plato returns to these metaphysical and epistemological matters in Books VI and VII, when he presents his famous account of the good. The good, he says, is the object of the highest study and the source of all value (504d—505b); the philosophers must master this study if they are to rule well. But what is the good? Alas, no one knows: the many think it is pleasure, whereas the wise think it is knowledge. But neither answer will do: for there are bad pleasures, and what could the knowledge that is good be about except the good (505b—c)? Socrates disclaims knowledge of the good (506c), so the outlook looks fairly bleak, but he does agree to offer some analogies, what he calls "interest" on the account owed, to explain its nature. These are the analogies of the sun, line and cave, and they are probably the best-known passages in Platonism. Before I turn to them, however, let me note one thing. Plato is often regarded by his critics as an authoritarian, a philosopher willing to give absolute power to an elite class based on their superior genetic endowment and training. If this is so, it is only to a group who know what the good is and, since even Socrates denies he knows this, it is likely to be a *very* small group. It is only people with this knowledge that Plato is willing to put in positions of authority and he is not willing to grant people absolute power unless they have absolute understanding.

The first analogy Socrates offers is with the sun. He begins with a recapitulation of the metaphysics and epistemology discussed above: there are many beautiful things, but only one form of beauty, and so on for other classes of things. We see the many particulars, but understand (*noeisthai*) the forms (507b). The sun is the source of light, and thus the cause of our ability to see things in the world of particular things (508a). It is also the cause of the generation and growth of these things (509b). The good is in the intelligible world what the sun is in the sensible

> This, then, which provides truth for the things that are known and gives the power of knowing to the one who knows, you must say is the idea of the good. It is the cause of knowledge and truth, as known by reason, and as fine as these are, knowledge and truth, if you believe that it is different from and even finer than these, you will believe correctly. (508e)

As it is beyond knowledge and truth while being their source, it is "beyond being" while being the source of the being of the other forms (509b). Plato does not explain this cryptic remark, but it is clear that the form of the good is in his mind the highest of the forms and in some sense the cause of all the others.

From the mysteries of the sun analogy Plato turns to the clear analysis of the divided line. He begins by dividing a line into two unequal sections, one corresponding to the visible world, the other to the intelligible world of the forms. The longer section is given to the intelligible world, as an indication of its greater clarity. These two sections are divided again in the same ratio, so that a line with four sections results

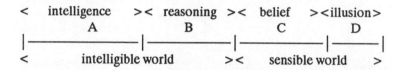

The shortest section of the line (D) contains the images of sensible objects, such as shadows and reflections. Plato refers (511e) to the mental state that apprehends things in this realm as "illusion" (*eikasia*), perhaps because he is thinking of someone viewing an image as being deceived by it, and mistaking it for its original. The next section (C) contains the sensible objects that are the originals of the images in section D, apprehended by "belief" (*pistis*). The relation of image to original is the same as that of the sensible and intelligible worlds in general (510a), so just as the things in section C are more intelligible than their images in section D, the things in sections A and B (forms) are more intelligible than those in C and D. Further, just as sensible objects are originals of images, forms are originals in relation to sensible objects, which are in this respect images. As Plato explains, geometers

> make use of visible shapes and make arguments about them, not thinking about them but about those other things that these are like, making their arguments for the sake of the square itself and the diagonal itself, not the one that they draw, and likewise in the other cases. The things that they form and draw, which themselves have shadows and images in water, they use in turn as images, seeking to see those other things which

one may not see except with the mind. (510d—511a)

It is the difference between the methodology of the sciences, such as geometry, and philosophy that leads to the division of the intelligible portion of the line into two segments

> In one part of it (B) the soul is forced to reason from hypotheses, using the things imitated in the lower section (D) themselves as images, not proceeding to a first principle but to a conclusion; in the other part (A) the soul proceeds to an unhypothetical first principle, moving from hypotheses without using the images used in the other section but making use of forms themselves and pursuing its inquiry through them.
> (510b)

Geometry, in other words, takes certain things for granted (such as definitions, axioms, and postulates) and deduces conclusions (theorems) from them, with the help of visual aids (diagrams).

Philosophy, on the other hand, reasons from these assumptions back to some ultimate principle, without visual aids. Philosophy is completely conceptual, abstract, probably because the concepts with which the philosopher is concerned (the good, beauty, justice and the like) do not have appropriate visual images anyway. The first principle the philosopher seeks is, of course, the good. Plato refers to the method of philosophy as dialectic (511b, cf. 531d—534d); he says it is an operation of "intelligence" (*noesis*), whereas geometry and the other sciences are products of "reason" (*dianoia*). Elsewhere he does not retain this somewhat technical fourfold distinction among illusion, belief, reason and intelligence, but relies on the more general distinction between understanding and observation, discussed above.

The divisions of the line form the framework for the allegory of the cave, probably the most famous passage in philosophical literature. In the allegory of the cave the philosopher makes the ascent from the lowest to the highest section of the line, from illusion to intelligence. At the start, says Plato, we are to

> behold people in an underground dwelling like a cave . . . in which they have been from childhood, their legs and necks chained so that they must stay looking only forward, and

because of the chain are unable to turn their heads. Their light comes from a fire burning above and behind them at a distance. (514a—b)

People moving along a wall behind the prisoners carry wooden and stone models of people and objects whose shadows are projected by the light from the fire on the wall of the cave in front of them. The prisoners cannot see the persons behind them, they don't know that others are manipulating the images that they see. In fact, they mistake these shadows for genuine objects (515b). (Every modern reader notes the parallel between motion picture projection and television broadcasts but it is worth making Plato's point explicitly concerning them: the images seen in movies and on television are just that, images and not reality, and these images are the product of manipulation by unseen and generally unknown agents. This point is particularly apt for the televised speeches of politicians, but it applies to all forms of televised or projected images.)

The prisoners are "at home" in this environment, so much so that, if they were freed from their chains and led up from the cave to the world above they would find the process painful and would resist it (515c—516a). Once the freed prisoners became accustomed to the brighter light in the upper world, and became able to observe the originals from which the images in the cave are copied, including finally the sun itself, they would pity the prisoners in the cave and despise the honors that the prisoners bestow on those who are particularly adept at life there (516a—e). People who have been liberated would, if forced to return to the darkness of the cave, initially be unable to make out much in the images on the cave wall, and the cave-dwellers would despise them and try to kill them if they could (516e—517a, the reference is obviously to the trial and execution of Socrates). None the less, Plato argues that the guardians, who have experienced the liberation of ascending to knowledge of the good, must return to the cave to govern

Each of you must go down in turn into the common dwelling of the others and become accustomed to see in the dark. When you have become accustomed you will see thousands of times better than those there, and will recognize what each of the images are and what they are images of, because you have seen the truth concerning fine, just and good things. And so your city and mine will live a waking life and not a dream, as now the many live, by fighting over shadows and disputing over political authority, as if it were a great good. The truth, I suppose, is this: the city in which those who are going to rule are least enthusiastic about it will necessarily have the best and least factionalized government, and the one that has the opposite sort of rulers will have the opposite government. (520c—d)

The philosophers should rule, says Plato, for two reasons: first because they have knowledge of the true nature of reality, which ordinary people lack, and second because this knowledge leads them to a proper appreciation of the value of public office, which others also lack. Philosophers alone pursue a quest greater than the quest for power, so they alone are immune to its allures.

Plato connects the allegory of the cave with the other analogies

the abode that is apparent to sight you may compare to the prison dwelling, the light of the fire in it to the power of the sun, and you won't be mistaken if you liken the journey upward and the vision of those things above to the upward path of the soul into the intelligible realm. . . . In the intelligible realm the last thing to be seen, and only with difficulty, is the idea of the good, and once seen it must be rationally judged that it is the cause of all that is right and good in everything, . . . and that the person who is going to act rationally either in private or in public must see it. (517b—c)

The allegory of the cave and its companion analogies give a powerful portrait of the philosophical life. There is no doubt that they describe Plato's own experience in turning away from the political ambitions of his youth (ambitions that any talented Athenian could be expected to have) in favor of philosophy. Of course, the vision of the philosophical life is not a fair description of every form of philosophical activity carried on today, or even in Plato's own time; Plato did not intend for it to be. It is an account that depends for much of its plausibility on the truth of Platonic metaphysics, for if Plato's theory of forms were false, the account would have to be altered significantly. It is an "elitist" account, in that Plato expects that only a few people will be able to make the ascent from the cave to the upper world but, given the difficulties of knowing the good described above, it is hard to see how it could be anything but elitist. Plato goes on to describe a curriculum for potential philosopher-kings that contains ten years of scientific and mathematical studies as a preface to the study of dialectic; since no one is to be compelled to study (536e—537a), we should again suspect that only a small, elite group will choose to take the path to philosophy.

Plato's portrait of the philosopher-king is that of a person equipped with the knowledge and the temperament suitable for a ruler. Since the philosopher-king is an ideal type, to which few, if any, actual individuals would correspond, it is impossible to determine by empirical study whether such a person would really desire knowledge more than power, and would really be able to rule better because of having such knowledge. There do seem to be people (intellectuals of all sorts, including scientists as well as philosophers) who prefer the pursuit of knowledge to that of power, but it seems impossible to find people who would satisfy Plato's conditions for having knowledge of the good. Nor is it clear that people possessing such knowledge would be particularly good at governing. In addition to the possession of wisdom and the absence of corrupting desires, Plato's rulers would need an interest in the day-to-day matters of government and the patience to deal with their less enlightened fellow citizens. Plato apparently relies on their sense of duty to the state to provide these attributes, but it is far from evident that they would come naturally to the sort of philosopher he has described.

Plato's account of the philosopher-king augments his description of the just individual in Book IV. Though Plato does not tell us precisely what knowledge of the good consists in, he does tell us that the wisdom of the just individual is derived from his or her knowledge of the good, and that this is rational knowledge of a form, an independently existing universal concept, rather than knowledge based on practical experience. If one wonders how knowledge of this sort leads to the other virtues of temperance, courage and justice, and to the harmony of the soul, two answers suggest themselves. The first is that, since the good is the source of all value and knowledge of the good is necessary for knowledge of the value of other things, by knowing the good the philosopher will come to know and appreciate the goodness of the virtues and will therefore choose to practice them. The second is that, since the desire to know the good is the ruling desire of the philosopher's life, he or she will not be motivated by the sorts of fears and passions that lead to cowardice, intemperance and injustice; one dedicated to the pursuit of the good will have little time for such things. Proper order of the parts of the soul would seem to require understanding of the value of the desires produced each part and this, thinks Plato, is what knowledge of the good provides.

Defective states and individuals: the comparison of lives

With this description of the nature and education of the philosopher, Plato completes his account of the just life. It remains for him to carry out the comparison of other lives and forms of government to the just ones, and this he undertakes in Books VIII and IX. These two books contain a brilliant analysis of different regimes and characters, an analysis in which Plato's theoretical understanding of the state and individual is combined with astute observation of people and governments. The analysis shows the effects of ignoring the principles of good government and psychological order articulated in Book IV, it thus applies and offers a confirmation of those principles. At times Plato seems to be straining to make each type of person correspond with the correlative form of government but in many cases his analysis is both insightful and plausible.

The first form of defective government is one in which the rulers pursue honor instead of wisdom; Plato calls it "timocracy" or "timarchy" (545b) from the Greek word for honor, *time*. (Plato depicts each successive government as arising from the decline of the previous one: thus, this regime is alleged to arise from the best state. I shall generally ignore this feature of Plato's account.) Critics of Plato often charge that his ideal state is based on the model of Sparta, but Plato makes it clear at 544c that it is this second state that resembles Sparta. The rulers resemble the auxiliaries of the ideal state, but lack the direction provided in that state by the guardians: they pursue honor and military virtue, but distrust intelligence and liberal education (547e—548c). Plato believes such rulers will introduce private property and will treat the economic class like serfs (547b—c). (Timarchy, as Plato describes it, in fact resembles the economic and social system of feudalism prevalent in the Middle Ages.) As the timarchic government represents the rule of the auxiliaries rather than the guardians, the individual of the timocratic type is one who is governed by the spirited part of the soul, the *thumos*, rather than reason.

In Plato's time most Greek city-states were divided into factions: the rich in general supported oligarchy, government by the few wealthy citizens, whereas the poor in general supported democracy. Plato notes (544c) that oligarchy is ranked above democracy, though this was probably the ranking only in the aristocratic circles Plato frequented; he adds, however, that it is "teeming with many evils." Plato defines oligarchy as a form of government "in which the rich rule and the poor person has no share of power" (550c—d). Wealth, he says, is an unsound basis for giving people political power, just as it would be for assigning people to be ship's captains (551c). Oligarchy not only divides the citizens into factions of rich and poor, but allows for people to live in poverty without performing any real work. (Plato calls such people "drones.") Crime emerges from this class.

If the timarchic state resembled feudalism, oligarchy resembles capitalism. Whereas the rulers of the timarchic state looked like members of the auxiliary class, the rulers of an oligarchy are the most industrious and successful members of the economic class, the leaders of business and industry. Such people tend to receive a good deal of admiration in modern Western societies, where wealth is the standard measure of success, so the modern reader is surprised to discover how little Plato thinks of them: they are squalid characters, greedy and uneducated, who behave well in public from fear of getting caught but who would cheat orphans without compunction if they could get away with it (554a—d). Such lives may appear respectable on the surface, but are filled with internal conflict because of the absence in them of genuine wisdom and courage.

If oligarchy and the oligarch are pretty poor stuff, they are none the less superior, in Plato's view, to democracy and the democratic person. Democracy results when the greed of the oligarchs stirs up a revolution among the poor: "when the poor have conquered they kill some of the wealthy and exile others, and grant to the remainder an equal share of citizenship and rule, the rulers in this city being elected for the most part by lot" (557a). Democracy is characterized by freedom: "the city becomes filled with liberty and freedom of speech, and it is possible in it to do whatever one wishes" (557b). An unlimited diversity of lifestyles results, and the sense of obligation to the state atrophies

> "There is no obligation to rule in this city," I said, "if one is capable of ruling, nor of being ruled, if one is unwilling; there is no need to fight in wartime, or to keep the peace when others are doing so." (557e)

Even convicted criminals flout the law, says Plato, walking the streets like innocent people (558a). Democracy ignores the education of its political leaders; they need only profess that they are "the people's friends" to be successful. Democracy, he concludes, is "a pleasant, anarchic and variegated form of government, distributing equality of a sort to equals and unequals alike" (558c).

The democratic person mirrors the variety and lack of discipline of the regime. He is as dedicated to the pursuit of pleasure as the oligarch (both would be in the economic class of Plato's state), but does not have the oligarch's ability to subordinate other pleasures to that derived from the attainment of riches. He can't distinguish necessary from unnecessary pleasures, says Plato, in true democratic fashion, he declares all pleasures equal (561b—c). This person flits from one pursuit to another, without plan or purpose

> First it's drinking wine and listening to flute music, then it's drinking water and dieting; now exercise, now idleness and a carefree life, and now philosophical pursuits. Often he takes part in political debate, and jumping to his feet says and does whatever occurs to him. Whenever he wishes to emulate certain military figures he is carried off in that direction; when it is businessmen, then it is in their direction. There is neither order nor constraint in his life, but he calls his life pleasant and free and blessed. (561c—d)

Plato's description of democratic society and the democratic individual is an indictment of the citizens and political life of Athens, if it is an accurate picture, it is a portrait of Athens at the end of the fifth century, after her defeat at the hands of Sparta in the Peloponnesian War. It is emphatically not a recognizable account of Athenian life at the time of the Persian invasions or even at the beginning of the Peloponnesian War. Plato's picture is not a fair or objective account of democratic government as such and it was probably not intended to be. If all the citizens of a state manifested the virtues of the philosopher-king, Plato would not object to their use of democratic decision procedures. The real object of his scorn is the careless hedonism of his "democratic man."

Unlike the person characteristic of the other forms of government, the "democratic man" is not depicted as a ruler in his society, but that is no surprise, for democracy as Plato describes it is a government in which no one rules, but each individual may "take to politics" on occasion and say "whatever comes into his head." (Note the violation of the Platonic principle of the division of labor: the democratic individual performs many jobs, as the mood suits him.) This is not a fair description of the democratic leadership of Pericles, which Thucydides (II.65) said resembled "government by the first citizen" more than democracy, but the Athenian assembly did allow all citizens to speak on topics of public policy. Of course, unbridled exercise of that right would lead to anarchy, but anarchy is not, in Plato's mind, very different from democracy, as noted above.

How much of what he says applies to modern western democracy? That is a question for the reader to determine, but there are some disturbing parallels between his account and contemporary life. Today's democratic citizens often seem as unconcerned with the public good and as devoted to the pursuit of the latest trend in pleasure-seeking as Plato claims and, like his "democratic man," many find nothing in principle wrong with such self-absorbed hedonism. To the extent that Plato's character resembles the citizen of a modern democracy, his criticisms are not ones we can simply dismiss as irrelevant to our current condition.

Plato thought that democracy degenerates into tyranny. As each successive government is ruled by progressively worse elements in the state, tyranny is the government of the worst cutthroats in the criminal class. Ironically, Plato thinks it is the extreme love of liberty among democrats that gives these "stinging drones" a chance to gain power. When they are in charge, they introduce a reign of terror, killing their enemies and confiscating the property of the rich. In order to remain in power, the tyrant must eliminate every person of virtue from the society, for such persons constitute a threat to his rule. The tyrant, Plato says, is the opposite of the good physician who administers a purge to his patient: "for doctors remove the worst element and leave the best, but he does the opposite" (567c).

As the tyrannical state is ruled by the worst elements in it, so the tyrannical individual is ruled by the worst elements in his soul. Like the oligarch and the democrat, the tyrant is devoted to pleasure, but unlike them, he knows no moderation or subordination in its pursuit. He pursues the most lawless and violent of the unnecessary pleasures

> "the ones aroused in sleep," I said, "when the rest of the soul is at rest, the rational and gentle and ruling part of the person, but the bestial and wild part, gorged on food or drink, springs up and, banishing sleep tries to go forth and satiate its customary desires. You know that in such a condition it dares to do anything, as if it untied and released from all shame and reason. It won't hesitate to try to have intercourse with its mother, as it thinks, or with anyone else, human, god, or beast, or to defile itself with bloody acts, and it will refuse no food. In a word, it will omit no act of folly and shame. (571c—d)

The good person, whose soul is properly ordered, is less troubled by such dreams than others, but Plato says that "there is a terrifying and wild and lawless form of desire in each of us, even in some of us who seem most temperate; and this becomes manifest in dreams" (572b). The waking life of the tyrant, however, resembles the worst nightmares of the philosopher. The tyrant is enslaved to some violent and lawless passion, which he will do anything to satisfy.

Plato's tyrant, in other words, is an addict, though the object of his addiction may vary. The depiction of such a person is realistic enough, and contains some impressive anticipations of Freudian psychology, but it is not easy to see a person of this sort as the leader of a state, because the addiction would make normal political activity impossible for him. The tyrant, that is, would be unable to rule by virtue of mental illness. None the less, it must be said that ancient tyrants were known to perform many of the violent and lawless acts Plato mentions, and at least Stalin and Hitler among modern tyrants seem to have been in the grip of some sort of psychopathology, if not quite that Plato describes.

Once the life of the tyrant has been described as a life of addictive pursuit of lawless pleasures, it is clear that no one would prefer it to the life of the philosopher described earlier. The earlier attractiveness of such a life is now seen to be a sham, based on external appearances only. Plato, however, adds several arguments to show that the philosopher is happier than the tyrant. The first is based on the analogy between the city and individual. Tyranny is clearly the worst of states, so the tyrant should be the unhappiest of people. As the populace of a tyranny is enslaved to the worst element in it, so is the tyrant. As the tyrannical state is impoverished, so is the life of the tyrant. Finally, as the citizens of a tyranny live in fear and anguish, so must the tyrant, who must live in constant fear of being overthrown (576c—580c).

The second argument makes use of the theory of the tripartite soul. Each part of the soul has its own particular pleasure: the appetite loves profit or gain; the spirited part loves honor; and the rational part loves knowledge and wisdom. There is a corresponding type of life for each set of desire: the life of acquisition, the life of honor and the life of the pursuit of knowledge (i.e. the life of the philosopher) . Each person will naturally prefer the type of life he or she has chosen to lead, whose preferences, then, are to be regarded as correct? In order to judge fairly, says Plato, we need experience, intelligence, and reason (582a). The philosopher, of course, is the expert in the use of intelligence and reason, he turns out as well to be the most experienced of the three. For the acquisitive type knows nothing of the pleasures of honor and wisdom, and the pursuer of honor knows nothing of the pleasures of the intellect. Only the philosopher, who will inevitably have experienced the lower pleasures as well as those of the mind, will be familiar with all three. Only the philosopher's judgment of the comparative values of the different pleasures, then, is sound.

The third argument concerns the reality of the different kinds of pleasures themselves. In addition to pleasure and pain, there is a neutral state between them. When we are relieved of pain and enter the neutral state, we often confuse this with pleasure, and likewise, when we cease to feel pleasure, we may confuse the neutral state with pain. Thus, the pleasures and pains we experience in these cases are apparent but not real. (Plato's account of the three states should be compared with Epicurus' doctrine that pleasure is the absence of pain, discussed in Chapter 5.) Some of our most intense bodily pleasures, Plato claims, result from the relief of pain: Plato calls these "pleasures of replenishment" (585b), and gives the pleasures of eating when hungry and drinking when thirsty as examples. The best and purest pleasures, on the other hand, are unaccompanied by pain, the pleasure of learning is among these. The pleasures of learning are more real than those of eating and drinking both in that they are less deceptive, less likely to be confused with the neutral state, and in that their objects (the forms) are more real than their physical counterparts.

Though Plato does not explicitly evoke the metaphysics of Book VII, it is clear that the pleasures of the body are those of the cave, and those of the mind are the pleasures of the liberated prisoner in the upper world

> Those, then, who are unfamiliar with practical wisdom and virtue, who are regular disciples of feasts and the like, are borne downwards and then barely back up to the middle, and in this region wander throughout their lives. They never either gaze at or are borne in the direction of what is really above, going beyond this limit, and never are really filled with reality or taste solid and pure pleasure. Instead, like cattle with their gaze ever turned downward and bent toward the earth they graze, feasting at their tables, and copulate, and out of greed kick and butt each other with horns and weapons of iron, and kill each other from insatiable desire, because they are filling an unreal receptacle in themselves with unreal things.
>
> (586a—b)

These three arguments (I omit a fourth designed to show that the philosopher is 729 times happier than the tyrant), like the arguments used by Socrates against Thrasymachus in Book I, are too brief in themselves to be convincing. They rely, as noted above, on the tripartite theory of the soul and the metaphysics of the sun, line and cave for their plausibility. The real argument for the superiority of the just life to the unjust, of the philosopher's life to that of the tyrant, is in fact the main body of the *Republic* itself, which these arguments only amplify and recapitulate. It is only fitting that Plato conclude his argument with an imaginative analogy of the tripartite soul: a many-headed beast, representing the appetites; a lion, representing the spirit; and a man, representing reason, all combined in a single human form. Plato remarks

> Let us say, then, to the one who says that it benefits a person to do wrong, and that right action is not beneficial, that he says nothing other than that it benefits one to make the beast of many natures strong by feasting and the lion and its concerns, but to starve the man and weaken him so that he can be dragged wherever either of the others pull him. . . . The one who says that just actions are beneficial would be saying that one must do and say those things that give the man within as much control of the whole man as possible, and that he must care for the many-headed creature like a farmer, nourishing and domesticating its gentle aspects, but preventing the wild ones from growing, and that he must make the nature of the lion his ally and bring them up with a concern for their common good, making them friends of each other and himself.
>
> (588e—589b)

It is clear which option Plato thinks is best for us to adopt.

The critique of literature and education

By the end of Book IX, the case for the superiority of justice over injustice is complete. I have so far omitted one aspect of Plato's argument, however, which I want now to consider. This is his critique of poetry and traditional Greek education, which constitutes his answer to Adeimantus' challenge in Book II. The reader will recall that, while Glaucon had posed a philosophical problem to Socrates, that of showing that justice was a good of the highest sort, Adeimantus had added to Glaucon's case the evidence of the poets, who had praised justice only for its consequences and not for its intrinsic nature. Plato's account of the just individual, the philosopher-king, is an attempt to meet Glaucon's challenge, while his critique of poetry answers Adeimantus. The two answers are related. Plato believes that the poets are wrong because he thinks his own views about the nature of human excellence are correct, and he thinks the poets are ignorant because his own epistemological and metaphysical theories indicates that they are. His own views, moreover, are developed in response to those of the poets, so it is not surprising that he should indicate his differences with them directly.

Plato's critique of poetry is instructive in that it places his own view into the context of traditional Greek views about the good life sketched in Chapter 1 above. Socrates, as we saw in Chapter 2, had set forth his own conception of the good life, both in words and by example. Socrates believed that the good life was the virtuous life, and that virtue was sufficient to make a person happy (*eudaimon*). He had also argued that the virtues were all forms of knowledge, and that possession of one virtue entailed possession of all. In these respects he differed from the views articulated by the poets: they had seen the virtues as distinct, wisdom (or knowledge) as one virtue among many, and virtue as insufficient as a guarantee of happiness. Socrates had not, however, explicitly contrasted his view with that of the poets. Such a contrast would have been ruled out by the constraints of his method, which forbade lengthy exposition. He lets us know in the *Apology* and elsewhere that he thinks the poets have no knowledge, and he dismisses the discussion of poetry in the *Protagoras* (347c—e) as unworthy of serious intellectual conversation. He makes frequent approving references to the poets, however, and compares himself in the *Apology* to the greatest of the Greek heroes, Achilles. Beyond this, though, he does not go; it is the task of Plato to set the philosophical conception of the good life in contrast with that of the poets.

I noted at the beginning of this chapter that Plato's views in the *Republic*, though indebted to those of Socrates, differed from them in many ways. His ideal of the good life as a harmonious integration of the rational and irrational parts of the soul is a major advance on the intellectualist position of Socrates. With respect to the sufficiency of virtue for happiness and the ignorance of the poets, however, he is at one with his master. The critique of poetry Plato offers in the *Republic* is, in the main, the sort of critique we might have expected from Socrates.

This critique is particularly relevant to the political project of the *Republic*. The modern reader is apt to forget that the Greeks regarded the poets not just as producers of aesthetically valuable works, but as civic and religious educators, the best sources of information about the gods and human nature. It is in this capacity as educators that Plato criticizes them. He does not deny the aesthetic appeal of their works, rather, he thinks that this power to delight the audience, when used to present a false picture of reality, is the source of great harm to the state (cf. 387a). In order for the state to be properly founded on a true basis, the distorted views of the poets must be replaced by the correct views of the philosopher.

In the latter part of Book II and the first part of Book III Plato indicates the places where he thinks the poets have gone wrong. The issue that prompts the discussion is the education of the guardians. Members of this class must be courageous and wise, swift and strong; how can they be trained to develop these traits? They must receive physical education to develop their bodies and education in literature (*mousike*, not "music" but the liberal arts in general) to develop their minds. The earliest form of this education occurs in the telling of stories (377a), and most current stories are unsuitable for children to hear.

The stories of the poets go wrong in two areas: their depiction of the gods, and their depiction of heroes. The first story Plato selects for criticism is the tale of the castration of the god Ouranos at the hands of his son Cronos, and the latter's deposition by Zeus. It is unworthy of the gods to behave in such a manner, such stories must not be told to the young

> Nor shall it be said to a young listener that he would be doing nothing remarkable by committing the greatest injustices, or punishing an unjust father in any way, but that he would only be doing what the first and greatest of the gods had done.
>
> (378b)

This is a criticism Plato owes to Socrates: in the *Euthyphro*, Euthyphro is pictured as defending his prosecution of his father on a charge of murder by arguing that Zeus and Cronos had treated their fathers thus (5e—6a), to which Socrates replies that he disapproves of such stories, and that this is perhaps the reason why he is being prosecuted for impiety. Socrates, unlike most ancient Greeks, conceived of the gods as highly moral (thus his refusal to believe that the oracle of Apollo might have lied when it said no one was wiser than he), and Plato is here following his lead.

Accordingly, all stories about the gods that represent them as quarreling with one another must be rejected. "The god must always be represented as he happens to be," writes Plato, "whether in epic, lyric or tragedy" (379a). In reality, god is good, and as such can only be the cause of good, not of evil

> "The god," I said, "since he is good, could not be the cause of all things, as the many say, but is the cause of a few things among humans, and is not responsible for many. For there are far fewer good things than evils among us, and though no other cause should be assigned to the good, we must seek other causes of the evils than the god." (379c)

Nor are the gods to be depicted as changing form: "Each god, being the finest and best being possible, remains in its own form forever" (381c). The gods detest falsehood, and do not use it to deceive humans (382c), despite what Homer and other poets have written.

When it comes to the depiction of heroes, the poets fare no better. Since the guardians of the state must be brave, and since courage requires that they not fear death, stories that portray the after-life as gloomy and heroes as fearing death must be forbidden

> We must, it seems, take charge of those who try to tell stories about these things and ask them not to denigrate generally the conditions in Hades but rather to praise them, on the grounds that such remarks are neither true nor beneficial to those who are going to be warlike. (386b—c)

This point also originates with Socrates, who had argued in the *Apology* that no one knows whether death is evil and who had portrayed the after-life as highly desirable. A large part of the tragic perspective of Greek poetry derives from its treatment of death as a terrible loss for the individual, and Plato's refusal to portray the death of Socrates as a tragedy results, as we saw in Chapter 2, from his refusal to accept that view of death.

If death is not to be feared, the hero should not lament the death of a comrade. "A person of this sort," writes Plato, "is especially sufficient in himself with respect to living well" (387d—e), so he will bear the loss of a friend or relative calmly rather than weep and wail disconsolately, as Achilles does over the death of Patroclus. Similarly, the hero should not be portrayed as given to fits of laughter, lies or losses of self-control. Rather, the hero should be shown as obedient to his superiors, truthful and enduring in the face of temptation, as was Odysseus when he "struck himself on the chest and spoke to his heart and scolded it." (Plato quotes this line from *Odyssey* 20, 17 at 390d and again at 441b; cf. above, p. 107.) It is all right for the young guardians-to-be to hear and imitate such examples of heroic conduct, but not those that portray heroes as vicious or mean-spirited.

Plato's method for ensuring that only the right tales will be told to children in his state is censorship, a solution that always repels modern readers, who reject it out of hand. It is necessary in this context to note two features of Plato's view that are easily overlooked. Though he speaks of banishing the false views of the poets from the state altogether, his concern is with the education of the young. His view is that they should not be exposed to ugly falsehoods, because that would damage their souls. Most parents in fact adopt this attitude and control (or attempt to control) the material children are allowed to read or (more commonly today) see on television. The arguments these parents use to "censor" the stories told to their young are very similar to those used by Plato. The differences between Plato's view and ours are that Plato believed that excision of such material from society as a whole is the only effective method of preventing children from being exposed to it (a point on which he may well be correct), and he does not have our confidence that even adult minds are capable of withstanding the allure of the poets. Moreover, he does not conceive of a fundamental right of free speech, which guarantees that adults may be exposed to a variety of views. If he is wrong on any of these points, then his argument for censorship fails, but that is not to say that he fails to raise serious and legitimate problems about the availability of certain literature to the young.

The second point on which Plato differs from us is in his conception of censorship itself. We view censorship as a method of suppressing information that may be dangerous to a regime or other institution because it is or may be true, and we oppose censorship because we believe that we have an obligation to see that the truth come to light. Plato, however, wants to censor material he claims to know is false, and dangerous precisely because it conveys false ideas about the gods and human beings. We are prone to reject the idea of a definitive truth in matters of this sort, or at least the idea that literature should be restricted to the expression of such truth. Plato, however, is looking at the poets as educators. He regards the views of Homer in the way that evolutionary biologists regard the views of "creation scientists." Biologists see such views as an unscientific attack on scientific truth, and do not feel obliged to give creationism equal time in the classroom with the theory of evolution. The reader may well think that Plato is not entitled to claim for his own views equal status with scientific biology, but the question could surely be asked, whether censorship of competing views would be justified if they did have that status. This question, I think, leaves us uneasy, perhaps because we think that scientific truth differs in some fundamental way from philosophical or literary truth, but it is quite difficult to spell out that difference without giving up the concept of philosophical and literary truth altogether, and thus begging the question against Plato, who assumes that matters can be known to be true in these areas.

Plato goes on to discuss the rhythms and genres of poetry that will be acceptable in his state. He remarks that the discussion of education is so far incomplete: he has not been able to show what is wrong with the treatment in poetry of ordinary people, because the answer has not yet been found to the question whether justice or injustice is better for such people (392a—c). When he returns to the discussion of poetry in Book X, that question has been answered in favor of justice, and Plato does not bring it up again. Instead, he uses the metaphysical theory of forms and the doctrine of the tripartite nature of the soul, philosophical positions that have been developed after the earlier critique of poetry, to reformulate the case against poetry.

Plato puts forward two arguments against poetry in Book X. The first is based on his metaphysics. We assume the existence of a single form for every set of particular things having the same name. There is thus one form of bed, and another of table. The craftsman who makes individual tables and beds looks to this form in doing so (596a—b). The artist in turns looks to the bed or table made by the carpenter when he produces a representation or imitation of it; he makes an image of the craftsman's bed, a copy of a copy, a thing "at third remove from reality" (597e; we would say "at second remove," omitting the first stage itself). The artist does not even attempt to represent the nature of the carpenter's bed, but only its appearance. Thus, it is not necessary for the artist to know the nature of the bed the carpenter makes to do his job well, let alone the form of bed.

Plato goes further. The fact that the artist creates images is proof that he is ignorant of the nature of things

> I think that if he truly had knowledge of the things he imitates, he would much prefer to concern himself with the actions than with their imitations, and would try to leave behind many fine actions of his own as a memorial, and would be eager to be the one praised rather than the one who praises. (599b)

Poets, like painters, are imitative artists of the type Plato has just described: he goes on to apply his criticism to Homer (599b—601a). Thus, the poet has no knowledge of the things he represents, as Socrates had argued in the *Apology* and elsewhere. Therefore, the poets are not qualified to be educators, and may safely be excluded from the state.

This argument is problematic in several respects. First, it depends on the truth of Platonic metaphysics. It is in fact a fairly straightforward application of the theory of the divided line: the artist works in the bottom segment, that of illusion; the craftsman works in the second, that of belief; and the top two segments are reserved for the mathematician and the philosopher. Even within this metaphysics, however, one may question the concept of the artist as merely imitative, or the idea of imitation as ignorant rendering of appearances. The artist, one might suggest, needs to know something about the form of man in order to represent human nature adequately in his compositions and the success of Homer and others is proof that they had such knowledge. Third, one may question Plato's assumption that it is better to perform deeds than to represent them. We have a very high opinion of the "fine arts," such as painting, and would say that a painting of a bed by a great master is a far more valuable work than the bed itself.

Even the Greeks, who did not distinguish the fine arts from the crafts in the way that we do, would have thought that a painting by one of their great artists, such as Zeuxis or Appeles, more valuable than the object painted in it. Even if we limit the question to the sorts of political topics that are of immediate concern to Plato, it is not clear that he is correct. Is it better to be Achilles and do great things, or Homer and write great poetry? Plato may think the answer should be clear, but it is not.

Plato is on surer ground with his second argument. Art, and poetry in particular, appeals to our senses and our emotions, rather than our reason. Tragedy, the form of art originated by Homer and perfected by the Athenian tragic poets, thrives on human suffering and conflict. If someone who is good in the Platonic sense suffers misfortune, such as the loss of a son, he will bear this misfortune as calmly as possible, resisting and restraining the grief that he will inevitably feel; he will not engage in public displays of sorrow, but will attempt to cure his sorrow by suppressing it (604d, another example of the Platonic asceticism I spoke of earlier in the chapter). But the tragedian cannot depict such a person on the stage because drama requires characters who freely express their emotions. We naturally admire such representations and feel pity for the characters thus portrayed (think here of Achilles grieving over the loss of Patroclus, and of Oedipus lamenting his fate), but this is dangerous

> I think few people are capable of reasoning that what we enjoy in others necessarily affects us, and that if our pity for others is nourished and grows strong it will not be easy to restrain in the case of our own sufferings. (606b)

The same is true in matters of comedy as in the case of tragedy

> As concerns sex and anger and all of the emotions and pleasures and pains in the soul, which we say follow every action, these are the sorts of things imitative poetry arouses in us. For it nourishes and fosters these things which it ought to let wither, and establishes them as rulers in us when they ought to be ruled in order that we may be better and happier instead of worse and more wretched. (606d)

This argument recapitulates the case made against the poetic depiction of heroes in Books II and III. As earlier, Plato may be criticized for discounting entirely the legitimate aesthetic value such works of art have, in proposing to deprive the citizenry of his state of works like the *Iliad* and *Oedipus the King* because of moral values alone. This is a criticism Plato would no doubt answer by saying that moral values are so important to the welfare of the state that they justify such an extreme response. He could also be criticized for claiming that poetry appeals only to our emotions; surely some poetry, including the sort he would abolish, leads people to think about the human condition. Perhaps Plato's real objection to Homer and the tragedians is that they lead people to think the wrong thoughts, not that they produce emotional responses. Still, when these objections have been removed, the fact remains that poetry, and tragedy in particular, does arouse strong emotions, and that it does so by its very nature. If one is to defend poetry against Plato's criticism, one must show that this is not in itself harmful.

Plato in fact leaves room for the reintroduction of poetry into the state, if it can answer his charges (607c—e). Though the reader may feel that the cards are stacked against poetry, there is a certain kind of literature that Plato is willing to retain. That is literature that fosters the aims of the state, that is politically beneficial as well as beautiful. When we hear this, we are apt to think that Plato would approve only the kind of propaganda employed by the totalitarian states of this century, but Plato is himself too good an artist to find this sort of literature acceptable. I think that Plato himself offers a better example of what he has in mind in the "Myth of Er," with which the dialogue ends. He does not explicitly put this story forward as an example of the kind of literature he has in mind, but the myth does display the heroes of the Greek tradition acting in ways he would approve, so it meets the criteria of acceptability he had put forth in Books II and III. Plato in fact includes myths, usually about the after-life, in several of his dialogues, including the *Gorgias*, *Phaedo* and *Phaedrus*. These myths may be his attempt to use the techniques of imaginative literature to deal with topics not well suited to philosophical exposition (Socrates, after all, had pointed out in the *Apology* that no one had philosophical knowledge of the after-life).

In the "Myth of Er" (which follows an argument for the

immortality of the soul), Plato depicts the punishment for wrongdoing and the rewards for goodness that await people after death. According to the story, those who are incorrigibly wicked are destroyed, while those who are capable of reform pay a tenfold penalty for their wrongs. The virtuous receive corresponding benefits for their good deeds (615a—616a). At the end of their period of purification, the souls of the dead choose new lives and undergo reincarnation. Each individual is responsible for the life he or she chooses (617d—e). While others choose lives in response to their previous situations in life, sometimes with disastrous results, Plato depicts Odysseus as choosing last

> Memory of his previous labors had released him from the pursuit of glory, and he looked around for a long time for the life of a private man uninvolved in affairs of state and found it with difficulty, lying somewhere disregarded by the others, and he chose it gladly, saying when he saw it that he would have done the same if he had had the first choice. (620c—d)

Since the story is set in the distant past and is being told by Socrates, Plato cannot depict the choice that would have been made by his model philosopher. Instead, he selects the hero from literature most renowned for his wisdom and has him repudiate the heroic ideal. Like Achilles in the *Iliad*, Odysseus has the choice between lives of glory and a life of quiet anonymity but unlike Achilles he chooses the latter. Plato cannot praise the philosophical virtues of this life, because, as he describes the choice of lives, the individual soul brings its own qualities of character to the life (618b). One feels, however, that Plato regards Odysseus' choice as a worthy one for a philosophical temperament, at least if the choice of being a philosopher-king is not available.

Plato's critique of poetry and his own attempt at poetic myth reveal both the strengths and weaknesses of the *Republic* as a whole. His theory may be criticized as unrealistic, because it is based on a controversial metaphysics, as somewhat over ascetic and narrow in its focus and as overzealous in its defense of some goods at the expense of others. None the less, it represents a major advance over its predecessors in comprehensiveness and plausibility and, in its theory of the three-part soul, it provides for the first time a psychological theory suitable for the articulation of the virtues. Aristotle, whom we shall study in the next chapter, was heavily indebted to Plato's psychology and theory of the virtues, though he disagreed with the metaphysical theory of the *Republic*. Finally, it must be noted that Plato is one of the few philosophers who have attempted to justify morality to the skeptic (in this case Thrasymachus) by showing that justice is good for the individual. Despite the weaknesses of his answer noted above, it remains one of the most nearly satisfactory attempts to answer this question in the history of philosophy.

4

ARISTOTLE'S
NICOMACHEAN ETHICS

Aristotle is one of history's greatest philosophers, and his *Nicomachean Ethics* is one of the greatest works in moral philosophy. The history of Greek philosophical thought about virtue reaches its culmination in the ethical theory of Aristotle.

Aristotle's life and works

Aristotle was born in 384 BC in the northern Greek town of Stagira. His father was a medical doctor, and Aristotle probably derived from him the lifelong interest in biology which pervades most of his writings, including his ethics. His father was court physician to Amyntas III, king of Macedonia. Amyntas was the father of Philip, who was in turn the father of Alexander the Great. Because of his father's position in the Macedonian court, Aristotle was associated from his earliest days with the most powerful dynasty in the Greek world.

In 367 BC Aristotle became a student in Plato's Academy. He remained there until Plato's death in 347. We have little knowledge of how Aristotle spent these years; however, it seems clear from his later writings that he respected and admired Plato but was hardly a slavish disciple. Aristotle generally treats Plato's philosophy as a foil, in contrast to which he develops his own view. When Plato died in 347 Aristotle left Athens for a dozen years. During this time he traveled in the area of the Aegean Sea, conducted biological research, married, and for a time tutored the young Alexander. If we may judge from the great differences between Alexander's vision of a world-state and the traditional *polis* or city-state described in Aristotle's *Politics*, Aristotle apparently had little philosophical influence on Alexander.

In 335 BC Aristotle returned to Athens and founded his own school, the Lyceum. If Plato's Academy may be called the Western world's first institution of higher education, the Lyceum seems to have been the first research university. It was during this period that most of the Aristotelian works we still possess were written. Aristotle apparently maintained friendly relations with Alexander during this period, for when Alexander died in 323 the Athenians expressed their anti-Macedonian sentiments by charging Aristotle with the stock accusation of impiety. Unlike Socrates, Aristotle left Athens rather than face trial, so that the Athenians, as he is reported to have said, might not "sin twice against philosophy." He died the following year.

Aristotle's writings fall into two broad classes. Of his dialogues, which were praised in the ancient world for their style, only fragments remain. Most of what we possess from Aristotle's pen are treatises. These works are terse and even cryptic in style, and were probably not intended for wide distribution. They may have been Aristotle's own notes for lectures he gave in the Lyceum. Of the four treatises in the traditional Aristotelian corpus devoted to ethics, one (*On Virtues and Vices*) is certainly not by Aristotle and another (*Magna Moralia*) is of doubtful authenticity. The *Eudemian Ethics* is generally accepted today as an Aristotelian work, probably written before the *Nicomachean*. There has never been any doubt that the *Nicomachean Ethics* was written by Aristotle. Historically, the *Nicomachean Ethics* has been by far more studied and more influential than the *Eudemian*; it remains today the work to which philosophers turn for the definitive statement of Aristotle's views on ethics.

The structure of the *Nicomachean Ethics*

Like most of the Aristotelian treatises, the *Nicomachean Ethics* owes its present form to the work of editors (the *Ethics* is named for Aristotle's son Nicomachus, either because it was dedicated to him or because he edited the work). Three of its books (V—VII) are also found in the *Eudemian Ethics*, and the work contains two discussions of pleasure (one at the end of Book VII and another at the start of Book X). Nevertheless, the work exhibits a generally tight overall structure.

The *Ethics* begins in Book I with an investigation of *eudaimonia*, happiness or the good life, the end for the sake of which Aristotle believes we cultivate the virtues. Aristotle defines this life in terms of *arete*, virtue, so it is natural that a discussion of virtue in general should ensue in Book II. In defining virtue, Aristotle in turn makes use of the concept of *prohairesis*, choice or preference, which is then discussed in the first part (Chapters 1—5) of Book III. The latter part of Book III, all of Book IV and Book V are devoted to a detailed discussion of particular moral virtues. The moral virtues require the intellectual virtue of *phronesis*, practical wisdom, for their proper exercise. Aristotle accordingly discusses this in Book VI, and moral weakness (a failure of *phronesis*) in Book VII. Books VIII and IX are devoted to the study of friendship, a key concept in ancient theories of ethics and politics and Book X concludes the work with a discussion of pleasure and a reconsideration of the good life.

Aristotle's methodology

The early books of the *Ethics* contain, alongside discussions of the substantive material outlined above, many remarks on the proper method of ethical investigation. Aristotle divided the sciences into three kinds: theoretical sciences, such as mathematics, physics and metaphysics; practical sciences, which include ethics and politics; and productive sciences, such as carpentry or pottery. The theoretical sciences, he thought, dealt with matters that are eternal, unchanging and necessarily the way they are. This unchanging subject matter gives the theoretical sciences, in his view, a stability and precision not to be found in either the practical or productive sciences.

The practical and productive sciences, on the other hand, deal with matters that can be changed by our own efforts. In the practical sciences actions are performed and the character of the agent is developed, but no separately existing product results; in the productive sciences, however, a product, a work of art, is created. Because the subject matter of the practical sciences is changeable, Aristotle thinks that these sciences themselves must be less precise than the theoretical sciences

Problems of what is noble and just, which politics examines,

146

present so much variety and irregularity that some people believe that they exist only by convention and not by nature. The problem of the good, too, presents a similar kind of irregularity, because in many cases good things bring harmful results. There are instances of men ruined by wealth, and others by courage. Therefore, in a discussion of such subjects ... we must be satisfied to indicate the truth with a rough and general sketch: when the subject and the basis of a discussion consist of matters that hold good only as a general rule, but not always, the conclusions reached must be of the same order. (I.3, 1094b 14—22; cf. I.7, II.2. Ostwald's translation.)

These remarks point out a major difference between Aristotle's concept of ethics and Plato's. Plato would have rejected the distinction Aristotle insists on between the theoretical and practical sciences, and the corresponding difference in precision between them. As the discussion between Socrates and Cephalus in *Republic* I shows, Plato would not have been satisfied with ethical principles that held only as a general rule, rather, he sought an account of virtue and goodness as precise and as philosophically respectable as anything in mathematics. Ethics was for Plato the investigation of certain eternal, unchanging forms, an enterprise as "theoretical" as any of Aristotle's theoretical sciences.

This difference in methodology leads to one of Aristotle's criticisms of Plato. In I.6 Aristotle discusses Plato's view of the good. The good of Platonic philosophy, he states, "evidently is something which cannot be realized in action or attained by man. But the good which we are now seeking must be attainable" (1096b 33—5). If the Platonists should argue that the good, though unattainable itself, is valuable as a standard against which the various attainable goods can be judged, Aristotle responds

This argument has, no doubt, some plausibility; however, it does not tally with the procedure of the sciences. For while all the sciences aim at some good and seek to fulfill it, they leave the knowledge of the absolute good out of consideration. . . . One might also wonder what benefit a weaver or a carpenter might derive in the practice of his own art from a knowledge of the absolute Good, or in what way a physician who has contemplated the Form of the Good will become more of a physician. (1097a 3—11)

As this quote indicates, the actual practices of the sciences are more important to Aristotle than they are to Plato. So also are common opinions. Aristotle does not simply derive his ethical theory from popular opinions but he does take such views seriously as material for ethical reflection. Rejecting the external standard of ethical conduct contained in Plato's theory of forms, Aristotle seeks the principles of ethics within ethical practices and opinions themselves.

This difference in methodology has practical consequences. Plato, believing he had access to an independent standard by which human actions could be judged (i.e. the forms), was quite willing to reject ordinary views as misguided. Thus he was able to reach radical conclusions, for instance on the equality of women and the abolition of the family, which were often quite at variance with the beliefs of Greeks of his time. No such radical conclusions will be found in Aristotle, precisely because of his reliance on the views of ordinary Greeks.

Clearly, neither Aristotle's respectful observance of the moral tradition in which he worked nor Plato's willingness to reject that tradition when it suited his purposes is a perfect methodology. Aristotle's approach yields insight in those cases where the tradition is fundamentally sound, but error when the tradition is flawed. Plato is more able than Aristotle to see and correct the shortcomings of Greek thought, but also more likely to dispense with something of value, to "throw the baby out with the bath-water."

The good: *eudaimonia*

Aristotle's general approach to ethics is, like Plato's, *teleological*: Book I of the *Ethics* begins with the claim that "every art or applied science and every systematic investigation, and similarly every action and choice, seem to aim at some good" (I.1, 1094a 1—2). Unlike Plato, however, Aristotle believes in a variety of ends: "Since there are many activities, arts, and sciences, the number of ends is correspondingly large" (1094a 6—8). Each activity or science, whether it is medicine, shipbuilding or military strategy, has its own end. How can a single good be found which is the object of all human endeavor, and thus a suitable end for ethics?

Aristotle solves this problem by noting that some activities and their ends are subordinated to others: the art of bridlemaking subserves the ends of horsemanship, while horsemanship (which in Aristotle's time was a military art) serves the interests of strategy. Thus, though there is a multiplicity of ends, it is hierarchically ordered. So there will be a single, ultimate good if there is a single science at the top of the hierarchical pyramid.

Aristotle believes that there is such a master science in the realm of action, and that it is politics

> For it determines which sciences ought to exist in states, what kind of sciences each group of citizens ought to learn, and what degree of proficiency each must attain. (I.2, 1094a 28—b 2)

Modern readers find it strange that Aristotle should begin a work on ethics with the claim that politics, rather than ethics, is the master practical science. Aristotle, though, like most Greeks, thinks that politics and ethics have the same end, "the good for man"; politics is superior to ethics only because it is a "greater and more perfect thing . . . nobler and more divine" (1094b 8—10) to secure and maintain the good life for an entire state than for a single individual.

Having established that there is a master practical science, and thus a single ultimate end of all human activity, Aristotle proceeds to ask what this end is.

> As far as its name is concerned, most people would probably agree: for both the common run of people and cultivated men call it happiness, and understand by "being happy" the same as "living well" and "doing well." (I.4, 1095a 17—20)

The word translated "happiness" here is *eudaimonia*, and, just from what Aristotle tells us about *eudaimonia* here we can see that it differs in meaning somewhat from the English translation. As I indicated in the Introduction, the English word "happiness" suggests a state of psychological contentment, pleasure or joy and, though this subjective component is not absent from the Greek *eudaimonia*, it is not its primary connotation. We might say of severely retarded persons living in pleasant circumstances that they were happy, though their lives were devoid of high intellectual activities, further, it does not seem an abuse of the English language to say that a child molester is happy when molesting children. Neither Aristotle nor any other Greek would call such people *eudaimon*, however, for, as Aristotle notes, people understand by *eudaimonia* "living well" and "doing well."

The concept of *eudaimonia* has connotations of achievement, success and moral excellence lacking in the concept of happiness. The word is derived from the Greek prefix *eu-*, which means "good," and *daimon*, which means "spirit", accordingly, *eudaimonia* is the state or condition of having a good spirit or psyche. Living well or doing well in an objective sense is only possible for one whose soul is in a good condition, so the investigation of *eudaimonia* will require the determination of just what a good condition of the soul consists in. Aristotle thought (and most Greeks would agree) that the good condition of the soul would produce the contentment and joy which are associated with "happiness" in English, so that everyone who is *eudaimon* in Aristotle's view would also be happy, but not everyone who is happy would be *eudaimon*. "The good life" might be a closer English translation of *eudaimonia* than "happiness."

Despite verbal agreement that the human good is *eudaimonia* and that this is equivalent to living well, the ancient Greeks disagreed about what this consisted in, just as we disagree today about what the good life consists in. Aristotle thinks there are three main candidates for the title of the good life: the life of pleasure or enjoyment, the political life and the contemplative life.

Aristotle does not think much of the life of pleasure: he says it is the choice of "the common run of people," who "betray their utter slavishness in their preference for a life suitable to cattle" (I.5, 1095b 19—20). Aristotle understands by "the life of pleasure," not any life filled with pleasant experiences, for he thinks the good life is pleasant in that sense, but rather, a life devoted to the pursuit of the pleasures of eating, drinking and sex. Such a life *is* in fact suitable to cattle, according to Aristotle's account of the soul. For according to this account, there are several different psychic capacities, arranged in a hierarchy. The most basic capacity is that of nutrition and reproduction, which is shared by all living things, including plants. Next up the scale are the capacities of sensation and locomotion, which distinguish animals from plants. Some animals possess the powers of memory and imagination, but only human beings possess reason. Living the life of pleasure requires the use of the nutritive, reproductive, sensitive and probably the imaginative faculties, but not reason. Thus it may be worthy of lower animals, but is beneath human dignity.

Honor, the end of the political life, is superior to pleasure at least in that it can only be pursued by human beings. But honor is defective as an end also

> for honor seems to depend on those who confer it rather than on him who receives it, whereas our guess is that the good is a man's own possession which cannot easily be taken away from him. Furthermore, men seem to pursue honor to assure themselves of their own worth; at any rate, they seek to be honored by sensible men and by those who know them, and they want to be honored on the basis of their virtue or excellence. (1095b 24—9)

The life of excellence itself, however, is not the good life either, for one might possess excellence

> while asleep or while being inactive all his life, and while, in addition, undergoing the greatest suffering and misfortune. Nobody would call the life of such a man happy, except for the sake of maintaining an argument. (1095b 32—1096a 2)

Almost as an after-thought, Aristotle adds to his list the life of wealth, which he dismisses in a sentence: "clearly, wealth is not the good which we are trying to find, for it is only useful, i.e., it is a means to something else" (1096a 6—7). It is surely one of the most remarkable features of the *Nicomachean Ethics* that Aristotle feels the need to devote no more space than this to the view of the good most common in the developed world today.

After reviewing these various candidates for the good life and finding them all wanting, Aristotle proceeds in I.7 to offer his own account of *eudaimonia*. His answer is based on the concept of a distinctively human "function" just as the goodness and performance of a flute player, a sculptor, or any kind of expert, and generally of anyone who fulfills some function or performs some action, are thought to reside in his proper function, so the goodness and performance of man would seem to reside in whatever is his proper function. It is then possible that while a carpenter and a shoemaker have their own proper functions and spheres of action, man as man has none, but was left by nature a good-for-nothing without a function? (1097b 25—30)

The English word "function" strongly suggests that the object in question must be an instrument of some sort, fulfilling the purpose of an agent who uses it: automobiles serve the function of taking us where we want to go. "Function," thus understood, seems inappropriate for the agent who uses the instrument, however: "whose purposes do we satisfy?", we are inclined to ask. The Greek word *ergon*, which "function" translates, is much less narrow in its meaning. *Ergon* literally means "work" and, though instruments do indeed perform work for us, we ourselves perform work, and can do so well or badly, without serving as instruments. Even "work" is slightly misleading in its connotations as a translation of *ergon*, for it connotes for us labor done for pay whereas what Aristotle is looking for in seeking the *ergon* of human beings is the sort of activity they characteristically engage in. It may be that human beings have an *ergon*, a characteristic activity, though they lack a "function."

Aristotle indeed thinks that there is a characteristically human activity.

What can this function possibly be? Simply living? He shares that even with plants, *but we are now looking for something peculiar to man.* Accordingly, the life of nutrition and growth must be excluded. Next in line there is the life of sense perception. But this, too, man has in common with the horse, the ox, and every animal. There remains then an active life of the rational element. (1097b 33—1098a 4, my emphasis)

This passage contains perhaps the most crucial argument in all of Aristotle's ethics. He approaches the question like the biologist he is, and invokes the same hierarchy of psychological faculties I brought up earlier. We need not be biologists, however, to see that the attributes he rejects could not help us in determining the nature of the good life. We would not say that someone was a good person if he or she excelled at eating, reproducing or using his or her senses.

Is Aristotle right to infer, however, that the human *ergon* must reside in the faculty of reason? It seems not, for several reasons. First, we should note that an activity which characterizes human existence need not be one which distinguishes it from that of other species but Aristotle has found (or so he believes, note emphasized passage above) a *distinguishing* feature of human existence. To illustrate: the human species could be distinguished from all others by a trait that tells us virtually nothing about our essential nature, as in the Platonic definition of man as a featherless biped. On the other hand, suppose that the most important human trait, the one that essentially characterizes our lives, *is* reason; this point would not be at all affected by the discovery that other species such as whales and dolphins were also rational.

There are two further possible objections to Aristotle's conclusion. The first is that his argument is an argument by elimination (like Plato's argument in *Republic* IV that justice must be doing one's own job), and like any such argument depends on Aristotle's having canvassed all the relevant human traits and Aristotle, like his predecessors, seems to have overlooked at least two. The first of these is the will, which Christian philosophers such as Augustine saw as central to human existence and as the source of good and evil; the second is moral sentiment or emotion, which Hume and other Enlightenment philosophers saw as the source of morality. It could be that the essential human characteristic, at least from the standpoint of morality, is manifested in our acts of will or in our compassionate responses to the suffering of others, rather than in our rational activity.

The second objection is that the human *ergon* may not be found in the activities of one psychological faculty but in their harmonious integration (the view defended by Plato in the *Republic*). Our humanness may be shown not only or even most distinctively in acts of pure thought, but in our use of reason to accomplish the aims of the nutritive, reproductive and sensitive faculties. Aristotle actually seems to describe this option in his account of practical wisdom; none the less, when he discusses in

Book X the best form of human existence he chooses the life of pure, unimpeded, theoretical reason over the harmonious, integrated life of practical reason. The explanation for this conclusion, I think, is to be found in the present argument that rational activity in itself is the human *ergon*. Aristotle's conclusion that rational activity is the human *ergon* is thus not justified by his argument. This is not to say, however, that Aristotle is profoundly mistaken. Rational activity is at least one of the features that characterize human life and the vast majority of later philosophers have followed Aristotle in focusing on rational activity as the key to ethics. Even if the good life cannot be completely defined as the life of reason, we can expect his clarification of the role of reason in ethics to be of great value.

Let us return to Aristotle's argument. If the distinctively human life is the life of reason, then the good life will be that in which reason is exercised well, as it would be by "a man of high standards", for "a function is well performed when it is performed in accordance with the excellence appropriate to it" (I.7, 1098a 15). From this Aristotle's official definition of *eudaimonia* follows

> the good of man is an activity of the soul in conformity with excellence or virtue, and if there are several virtues, in conformity with the best and most complete. (1098a 16—18)

In order to understand this definition fully we must interpret it in light of the conclusion about reason he has already reached. The human good is not *any* activity of the soul that conforms to virtue, for eating is an activity that can conform to the virtue of temperance, but it is an activity of the lowest faculty of the soul, the nutritive faculty. The human good consists in the activity of the highest faculty of the soul, which as we have seen is reason. The excellence or virtue which is "the best and most complete" is the excellence of the rational faculty. Thus the good life is not that in which we eat, reproduce, sense, move, remember or imagine well, but that in which we exercise reason well.

The conclusion that the good human life is that in which we reason well does in fact follow from the premise that the human *ergon* is rational activity and the premise that something is a good thing of its kind if it performs the *ergon* of that kind of thing well. The second premise seems uncontroversial, thus any problems that exist in the argument must arise from the first premise, which we have already discussed.

With this definition of the good life, Aristotle's account of *eudaimonia* is essentially complete. He goes on to add the qualification that *eudaimonia* must be evaluated "in a complete life" (1098a 18), rather than over a brief period; a qualification that recalls for us the fact that Aristotle, like other Greek moral theorists, is primarily interested in the evaluation of lives, not of acts or other episodes in them.

Though Aristotle's formal account of *eudaimonia* is complete at the end of I.7, many questions remain. We know that Aristotle believes the good life to be that in which we reason well, but what forms can this good rational activity take? Reasoning well means exercising virtue, but what kind of virtue? How do the traditional virtues of Greek philosophy fit with Aristotle's notion of the good life? And what is the relation between virtue, as Aristotle understands it, and the good life? To answer these questions we must turn to Aristotle's discussion of *arete*, excellence or virtue.

Arete: moral excellence or virtue

All of Book II of the *Ethics* is devoted to the analysis of moral virtue, but the discussion actually begins in the final chapter of Book I. Aristotle there divides the soul into two parts, one rational, the other irrational. The irrational part he again divides in two. One part, the nutritive, is "vegetative" in nature and has nothing to do with virtue. The other part, "the seat of the appetites and of desire in general" (I.13, 1102b 30), can be described as either rational or irrational. It is irrational to the degree that it "opposes and reacts against" the dictates of the rational element, and rational "insofar as it complies with reason and accepts its leadership" (1102b 30—1).

Aristotle's account of the soul is similar but not identical to that given by Plato in the *Republic*. The rational part of the soul is the same in both theories, and so is the appetitive, but Aristotle introduces the vegetative part of the soul, which Plato omits, and does not separate the "spirited" part from the appetitive. Like Plato, Aristotle uses the language of persuasion to describe the influence of reason on appetite: "That the irrational element can be persuaded by the rational is shown by the fact that admonition and all manner of rebuke and exhortation are possible" (1102b 33—1103a 1).

Once the parts of the soul have been thus distinguished, the virtues can be divided in a corresponding manner

> Virtue, too, is differentiated in line with this division of the soul. We call some virtues "intellectual" and others "moral": theoretical wisdom, understanding, and practical wisdom are intellectual virtues, generosity and self-control moral virtues.
> (1103a 3—7)

Clearly, Aristotle intends the intellectual virtues to be seen as belonging to the rational part of the soul, and the moral virtues or virtues of character to the irrational part, insofar as it has accepted the persuasion of the rational. This entails that the intellectual virtues are the primary contributors to the good life, since Aristotle has defined this life in terms of rational activity; the moral virtues contribute to the good life only indirectly, insofar as they reflect the conformity of the lower parts of the soul to the direction of reason. It is easy to forget this point, since Aristotle devotes a great deal of care to the analysis of the moral virtues in Books II—V of the *Ethics*.

Aristotle deals with the moral and the intellectual virtues separately. He treats of the moral virtues first, and only in Book VI does he take up the intellectual virtues, including practical wisdom. This results in a somewhat one-sided picture of moral virtue. It is important to remember that the moral virtues are crowned or completed by the intellectual virtue of practical wisdom, and that what he says about them independently of practical wisdom must be supplemented by the later account of that virtue. For instance, Aristotle begins his account of the moral virtues by noting that they are "formed by habit" (II.1, 1103a 17). This makes it sound as if the moral virtues are acquired without reflection, by rote, but this does not do justice to the dialectical relation between the rational and irrational parts of the soul already described in I.13. If we are habituated into acting justly, it is at the direction of practical wisdom and with the compliance of our irrational souls.

Aristotle notes that

> the virtues are implanted in us neither by nature nor contrary

to nature: we are by nature equipped with the ability to receive them and habit brings this ability to completion and fulfillment. (1103a 23—6)

Thus we are by nature neither good nor evil, but we have the capacity to become either through training. (Aristotle later, in VI. 13, allows that we may have natural propensities toward one virtue or another, and that these may differ from individual to individual.) Though he does not stress the point here, the same capacity that can lead to virtue through proper training can lead to vice when improperly conditioned, therefore he insists that

it is no small matter whether one habit or another is inculcated in us from early childhood; on the contrary, it makes a considerable difference, or, rather, all the difference.

(1103b 23—5)

According to Aristotle, then, we acquire the moral virtues through training; we form virtuous habits by performing virtuous acts. Aristotle, however, identifies virtuous acts in relation to virtuous agents

acts are called just and self-controlled when they are the kind of acts which a just or self-controlled man would perform; but the just and self-controlled man is not he who performs these acts, but he who also performs them in the way just and self-controlled men do. (II.4, 1105b 5—9)

This means that if I wish to become virtuous, I must find a virtuous person and imitate his actions. For Aristotle the moral agent, rather than a set of moral principles, is the primary source of moral knowledge. Though Aristotle's approach to moral education differs from that of most modern ethicists, it does reflect the fact that children do acquire many of their good and bad habits by imitating their elders. Furthermore, though it may be difficult to identify the proper role models for young people to imitate, it is probably no more difficult than identifying the correct moral principles to inculcate.

There is more to being virtuous than the mere imitation of virtuous acts: as the passage above indicates, the virtuous agent

157

performs those acts in a certain way. Aristotle states that

> in the case of the virtues an act is not performed justly or with
> self-control if the act itself is of a certain kind, but only if in
> addition the agent has certain characteristics as he performs it:
> first of all, he must know what he is doing; secondly, he must
> choose to act the way he does, and he must choose it for its
> own sake; and in the third place, the act must spring from a
> firm and unchangeable character. (1105a 28—34)

It is easy to understand why the possession of virtue requires
more than the performance of virtuous acts. Suppose I am standing
on a subway platform when a small child falls onto the tracks. I
leap down and rescue the child, pulling him just in the nick of time
from in front of an onrushing train. This is unquestionably a
courageous act, but am I therefore a courageous person? No, for I
might have been ignorant of the danger I was in (not hearing or
seeing the train), or I might have had an ulterior motive for
performing the act (perhaps I expected a large reward), or I might
have acted out of character (my normal behavior being cowardly
rather than courageous). Only if I act in the way Aristotle describes
above can I, as well as my action, be called courageous.

At the outset, it is repetition of virtuous actions that causes the
person to form a virtuous character; once that character is formed,
however, it is no longer the effect but now the cause of the agent's
virtuous actions. As Aristotle puts it

> Not only are the same actions which are responsible for and
> instrumental in the origin and development of the virtues also
> the causes and means of their destruction, but they will also be
> manifested in the active exercise of the virtues. . . . Strength is
> produced by consuming plenty of food and by enduring much
> hard work, and it is the strong man who is best able to do these
> things. The same is also true of the virtues: by abstaining from
> pleasures we become self-controlled, and once we are self-
> controlled we are best able to abstain from pleasures. So also
> with courage: by becoming habituated to despise and endure
> terrors we become courageous, and once we have become
> courageous we will best be able to endure terror. (II.2, 1104a
> 27—1104b 3)

If we now have an account of how moral virtue is acquired, we are still in need of an account of what it is. Aristotle begins his definition of virtue in II.5 by explaining the general kind of thing virtue is: a *hexis*, i.e. a characteristic or state of character. His argument for this conclusion is another argument from elimination, of the sort we saw earlier in his definition of *eudaimonia* (I.7), and it is no better than that earlier argument. The virtues must be states of character, he says, because they are neither capacities nor emotions, but the reader is not told why our choices must be limited to these three. Yet though the argument is bad, the conclusion seems correct: the moral virtues *are* states of character.

But if the virtues are states of character, which states are they? To begin with, every virtue "(1) renders good the thing itself of which it is the excellence, and (2) causes it to perform its function well" (II.6, 1106a 16—17). Since the function of human beings is rational activity, human virtue will, we expect, be a characteristic that makes us good human beings by enabling us to reason well.

Aristotle goes on to give an explicit definition of virtue

> We may thus conclude that virtue or excellence is a characteristic involving choice, and that it consists in observing the mean relative to us, a mean which is defined by a rational principle, such as a man of practical wisdom would use to determine it. It is the mean by reference to two vices: the one of excess and the other of deficiency. (1106b 36—1107a 3)

When Aristotle says that virtue is a characteristic involving choice, he is actually anticipating the discussion of choice which takes place in Book III. It is sufficient for the present to note that, for Aristotle, choice is the product of deliberation, which is the rational activity appropriate to practical matters, thus, to say that virtue involves choice is to mark it as a rational characteristic.

What is the choice involved in virtue? It is the choice of an action which observes "the mean relative to us." What, then, does this mean? In the preceding portion of II.6 Aristotle has explained the concept of a mean or a median, and distinguished between two sorts of mean: one relative to the thing itself, and one relative to us. Aristotle defines the mean in terms of equal parts of a

continuous entity. Consider a line

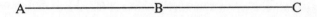

A————————————B————————————C

The line is a continuous length, A and C are points which mark its extremes. B is the median or mean: it is halfway between the extremes, and divides the line into two equal parts. This definition makes clear the idea of a mean relative to a thing, but what about the mean relative to us? This is the way Aristotle distinguishes the two

> By the median of an entity I understand a point equidistant from both extremes, and this point is one and the same for everybody. By the median relative to us I understand an amount neither too large nor too small, and this is neither one nor the same for everybody. To take an example: if ten is many and two is few, six is taken as the median in relation to the entity, for it exceeds and is exceeded by the same amount, and is thus the median in terms of arithmetic proportion. But the median relative to us cannot be determined in this manner: if ten pounds of meat is much for a man to eat and two pounds little, it does not follow that the trainer will prescribe six pounds, for this may in turn be much or little for him to eat; it may be little for Milo and much for someone who has just begun to take up athletics. (1106a 29—1106b 4)

It is clear from this passage that "the mean relative to us" means simply "the right amount for a given individual." Aristotelian ethics is thus relativistic: the right thing to do in a particular situation might not be the same for different people, just as the right amount of meat to eat may not be the same. This explains why Aristotelian ethics, like Platonic ethics, cannot be reduced to a set of rules that can be applied universally. Aristotle's relativism is not complete, however. In the first place, the Aristotle believes there is an objective answer to the question "what should I do in this situation?", just as there is an answer to the question how much meat I should eat. Moreover, he does not think that the answer depends on the judgment of the individual in question: what is best for Charlie is not necessarily what Charlie thinks is best for him. Rather, the right action is the one that would be "defined by a rational principle, such as a man of practical wisdom would use to determine it."

The "man of practical wisdom," the *phronimos*, thus provides an important limitation for Aristotelian relativism. Who is the *phronimos*? He (and Aristotle surely thought of the *phronimos* as a male, and indeed as a Greek gentleman, though there is no reason why we need to follow him in these respects) is simply a person who is able to reason correctly about ethical matters, a person who can see the correct course of action for someone to take. That someone need not be himself; the *phronimos*, given enough information about Charlie, could tell, perhaps better than Charlie himself, what Charlie should do in a given situation. The *phronimos* could determine the correct rational principle on which Charlie should act, but this would be a rational principle specific to Charlie and his situation, not a universal ethical rule valid for everyone. Aristotle does not really give the reader much information about the *phronimos* until Book VI and we shall therefore defer a detailed discussion of him till later. For now we merely note that the *phronimos* is the objective standard or yardstick against which individual conduct is measured. The "right thing to do" in a certain situation is just what the *phronimos* would do in that situation, and nothing more or less.

If the "mean relative to us" is simply "the right amount for a given individual," why does Aristotle insist on describing this amount as a mean? He does so because he believes that this "right amount" always in fact is a mean between two extremes. Here is how he applies the doctrine of the mean to moral virtue

it is moral virtue that is concerned with emotions and actions, and it is in emotions and actions that excess, deficiency and the median are found. Thus we can experience fear, confidence, desire, anger, pity, and generally any kind of pleasure or pain either too much or too little, and in either case not properly. But to experience all this at the right time, toward the right objects, toward the right people, for the right reason, and in the right manner—that is the median and the best course, the course that is the mark of virtue. (II.6, 1106b 16—23)

Though the point is made here with respect to emotions, Aristotle goes on to repeat it for actions.

Aristotle's "doctrine of the mean" is one of the best-known but most criticized and (I think) least well understood aspects of his ethics. Aristotle is not an advocate of mediocrity or of mere moderation: he notes that "in respect of its essence and the definition of its essential nature virtue is a mean, but in regard to goodness and excellence it is an extreme" (II.6, 1107a 6—8). He defines virtue as a mean because he believes that is where the acme of excellence can be found. If we ask why he believes this, I think the likeliest guess is that Aristotle has made a generalization based on an empirical study of many different virtues. He discovered that this deficiency—mean—excess model fitted tolerably well the major moral virtues he wanted to discuss, and therefore he generalized the model and used it to characterize virtue in his formal definition of it.

Aristotle regards the doctrine of the mean as a valuable classificatory tool, but I doubt that he thinks of it as a very precise instrument of ethical reasoning. He knows, first of all, that it only applies to those actions or emotions which contain a range of possibilities, at least some of which are good

> Not every action nor every emotion admits of a mean. There are some actions and emotions whose very names connote baseness, e.g. spite, shamelessness, envy; and among actions, adultery, theft, and murder.... In cases of this sort, let us say adultery, rightness and wrongness do not depend on committing it with the right woman at the right time and in the right manner, but the mere fact of committing such action at all is to do wrong. (1107a 8—15)

Second, Aristotle is aware that the concept of a "mean relative to us" does not determine the correct choice of action in any very precise way, as he notes in VI.1

> it is indeed true to say that we must exert ourselves or relax neither too much nor too little, but to an intermediate extent and as right reason demands. But if this is the only thing a person knows, he will be none the wiser. (1138b 27—30)

If virtue consisted in finding a mean relative to a thing, the concept of the mean could perhaps be used as a precise way of determining the correct course of action. As the mean is relative to the individual, however, all the doctrine of the mean tells the *phronimos* is that he should avoid the extremes of excess and deficiency in emotion and action: he should neither "take it too easy" nor "overdo it." In order to determine precisely what action or emotion is called for in a given situation we must supplement Aristotle's general account of virtue with his account of the particular moral virtues.

The particular virtues: courage and temperance

This account begins at the end of Book II, in ch. 7; it continues, after an interruption at the beginning of Book III for a discussion of choice and related concepts (which we will consider below, under **Deliberation, choice, and practical wisdom**) from ch. 6 of Book III to the end of Book V. The account of the particular virtues aims to show that each virtue conforms to the deficiency—mean—excess pattern Aristotle has used to define virtue. Aristotle accepts a much larger list of virtues than did his predecessors (see chart below). Whereas Plato and Socrates had discussed four or at most five primary virtues (wisdom, courage, temperance, justice and sometimes piety), Aristotle discusses a dozen. Moreover, several of Plato's virtues are absent from this list. Justice is missing, but Aristotle promises to discuss it later, and it is clear that he believes it is also a mean between two vices. Wisdom is missing because in Aristotle's scheme of classification it is an intellectual, not a moral virtue and thus to be considered in Book VI, along with the other intellectual virtues. Piety is simply missing, with no explanation for its absence offered.

Aristotle also defines the field of operation of the virtues much more precisely than did Socrates or Plato. Of course, since it was Socrates' view that the virtues were one, he had no interest in discriminating the particular virtues according to their areas of operation. Plato assigned the cardinal virtues to different parts of the soul: wisdom to reason, courage to spirit, temperance and justice to the three parts in relation to one another, but he made no attempt at a finer discrimination than that. Aristotle, in contrast, is quite restrictive in his specification of the scope of the individual virtues.

Aristotle's discussion of the individual virtues reveals some limitations in the defect—mean—excess scheme he is illustrating. The first sign that the facts are being squeezed slightly to fit this pattern comes when Aristotle mentions that there are no names for several niches in the scheme: the person who exceeds in fearlessness, the person deficient in pleasure (Aristotle invents the term *anaisthetoi*, "insensitive" for these people, who, he admits, "are not often found" II.7, 1107b 7), and several others. More serious than this, however, is an apparent confusion on Aristotle's part concerning spite and envy. Envy, as Aristotle defines it, is an excessive negative response to the good fortune of others. If spite were the opposite of envy, it would be a deficient positive response to that good fortune, but the trait Aristotle cites, *epichairekakia*, "spite," literally means rejoicing at the *bad* fortune of others. This, far from being the opposite of envy, is quite compatible with it: the same person who envies another who does well may rejoice when the other suffers misfortune.

These problems are relatively minor, however; the great strength of the deficiency—mean—excess scheme is that it goes beyond the bipolar opposition of virtue and vice and enables Aristotle to give a more detailed analysis of the virtues and vices than was previously possible. To see this, let us consider two of the virtues Aristotle examines, courage and temperance.

Aristotle discusses courage in Book III, chs 6—9. He begins by noting what the chart opposite shows, that courage is a mean with respect to two emotions, fear and confidence. The object of fear is evil, but not every evil is relevant to courage. The courageous person responds fearlessly not to the threat of disrepute, poverty or disease, but to death, and not to any sort of death, but only noble death, such as one faces in battle

> Properly speaking, therefore, we might define as courageous a man who fearlessly faces a noble death and any situations that bring a sudden death. Such eventualities are usually brought about by war. But of course a courageous man is also fearless at sea and in illness, though not in the same way as sailors are. Because of their experience, the sailors are optimistic, while the courageous man has given up hope of saving his life but finds the thought of such an <inglorious> death revolting. (III.6, 1115a 32—b 4)

ARISTOTLE'S CATALOG OF THE VIRTUES

Area	*Defect* (vice)	*Mean* (virtue)	*Excess* (vice)
fear and confidence	cowardice	courage	recklessness
pleasure and pain	insensitivity	self-control	self-indulgence
money: small amounts	stinginess	generosity	extravagance
large amounts	niggardliness	magnificence	gaudiness vulgarity
honor: large honors	small-mindedness	high-mindedness	vanity
small honors	being unambitious	unnamed	being ambitious
anger	apathy	gentleness	short temper
truth	self-depreciation	truthfulness	boastfulness
pleasantness: in amusement	boorishness	wit	buffoonery
in daily life	grouchiness	friendliness	obsequiousness
shame	shamelessness	modesty	being terror-stricken
the fortune of others	spite	righteous indignation	envy

The courageous person faces death bravely in such situations because it is noble to do so; he acts for the sake of nobility or honor. Aristotle compares this courageous attitude with several others that resemble it, including some that his predecessors had identified as courage. The citizen soldier faces death as the courageous person does, but out of obedience to the law rather than for the sake of honor. The professional soldier or in general the person experienced in facing danger appears courageous, and Aristotle notes that "Socrates for this very reason thought courage was knowledge" (III.8, 1116b 4—5). Such people run away rather than face superior opposition, however, so are not truly courageous. Nor is courage equivalent to a spirited temper (here Aristotle must be thinking of Plato's definition of courage in the *Republic*, though he does not mention him by name), but Aristotle says that a spirited temper "becomes true courage when choice and purpose are added to it" (1117a 4—5). Optimists are confident, like the courageous, but cannot handle adversity better than the experienced professional soldiers mentioned above: when things do not go according to plan, they run away. Finally, the ignorant may act with apparent courage, but we have already seen that they cannot be truly courageous.

Aristotle deals with self-control, temperance, in the same way he deals with courage. He first defines its sphere of operation. As his predecessors had thought, this is pleasure; but again, not any pleasure. Self-control concerns pleasures of the body, specifically the pleasures of eating, drinking, and sex. Aristotle admits that people who enjoy these pleasures less than they should "are scarcely ever found" (III.11, 1119a 6) and that people who go wrong with respect to these appetites do so "in only one direction, namely excess" (1118b 16). One may go wrong not only in enjoying satisfaction of one of the appetites to excess, but also by developing appetites for some particular thing not enjoyed by all

> everyone who is young and vigorous has an appetite for sexual intercourse. But when it comes to appetite for some specific food or sexual relation, not everybody shares it. (1118b 11—12)

The self-controlled person is one whose natural appetites are moderate, and who takes no delight in "unnatural" pleasures

But all the pleasant things that contribute to his health and well-being he desires moderately and in the way he should, and also other pleasures as long as they are neither detrimental to health and well-being nor incompatible with what is noble nor beyond his means. (1119a 16—18)

Self-control, as Aristotle sees it, is not successful combat against strong desire, but the satisfaction of moderate desire. Training the appetites to be moderate is what makes the self-controlled person temperate; the lack of such training is what makes the self-indulgent person unable and unwilling to control the appetites. This training, of course, results from reason's guidance, without which, Aristotle thinks, the appetites become insatiable.

How does this account of the nature of the moral virtues fit with Aristotle's view of the good life? The moral virtues are rational in that they obey the dictates of reason, as embodied in the *phronimos,* the "man of practical wisdom." It is because the moral virtues require rational activity that the life of practical wisdom is a form of *eudaimonia*; merely habitual control of the appetites and emotions would not be intrinsically valuable, on Aristotle's account. The traditional moral virtues of Greek ethics do contribute to living the good life, however, because they do involve essentially the proper exercise of reason. It is commonly said that virtue is a means to the end of happiness, but it would be more accurate to say that, for Aristotle, the life of the *phronimos*, provided only that it avoids extreme misfortune, is the life of *eudaimonia*, and that it is *eudaimon* precisely because of the excellent exercise of reason involved in such a life. Virtue and happiness are related not as means and (separable) end, but as a constitutive element in a complete whole.

Justice and friendship

Since Aristotle views the virtues as part of a good or happy life, he tends to regard the possessor of the virtues as the primary beneficiary of them. In the case of temperance, it is obvious that the temperate person benefits most from his or her own temperance. In the case of courage, however, this is not so clear, especially if we focus, as Aristotle does, on courage in battle. For, as Aristotle notes in I.3, people have been "ruined" by courage;

certainly the courageous death of a soldier in battle can benefit those whose lives he is defending, but it is hard to see how it benefits the soldier. Yet Aristotle in this case defends the difficult position that heroic death benefits the one who dies, since it brings him honor, and, given the close connection he wishes to maintain between *arete* and *eudaimonia*, it is easy to see why he would wish to do so.

There are two virtues that Aristotle thinks are basically altruistic, however, in that they consider the good of another as an end in itself rather than as a means to the agent's own end: justice and friendship. He devotes all of Book V to a discussion of justice, and two full books (VIII and IX) to friendship. These books counteract the impression given by the rest of the *Ethics* that Aristotle's moral philosophy is primarily egoistic. Even in the case of these virtues, however, a self-referential aspect still exists, as we shall see.

It should be clear from the outset of the *Ethics* that justice will turn out to be an important virtue, for Aristotle there chose politics as the master practical science. Man, as he notes in the *Politics*, is a "political animal," and justice is a key political virtue. If the good life can only be realized in a political community, and if all such communities require justice, justice will be essential to the good life.

Aristotle distinguishes in V.1 between two senses of "justice": justice in a general sense is obedience to the law, while particular justice is fairness in distribution and rectification. It may be surprising that Aristotle identifies justice in its general significance with what is lawful, for we immediately think of unjust laws. We must remember, however, that Aristotle thinks of legislation in terms of its proper end: "we call those things 'just'" he writes, "which produce and preserve happiness for the social and political community" (1129b 17—20). The law "commands some things and forbids others, and it does so correctly when it is framed correctly, and not so well if it was drawn up in haste" (1129b 24—5). Not every law is therefore just, but only those laws which succeed in achieving their aim.

This general justice, Aristotle says

is complete virtue or excellence, not in an unqualified sense but in relation to our fellow men. And for that reason justice is regarded as the highest of all virtues ... he who possesses it can make use of his virtue not only by himself but also in his relations with his fellow men; for there are many people who can make use of their virtue in their own affairs, but who are incapable of using it in their relations with others ... justice alone of all the virtues is thought to be the good of another, because it is a relation to our fellow men in that it does what is of advantage to others ... the best man is not one who practices virtue toward himself, but who practices it toward others, for that is a hard thing to achieve. Justice in this sense, then, is not a part of virtue but the whole of excellence or virtue. (1129b 26—1130a 9)

The reason justice is complete virtue is that it enjoins all the acts of the various virtues: it requires people to be brave, temperate, gentle and so on as well as just in the narrow sense. The reason it is not "virtue in an unqualified sense" is that it requires people to do these things not for their own benefit but for that of others: it requires that people be brave, for instance, not for the sake of their own honor but for the sake of the well-being of their community. Aristotle's remark that justice in this sense "is a hard thing to achieve" shows his recognition of the fact that people tend by nature to be egocentric, to look first after their own welfare and only later (if at all) after that of others. General justice, as Aristotle defines it, is similar to the social justice of Plato's *Republic*, but Aristotle, unlike Plato, does not try to show that justice is ultimately for the benefit of the just person. Instead he accepts the common-sense view that justice is "another's good."

Particular justice differs from general in that it is concerned not with all wrong-doing but with that which proceeds from the motive of greed. The person who is unjust in the narrow sense desires to get more than his or her share of good things and less than his or her share of evils. It is not the performance of a particular act that marks someone as just or unjust, but the presence or absence of this motive

if one man commits adultery for profit and makes money on it, while another does it at the prompting of appetite and spends and thus loses money on it, the latter would seem to be self-indulgent rather than grasping for a larger share, while the former is unjust but not self-indulgent, and obviously so because he makes a profit by it. (V.2, 1130a 24—8)

Aristotle distinguishes two kinds of justice in the narrow sense: justice in distribution and justice in rectification. Distributive justice is concerned with the allotment of public goods to the citizens of a state. A fair distribution of such goods (which might be honors, material goods or other benefits) is one that takes account of the merit of the recipients. Aristotle does not assume that every citizen is equal in merit but he does insist that a fair distribution should reflect such inequalities in merit as do exist. What is the basis of judgments of merit? Aristotle does not answer the question, merely noting that "democrats say it is free birth, oligarchs that it is wealth or noble birth, and aristocrats that it is excellence" (V.3, 1131a 27—9). This gives his account a neutrality lacking in specifically democratic or aristocratic theories of justice, but at the cost of making his explanation of distributive justice rather abstract and general.

Achieving the mean in distributive justice is distributing the goods in proportion to the merit of the recipients so the equality involved is proportional rather than numerical. In the case of rectificatory justice, however, the opposite is the case. In this branch of justice, which involves what we would call the civil and criminal law, the aim of the judge is to compensate the victim of crime or fraud for his loss and to punish the perpetrator by taking away his ill-gotten gain

> It makes no difference whether a decent man has defrauded a bad man or vice versa, or whether it was a decent or a bad man who committed adultery. The only difference the law considers is that brought about by the damage; it treats the parties as equals and asks only whether one has done and the other has suffered wrong, and whether one has done and the other has suffered damage. As the unjust in this sense is inequality, the judge tries to restore the equilibrium . . . by inflicting a loss on the offender, the judge tries to take away his gain and restore the equilibrium. (V.4, 1132a 2—10)

In other words, while merit must count in distributive justice, it must not in matters of rectification; while distributive justice may be aristocratic, rectificatory justice must be egalitarian.

Since justice, whether of the particular or general sort, is "another's good" and involves determining a "fair share" or a "fair penalty" for others, the question arises why one should want to be just. Aristotle does not answer the question directly, but two answers seem possible. The first is that, since justice in distribution and in rectification involve determining a mean, justice is an objective matter which can be determined by practical wisdom. Thus, to prefer an unjust to a just state of affairs is to prefer wrong to right because of some desire for personal advantage (greed). But this greed is incompatible with the highest part of our natures, the part that, in Aristotle's view, enables us to flourish, thus, no one with a correct apprehension of *eudaimonia* would ever allow himself to become greedy. The *phronimos* would act justly because practical reason determines what is just, and since the life of *phronesis* is one version of the good life, someone desiring the good life should desire to act justly rather than unjustly, even if it does not immediately benefit him. The second answer is hinted at by Aristotle in Book V. Justice is not simply an abstract ideal, it is embodied in the laws and customs of the city one lives in. We are not simply individuals desiring to be rational and happy, we are part of a political community. As he notes, "The just in political matters is found among men who share a common life in order that their association bring them self-sufficiency, and who are free and equal" (V.6, 1134a 25—7). If I desire the self-sufficiency, freedom and equality of political life, I have reason to be committed to the observance of the rules of justice which make that kind of life possible. To desire the benefits of social life without the burdens is as irrational as to desire to be both practically wise and greedy. Of course, if no political association offering these goods were open to me, then I would have no reason to be just, but, since Aristotle believes we are by nature social or political animals, he would still find it natural and proper for me to desire that such a political association should come into being so that I might obtain the above-mentioned goods by participation in it.

Aristotle considers *philia*, friendship, to be similar in function to justice but even more important for statesmen

> friendship also seems to hold states together, and lawgivers apparently devote more attention to it than to justice. . . .

> When people are friends, they have no need of justice, but when they are just, they need friendship in addition. (VIII.1, 1155a 22—7)

Philia is a term of broader significance than our "friendship"; a citizen of ancient Athens would have included his family and political and business associates among those who were "dear" (*philos*) to him, as well as others for whom he felt affection, whereas we are apt to distinguish our friends both from our family and from our "associates." This does not mean that affection is absent from the Greek concept of *philia*, though Aristotle notes that "affection resembles an emotion, while friendship is a characteristic or lasting attitude" (VIII.5, 1157b 28—9). Despite this distinction Aristotle bases his theory of friendship on the objects of affection: "we do not feel affection for everything, but only for the lovable, and that means what is good, pleasant, or useful" (VIII.2, 1155b 18—19). Since there are three kinds of objects of affection, there are three corresponding kinds of friendship, based respectively on utility, pleasure and goodness.

In the friendships based on utility and pleasure, Aristotle thinks, we do not love the friend so much as the pleasure or usefulness he or she provides

> when the motive of affection is usefulness, the partners do not feel affection for one another *per se* but in terms of the good accruing to each from the other. The same is also true of those whose friendship is based on pleasure: we love witty people not for what they are, but for the pleasure they give us. (VIII.3, 1156a 10—14)

In the friendship based on goodness, however, it is different

> The perfect form of friendship is that between good men who are alike in excellence or virtue. For these friends wish alike for one another's good because they are good men, and they are good *per se*. (1156b 7—9)

This perfect friendship is pleasant and useful as well, but since it is based on the good character of the friends, it is more lasting than those friendships based merely on pleasure or advantage. Anyone can form friendships of the lesser sorts, but only good people can be friends of the highest kind.

Aristotle thinks our friendly relations with others are based on self-love and we believe that friends

1 wish for and do what is good for their friends, for their
   friends' sake
2 wish for their friends' lives for their friends' sake
3 spend time in their friends' company
4 have the same desires as their friends
5 share sorrow and joy with their friends.

He then notes that "a good man has all these feelings in relation to himself" (IX.4, 1166a 10—11). He wishes for his own good and his own life, enjoys his own company, and has no conflicts in his desires, joys and sorrows. Bad people, in contrast, lack these traits and Aristotle views their lives as filled with conflict very much in the way Plato saw them in the *Republic*. Since a good person has the same attitude toward his friends that he has toward himself, Aristotle says that the friend "really is another self" (1166a 31—2).

By describing the friend as "another self" Aristotle is not making the psychological point that self-love is a necessary condition for love of another (though his own analysis leads to that conclusion). Rather he is saying that our love of another person is the same as our love of ourselves. His analysis really applies only to the "perfect" form of friendship. There the friends really do desire the good of the other for his or her own sake, as we all desire our own good for our own sake. Moreover, since only good people can enter into this kind of friendship, they will have the same wishes and desires, the same joys and sorrows, for these will be determined by the virtues that they, as good people, share. On Aristotle's view, therefore, two good people will like each other because each likes the same things.

Since friendship is based on self-love, Aristotle considers in IX.8 whether self-love is essentially selfish or egoistic. Typically, he answers this question by distinguishing different senses of egoism

those who use "egoist" as a term of opprobrium apply it to people who assign to themselves the larger share of material goods, honors, and bodily pleasures. . . . Those, therefore, who

173

try to get more than their share of these things, gratify their appetites, their emotions in general, and the irrational part of their souls, and most people are of this kind. Hence, the <pejorative> use of the term is derived from the fact that the most common form of self-love is base, and those who are egoists in this sense are justly criticized. . . . If a man were always to devote his attention above all else to acting justly himself, to acting with self-control, or to fulfilling whatever other demands virtue makes upon him, and if, in general, he were always to try to secure for himself what is noble, no one would call him an egoist and no one would find fault with him. (IX.8, 1168b 15—28)

It would seem, however, that such a person is actually a truer egoist or self-lover. At any rate, he assigns what is supremely noble and good to himself, he gratifies the most sovereign part of himself, and he obeys it in everything.

The most sovereign part of the individual is, of course, reason, and Aristotle even goes so far as to identify this element with the individual

Thus it is clear that a man is—or is in the truest sense—the ruling element within him, and that a good man loves this more than anything else. Hence it is he who is in the truest sense an egoist or self-lover. (IX.8, 1169a 2—4)

This ruling element often requires a person to act on behalf of others in matters of justice or friendship; doing what reason demands does not mean acting in one's narrow self-interest. Yet in the very act of self-sacrifice the agent satisfies the demands of reason and nobility, so that altruism and egoism do not oppose each other in such cases, but actually coincide.

Aristotle's identification of the "true self" with reason enables us to see how one could have a "self-interested" motive for obeying the impersonal commands of justice and friendship. Of course, it is easier to understand why one would act out of friendship than out of justice for, whereas justice may require me to act against my own interest and on behalf of a perfect stranger, friendship only requires that I act on behalf of someone I already know and like and whose interests are the same as mine. None the less, both kinds of action require me to act for the sake of another's well-being rather than my own, and Aristotle's account explains why I should be motivated to do so.

Aristotle's accounts of justice and friendship remain models of philosophical analysis. His account of friendship, to be sure, is incomplete, for it does not explain why I choose certain people as friends out of the many I know who share my interests, or in other words why I like some people who share my interests better than others. On the other hand, if Aristotle gives too little emphasis to the role of personal affection in friendship, he is right to emphasize the role played by shared values in such relationships, a feature of friendship that we are apt to overlook. Friendship (including family and business relationships) requires more than affection if it is to be stable; lasting friendships are based on common interests.

Deliberation, choice and practical wisdom

So far in our treatment of the moral virtues we have stressed the fact that they are rational, but have said little about the actual role of reason in virtuous activity. Aristotle discusses the way reason works in Book III, chs 1—5 and Book VI of the *Ethics*. In Book III his aim is to show that we are in general responsible for our actions; in Book VI he describes the intellectual virtue of practical wisdom. Thus the emphasis is different in the two discussions, none the less, a general picture of the nature of action emerges from them.

Aristotle begins Book III with a discussion of voluntary action. "A voluntary action" he writes, "would seem to be one in which the initiative lies with the agent who knows the particular circumstances in which the action is performed" (III.1, 1111a 22—4). An involuntary action, in contrast, is one in which the agent "contributes nothing" to the act or is ignorant of some aspect of the action. Thus, there are two necessary ingredients of voluntary action: initiative and knowledge of the circumstances of the act. Aristotle makes it clear in the subsequent discussion of action that the initiative in question is always a desire of the agent to achieve a certain end, and that the knowledge of particular circumstances is the result of a faculty he calls "perception." Thus, the simplest sort of action would be described like this

```
desire    ⌉
          ├action——>end
perception ⌋
```

Not every action is one in which the agent simply desires a certain result and spontaneously acts to achieve it, however: many actions involve deliberation and choice as well. Aristotle explains choice (*prohairesis*) in III.2. The Greek word literally means "preference," and strongly suggests a selection from at least two alternatives, as Aristotle notes at the end of the chapter. This in turn suggests a selection process in which the alternatives are weighed, which Aristotle refers to as deliberation. Aristotle does not stress the existence of alternatives in matters of choice, but points out instead the connection between choice and deliberation and the rationality of the deliberative process. It is in deliberation that reason enters human action.

Aristotle begins his discussion of choice by noting that "choice seems to be very closely related to virtue" (1111b 5—6); this recalls the fact that he had previously defined virtue as a characteristic involving the choice of a mean according to a rational principle. Choice is voluntary, but not all voluntary actions are chosen. Children and animals act voluntarily, but do not exercise choice, though Aristotle does not say why this is so, the reason is clearly that children and animals do not deliberate about what they will do, but act on impulse. Choice is further defined by two additional characteristics: it is limited to things which we are able to achieve through our own agency, and it is directed at means rather than ends

> we *wish* to be healthy and *choose* the things that will give us health. Similarly, we say that we *wish* to be happy and describe this as our wish, but it would not be fitting to say that we *choose* to be happy. (1111b 27—9)

Choice turns out to be "the result of preceding deliberation," and something that "involves reason and thought" (1112a 15—16). Later, Aristotle states that

> Choice is the starting point of action. . . . The starting point of choice, however, is desire and reasoning directed toward some

176

end. That is why there cannot be choice . . . without intelligence and thought. (VI.2, 1139a 31—4)

He there describes choice as "either intelligence motivated by desire or desire operating through thought" (1139b 4—5) and, more succinctly, as "deliberate desire" (1139a 23).

What then is deliberation? Like choice, it is directed toward things within our power and toward means rather than ends; in deliberation

> we take the end for granted, and then consider in what manner and by what means it can be realized. If it becomes apparent that there is more than one means by which it can be attained, we look for the easiest and best; if it can be realized by one means only, we consider in what manner it can be realized by that means, and how that means can be achieved in turn. We continue that process until we come to the first link in the chain of causation, which is the last step in order of discovery . . . if in the process of investigation we encounter an insurmountable obstacle, for example, if we need money but none can be procured, we abandon our investigation; but if it turns out to be possible, we begin to act. (III.3, 1112b 15—27)

Deliberation is therefore a rational process of calculating the best means for achieving an end we desire. In the passage quoted Aristotle suggests that deliberation culminates in action: when we find an action that is a means to our desired end and that is within our power, we perform that action. It would be more proper to say that deliberation culminates in choice, which in turn leads to action, however, because choice is the *state* in which the *process* of deliberation terminates. As Aristotle puts it, "the object of deliberation and the object of choice are identical, except that the object of choice has already been determined . . . on the basis of deliberation" (1113a 2—5).

The conclusion of a process of deliberation is the rational choice of a particular action to be performed. Thus deliberation is concerned not only with universal principles but also, even primarily, with concrete particulars. Aristotle says of practical wisdom that it is concerned with ultimate particulars, since the actions to be performed are ultimate particulars . . . practical wisdom has as its object the ultimate particular fact, of which there is perception but no scientific knowledge. (VI.8, 1142a 24—7)

Since practical wisdom involves excellence in deliberation, what Aristotle says about it applies to deliberation as well. Deliberation culminates in my choosing to do this particular thing in this particular situation. My recognition that this is the appropriate thing to do is something of which Aristotle says I can have perceptual, but not scientific, knowledge. We might say that I have an intuition of what I should do, but this intuition will necessarily involve the kind of knowledge of what I am doing that Aristotle mentioned as a necessary condition of voluntary action. Thus, modifying our picture of voluntary action to include deliberation and choice, we get the following diagram

$$\left.\begin{array}{l} \text{desire} \\ \\ \text{deliberation} \longrightarrow \text{perception} \end{array}\right\} \text{choice} \longrightarrow \text{action} \longrightarrow \text{end}$$

With this picture in mind we can turn to Aristotle's discussion of practical wisdom in Book VI. Book VI is devoted to an account of the intellectual virtues. As he had earlier divided the entire soul into a rational and an irrational part, Aristotle now divides the rational part of the soul into a "scientific" and a "calculative" part. With the scientific part, "we apprehend the realities whose fundamental principles do not admit of being other than they are" (VI.1, 1139a 6—8); with the calculative part we apprehend those things which are subject to change. This division corresponds to the division of the sciences we mentioned above (under **Aristotle's methodology**): the theoretical sciences are studied by the scientific element, the practical and productive sciences by the calculative.

As the virtues of the irrational part of the soul were called "moral" virtues, the virtues of the rational part of the soul are called "intellectual" virtues. Each division of the rational part of the soul has its own virtue. The virtue of the scientific element is theoretical wisdom (*sophia*). *Sophia* requires both knowledge of the first principles of science (which Aristotle says is produced by "intelligence," or *nous*) and the ability to construct valid syllogisms

178

from these first principles, that is to demonstrate scientific theorems (a faculty he calls *episteme*). The object of theoretical wisdom is truth, and specifically truth about "the things that are valued most highly" (VI.7, 1141a 20), i.e. God and the eternal objects of nature, but *not* the truths of ethics and politics: "For it would be strange," Aristotle writes, "to regard politics or practical wisdom as the highest kind of knowledge, when in fact man is not the best thing in the universe" (1141a 20—2). This claim that theoretical wisdom is superior to practical wisdom anticipates the claim of Book X that the life of theoretical wisdom is superior to that of practical wisdom.

The virtue of the productive sciences is art (*techne*); that of the practical sciences is practical wisdom (*phronesis*). Whereas the aim of theoretical wisdom is the understanding of truths about eternal objects, the aim of practical wisdom is the attainment of good in matters subject to our control. Practical wisdom aims not at mere understanding, but at action. Like theoretical wisdom, however, practical wisdom is complex: just as theoretical wisdom included both a knowledge of first principles and an ability to demonstrate, practical wisdom includes both a correct desire for the ultimate end of conduct and an ability to calculate the proper means to that end. Now calculation of the means to an end is deliberation, as we have seen (and Aristotle says at VI.1, 1139a 12—13, "deliberating and calculating are the same thing") thus, practical wisdom involves excellence in deliberation: "a man of practical wisdom," he writes at VI.5, 1140a 31, "is he who has the ability to deliberate," "the most characteristic function of a man of practical wisdom is to deliberate well" (VI.7, 1141b 9—10).

Since deliberation is the matching of means to a desired end, we might suspect that excellence in deliberation would be the ability to discover the best means to such an end. This ability is only part of practical wisdom, however. As Aristotle notes

There exists a capacity called "cleverness," which is the power to perform those steps which are conducive to a goal we have set for ourselves and to attain that goal. If the goal is noble, cleverness deserves praise; if the goal is base, cleverness is knavery . . . the capacity alone is not practical wisdom, although practical wisdom does not exist without it. Without virtue or excellence, this eye of the soul <intelligence,> does

not acquire the characteristic <of practical wisdom>. . .
whatever the true end may be, only a good man can judge it
correctly. For wickedness distorts and causes us to be
completely mistaken about the fundamental principles of
action. Hence it is clear that a man cannot have practical
wisdom unless he is good. (VI.12, 1144a 23—b 1)

The kind of excellence in deliberation that is involved in practical
wisdom is not mere cleverness but something more, it is skill in
finding the means to morally good ends

> the capacity of deliberating well about what is good and
> advantageous for oneself is regarded as typical of a man of
> practical wisdom—not deliberating well about what is good
> and advantageous in a partial sense, for example, what
> contributes to health or strength, but what sort of thing
> contributes to the good life in general. (VI.5, 1140a 25—8)

Now we have already seen that deliberation is concerned solely
with means and not with ends: what is it, then, that makes the man
of practical wisdom aim at the right ends? As the passage from
VI.12 quoted above indicates, it is moral virtue: as Aristotle says
elsewhere in the same chapter, "virtue makes us aim at the right
target, and practical wisdom makes us use the right means" (1144a
8—9; cf. VI.13, 1145a 5—6: "virtue determines the end, and
practical wisdom makes us do what is conducive to the end"). Thus,
practical wisdom would seem to have both a rational and a moral
component and though Aristotle does not describe it precisely this
way, it seems fair to say that practical wisdom is cleverness plus
moral virtue.

If this is correct, then Aristotle's classification of practical
wisdom as an intellectual virtue is somewhat misleading. It would
seem better to describe it as the synthesis of the intellectual virtue
of excellence in deliberation with the moral virtues. Just as the
moral virtues are perfected by deliberative excellence, so cleverness
is turned into a virtue by being directed toward the correct end by
moral virtue. Both need each other, practical wisdom is the trait in
which both find their necessary completion. This would seem to be
the conclusion Aristotle is leaning toward in VI.13. In this, the last
chapter of Book VI, Aristotle makes three claims about the

relation between practical wisdom and moral virtue

1 Virtue in the full sense requires practical wisdom. Though
   Socrates was wrong to think that virtue simply was wisdom,
   he was right to think that virtue requires wisdom.
2 Virtue is not merely *guided by* right reason (practical
   wisdom), it is *united with* right reason.
3 Though one may be endowed to a different degree with the
   various natural virtues, one cannot possess practical wisdom
   without possessing the other virtues in their perfected form.

These three claims indicate that practical wisdom and the moral
virtues (in their perfected, though not their "natural" state) imply
each other. Thus, Aristotle can maintain the Socratic thesis that
the virtues are unified without adopting the extreme view that they
are simply rational states or knowledge. If we return, therefore, to
our diagram of deliberative action, we can see how practical
wisdom enables us to act well

practical wisdom (= moral virtue + cleverness)

moral virtue——>right desire ⎤
                             ⎬right choice——>action——>end
cleverness——>right perception ⎦

Without a doubt, this scheme represents a closer integration of
reason and desire than even Plato achieved in the *Republic*. It does
have several troubling features, however. It is clear from Aristotle's
account that the only official role reason has in practical reason is
an instrumental one of determining the proper means to the right
end. Yet if the life of practical wisdom is (as Aristotle thinks) a
form of *eudaimonia*, the rational activity in it must be seen as
intrinsically, not instrumentally valuable. Can reason be both
instrumentally valuable in determining the means to an end and
intrinsically valuable as a constituent of that end?

Moreover, reason seems to play no role in shaping our desires,
yet it is our desires that give us our ends. Does this mean that
Aristotle believes that reason has no role in the evaluation of the
end of our actions? His own practice in Book I belies this claim, for
there Aristotle presented a rational evaluation of various

candidates for the good life. One would like Aristotle to provide a place in his theory as well as his practice, though, for the rational evaluation of ends; in this respect Plato's analysis of reason in the *Republic* seems superior to Aristotle's.

Finally, though Aristotle has claimed that moral virtue is united with right reason, when he speaks of moral virtue determining our ends and practical reason as determining our means he must be thinking of moral virtue as he had described it in Books II—V: as the product of habituation. Aristotle wants to claim that we are responsible for our actions, both good and bad, yet surely our early childhood training is not up to us: we are not free to choose, in every society, whether we will learn the virtues or the vices. But if we are trained in vice, as Aristotle indicates, we will acquire a misperception of the end of human existence: "For wickedness distorts and causes us to be completely mistaken about the fundamental principles of action" (VI.12, 1144a 34—6) If no rational evaluation of ends is possible, how can the person trained in vice hope to correct his or her conduct and what sense does it make to say that such a person is responsible for his or her bad character?

These problems, I think, reveal a limitation in Aristotle's account of practical wisdom. He needs to supplement his account of rational deliberation with an account of the rational evaluation of ends. He has given us, in other words, an excellent account of one of the ways in which reason plays a role in moral thought; but it is not and in terms of his own practice cannot be, the only way.

Moral weakness

Book VII of the *Ethics* is devoted to a discussion of moral weakness (*akrasia*). The connection with Book VI is close: there we saw that practical reasoning culminates in the choice of an action and that the action itself follows directly from the choice. In moral weakness, however, something interrupts the normally tight connection between choice and action; the morally weak person knows what is good but acts in opposition to this knowledge.

Aristotle begins Book VII with a typology of desirable and undesirable moral traits. The three traits to be avoided are vice, moral weakness and brutishness while opposite to these are three characteristics to be sought: virtue, moral strength, and what

Aristotle calls "superhuman virtue." The following chart displays their relationships

	Desirable trait	Opposite undesirable trait
most	superhuman virtue	brutishness
	virtue (temperance)	vice (self-indulgence)
least	moral strength	moral weakness

The most desirable trait, superhuman virtue, appears at the top of its list, as does the most undesirable trait, brutishness. It is not clear whether or not all six categories can be applied to every virtue. The domain of moral weakness is the same as that of temperance in that it is concerned with the appetites, and in particular those of eating, drinking and sex. (Aristotle notes the use of "moral weakness" in cases involving anger and profit, but thinks this usage is based on an analogy with moral weakness proper.) Thus the relevant vicious trait is self-indulgence, as the chart indicates and the corresponding virtue is temperance or self-control.

This typology expands and improves upon the previous typology of virtue and vice. First of all, it shows that there are other possibilities in conduct besides those two. Second, it makes clear a point that Aristotle insists on several times in the *Ethics*, that ordinary virtue is human virtue, something one does not require extraordinary powers to possess but which is rather within the reach of all normal people. Third, it makes an important distinction between moral strength and virtue. The modern reader is apt to bring to Aristotle the assumption that virtue is the successful resistance to strong appetites, and this is especially so in the case of temperance. Aristotle makes it clear that this trait is not virtue but moral strength

a morally strong man is the kind of person who does nothing contrary to the dictates of reason under the influence of bodily pleasures, and the same is true of a self-controlled man. But while a morally strong man has base appetites, a self-controlled man does not and is, moreover, a person who finds no pleasure in anything that violates the dictates of reason. A morally strong man, on the other hand, does find pleasure in such things, but he is not driven by them. (VII.9, 1151b 34—1152a 3)

Aristotle also distinguishes between ordinary vice and brutishness. The vicious person (in this case the self-indulgent person) does wrong deliberately and intentionally, because he or she has an incorrect apprehension of the good. The self-indulgent person acts from choice, but the brutish person does not exercise choice. Brutishness Aristotle thinks is due either to physical disability, habituation, or a "depravity of nature" (VII.5, 1148b 18). Aristotle lists insanity as a source of brutishness, and clearly what he is thinking of is a set of conditions we today would regard as pathological, as indicative of mental illness rather than moral choice. Indeed, people are called brutish just because they lack the power of rational deliberation and choice: they act from compulsion rather than deliberately. Thus Aristotle says that such people are "outside the limits of vice" (1148b 34—1149a 1). Brutishness is, says Aristotle, "a lesser evil than vice, but it is more horrifying" (VII.6, 1150a 1—2). It is less evil because "a bad man can do ten thousand times as much harm as a beast" (1150a 6—7), but it is more horrifying because it is caused by the absence or perversion of the best element in human nature.

Aristotle says little about superhuman virtue, except that it is "heroic and divine" (VII.1, 1145a 20) and, like brutishness, rarely found among men. Brutishness and superhuman virtue, though rarely found, are fairly straightforward and easy to understand, so are virtue, vice and moral strength. As we have seen in earlier chapters, however, moral weakness is problematic and Aristotle devotes the bulk of Book VII to explaining what it is and how it is possible.

The morally weak person is one who acts badly though in possession of knowledge of what is good. In action he or she resembles the vicious person, but in thought the virtuous or morally strong person. Aristotle recalls Socrates' view in explaining why this is difficult to understand

how can a man be morally weak in his actions, when his basic assumption is correct <as to what he should do>? Some people claim that it is impossible for him to be morally weak if he has knowledge <of what he ought to do>. Socrates, for example, believed that it would be strange if, when a man possesses knowledge, something else should overpower it and drag it about like a slave. In fact, Socrates ... did not believe that moral weakness exists. (VII.2, 1145b 21—6)

Aristotle says that Socrates' theory "is plainly at variance with the observed facts" (1145b 27—8) and his task, therefore, is to explain how one can know what is good and do evil in the face of that knowledge.

Aristotle attempts to solve the problem by distinguishing two senses of "to know"

the verb "to know" has two meanings: a man is said to "know" both when he does not use the knowledge he has and when he does use it. Accordingly, when a man does wrong it will make a difference whether he is not exercising the knowledge he has ... or whether he is exercising it. In the latter case, we would be baffled, but not if he acted without exercising his knowledge. (VII.3, 1146b 31—5)

His general strategy, then, will be to show that the morally weak person *has* knowledge which he or she does not *use* in a particular situation. So far, Aristotle's position seems trivially correct: no one thinks that the morally weak person exercises knowledge in acting weakly, for to exercise knowledge of the good would be to act correctly. The problem seems to be that the person has knowledge but does not employ it.

His next step is to note that there are two kinds of premise in a practical syllogism, a universal and a particular. The morally weak person may know the particular premise only as a universal. To use Aristotle's example, the morally weak person may know that dry food is good for all men and that a certain kind of food is dry, "but whether the particular food before him is of this kind is something of which <a morally weak man> either does not have the knowledge or does not exercise it" (1147a 7). Again, he says it would not be surprising if the morally weak person "knows" the truth in a general way, but it would be surprising if he knew it in its full particularity (namely that this particular act would be the right thing to do in this particular situation).

He goes on to state that "There is ... another way besides

those we have so far described in which it is possible for men to have knowledge" (1147a 10—11) but not to use it. To make this alternative clear he distinguishes two senses of "having a characteristic" as he had previously distinguished two senses of "to know"

> "having" a characteristic has different meanings. There is a sense in which a person both has and does not have knowledge, for example, when he is asleep, mad, or drunk. But this is precisely the condition of people who are in the grip of the emotions. Fits of passion, sexual appetites, and some other such passions actually cause palpable changes in the body, and in some cases even produce madness. Now it is clear that we must attribute to the morally weak a condition similar to that of men who are asleep, mad, or drunk. (1147a 12—18)

He also compares such conditions to that of beginning students, who "can reel off the words they have heard, but . . . do not yet know the subject" (1147a 21—2).

There remains one more explanation of moral weakness that Aristotle offers. It may be that a morally weak person is faced with conflicting opinions about what he or she should do

> suppose that there is within us one universal opinion for bidding us to taste < things of this kind >, and another < universal > opinion which tells us that everything sweet is pleasant, and also < a concrete perception >, determining our activity, that the particular thing before us is sweet; and suppose further that the appetite < for pleasure > happens to be present. < The result is that > one opinion tells us to avoid that thing, while appetite, capable as it is of setting in motion each part of our body, drives us to it. . . . Thus it turns out that a morally weak man acts under the influence of some kind of reasoning and opinion, an opinion which is not intrinsically but only incidentally opposed to right reason; for it is not opinion but appetite that is opposed to right reason. (1147a 31—1147b 3)

These three explanations of moral weakness are different from and independent of each other, they in fact seem to be explanations

explanations of different phenomena. The second explanation, in which the morally weak person is compared to someone mad, asleep or drunk, has been taken as the "official" Aristotelian account of moral weakness and indeed it is the account he uses when summarizing his view at the end of VII.3. Yet this account has a surprising consequence

> we seem to be led to the conclusion which Socrates sought to establish. Moral weakness does not occur in the presence of knowledge in the strict sense, and it is sensory knowledge, not science, which is dragged about by emotion. (1147b 14—17)

Given that Aristotle began his account with the claim that Socrates' position "is plainly at variance with the observed facts," it is awkward, to say the least, to find him endorsing the essence of the Socratic claim in his own conclusion. What has gone wrong?

Socrates did not make the distinctions Aristotle draws between general and particular, and potential and actual knowledge, but it seems clear that what he denied was the possibility of acting wrongly in the presence of actual, particular knowledge of what one ought to do. Moreover, in dealing with this problem we must distinguish between moral weakness and psychological compulsion. A person who does wrong in the face of knowledge of what is right because overpowered by irresistible impulse is not morally weak but psychologically compelled to act. We do not blame such people as we blame the morally weak, rather, we pity them. Thus, the classic problem of moral weakness is the problem how one can act wrongly while in possession of actual, particular knowledge of what one ought to do, and while psychologically able to do what one ought.

When the problem is stated in this way, it becomes clear that Aristotle's first two explanations fail to address it. His first account shows that one can go wrong when one knows only in a general way what one ought to do; his second, that one can go wrong when one has potential or dispositional, but not actual knowledge of what one should do. But neither of these cases is a case of moral weakness and it is no wonder that, in endorsing his second account, Aristotle fell back on the Socratic position he had earlier disparaged.

He need not have done so, for his third explanation not only

187

addresses but promises to solve the classic problem of moral weakness. According to the third solution the morally weak person has actual, concrete knowledge of what he or she ought to do, but acts in the face of that knowledge because moved by appetite. The appetite does not compel the person to act wrongly, however; it merely contributes one factor to the decision. The other factor is a process of reasoning opposed to the first and in favor of the wrong action. The morally weak person acts rationally but wrongly because appetite tips the scales in favor of the wrong action.

Aristotle's third explanation of moral weakness is a perceptive account of the psychology of the morally weak person. It distinguishes between moral weakness and psychological compulsion and makes it possible for us to understand why the morally weak person acts as he or she does. It is compatible with Aristotle's account of practical reason also, for it shows us that two things are necessary for morally weak action that is fully deliberate: there must be some reason for doing the act, and there must be an appetite for it. The man of practical wisdom cannot be morally weak because he lacks the bad appetite necessary and because the only reason that will occur to him is the one that explains what is the right thing to do. In light of these facts it seems fair to say that Aristotle does show how moral weakness is possible but it is somewhat surprising that he does so in an explanation that he himself did not regard as the major one.

The lives of theoretical and practical wisdom

In Book X of the *Ethics* Aristotle returns to the question of *eudaimonia* with which he had begun Book I. The book starts with a discussion of pleasure. Aristotle argues that pleasure is *a* good but not *the* good, and that pleasure is not a motion or a process, as Plato had thought, but an activity or state. Moreover, it is a state which *supervenes on* other activities, one cannot enjoy the pleasures of playing chess, for instance, without engaging in the actual activity of chess-playing. The pleasures associated with good human activities are good and add to or complete the goodness of those activities. Thus, though pleasure is a side-effect of good activity and not the end of that activity, it is a side-effect that contributes to the over-all goodness of the activity. Since the life of *eudaimonia* is a life of rational activity, we can expect it to be a pleasant life, for the pleasures appropriate to rational activity will accompany the activity itself.

Following the discussion of pleasure, Aristotle turns to the topic of the best human life. He considers only three lives as candidates for the best life: the life of amusement; the life of theoretical wisdom; and the life of practical wisdom. The life of amusement he quickly dismisses

> happiness does not consist in amusement . . . it would be strange if our end were amusement, and if we were to labor and suffer hardships all our life long merely to amuse ourselves. . . . Anacharsis seems to be right when he advises to play in order to be serious; for amusement is a form of rest . . . rest is not an end, for we take it for the sake of <further> activity. (X.6, 1176b 27—1177a 1)

Aristotle then reminds us that happiness is activity in conformity with the highest virtue, which is the virtue of the best and most divine part of us. This activity is *theoria*, contemplation, the activity of the scientific part of our intellect, and the activity whose virtue is theoretical wisdom. By *theoria*, incidentally, Aristotle does not mean the mental activity of scientific research or investigation, rather, he means the contemplation of the completed results of that activity, the synoptic vision of a finished scientific account of the world. To engage in *theoria* is to view the world from a "God's eye view," to see it, as Spinoza said, *sub specie aeternitatis*, under the aspect of eternity.

Why does the life of theoretical wisdom win out over that of practical wisdom, which has yet to be discussed? First because it is the highest kind of human activity, "for intelligence is the *highest* possession we have in us, and the objects which are the concern of intelligence are the highest objects of knowledge" (X.7, 1177a 20—1). Second, because it is the most *continuous* form of human activity, "we are able to study continuously more easily than to perform any kind of action" (1177a 21—2). Third, because it is the most *pleasant* kind of activity: "At any rate, it seems that . . . philosophy holds pleasures marvelous in purity and certainty" (1177a 25—6). Fourth, because it is *self-sufficient*

> a wise man is able to study even by himself, and the wiser he is

the more he is able to do it. Perhaps he could do it better if he had colleagues to work with him, but he is still the most self-sufficient of all. (1177a 32—b 1)

Fifth, because "study seems to be the only activity loved for its own sake" (1177b 1—2): the practical virtues bring some benefits beyond the activities themselves, but *theoria* does not. Sixth and finally, because contemplation is an activity of *leisure*, whereas the activities of practical reason depend on external events.

The life of *theoria* is worthy of the gods, whereas the life of *phronesis* is not

> We assume that the gods are in the highest degree blessed and happy. But what kind of actions are we to attribute to them? Acts of justice? Will they not look ridiculous making contracts with each other, returning deposits, and so forth? . . . a concern with actions is petty and unworthy of the gods. Nevertheless, we all assume that the gods exist and, consequently, that they are active. . . . Now, if we take away action from a living being, to say nothing of production, what is left except contemplation? (X.8, 1178b 8—21)

Aristotle notes that such a life "would be more than human" (X.7, 1177b 26—7); yet he does not regard this as a criticism of such a life

> We must not follow those who advise us to have human thoughts, since we are <only> men, and mortal thoughts, as mortals should; on the contrary, we should try to become immortal as far as possible and do our utmost to live in accordance with what is highest in us. (1177b 31—4)

This highest element, in fact, he identifies with the person: "intelligence, above all else, is man" (1178a 7).

The life of practical wisdom, *phronesis*, is also happy, but "in a secondary sense" (X.8, 1178a 9)

> some moral acts seem to be determined by our bodily condition, and virtue or excellence of character seems in many ways closely related to the emotions. . . . The fact that these

virtues are . . . bound up with the emotions indicates that they belong to our composite nature, and the virtues of our composite nature are human virtues; consequently, a life guided by these virtues and the happiness <that goes with it are likewise human>. The happiness of the intelligence, however, is quite separate. (1178a 14—22)

Thus, the superiority of the life of theoretical reason to that of practical reason consists in the fact that theoretical reason is divine, practical reason, human.

What are we to make of Aristotle's preference for the life of *theoria*? The reader is apt to suspect that, despite Aristotle's presentation of six reasons for the superiority of contemplation to action, he is merely expressing a preference for his own chosen lifestyle. Certainly the reasons he presents are not convincing. On the matter of self-sufficiency he seems confused: in claiming that happiness was self-sufficient in I.7 he had denied that this had anything to do with the isolation of the happy person from others.

We do not mean a man who lives his life in isolation, but a man who also lives with parents, children, a wife, and friends and fellow citizens generally, since man is by nature a social and political being . . . we define as "self-sufficient" that which taken by itself makes life something desirable and deficient in nothing. (1097b 8—15)

Here, however, he cites as a factor in favor of the self-sufficiency of *theoria* the fact that one could practice it alone.

Nor are his other reasons much better. Whether contemplation is more pleasant than practical activity would seem to depend on how well-trained in and adept at it one is and likewise with the continuousness of the activity. When Aristotle claims that only contemplation is engaged in for its own sake he seems to contradict what he had earlier said about the moral virtues. To prefer a life of leisure to one based on externally dictated activity seems to be to express a Greek preference not shared by many other cultures (including our own). Finally, even if it is true that we are not the finest things in the universe, it is not clear that contemplating things finer than ourselves contributes in any direct way to our happiness. What makes us happy should be the realization of our own nature or end, and this might be thought to involve contemplation of *that* rather than of the gods. The proper study of mankind, one might object to Aristotle, is man.

In fact, however, Aristotle's preference for the contemplative over the practical life is not merely personal prejudice but neither is it based entirely on the arguments presented here. It has its roots, as I indicated above (see **The good: eudaimonia**), in the argument of Book I that the human *ergon* was the activity of the highest element in the soul rather than the integration of the elements. Had Aristotle adopted an integrationist picture of the human *telos* rather than a separatist one, the very reason he cites in Book X for preferring *theoria* to *phronesis* (that it is divine rather than human) would be a reason for preferring *phronesis* to *theoria*.

One may wonder, moreover, why one has to choose between the life of *theoria* and that of *phronesis*. Even if we limit the argument to the intellectual virtues, and do not make a case for the inclusion of the virtues of the lower parts of the soul in a complete picture of the best human life, there are (if Aristotelian psychology is correct) two parts of the intellect and two corresponding virtues, theoretical and practical wisdom. Why should we accept the choice between developing one of these and the other; why should we not rather insist on both? Certainly the theoretical life will (as Aristotle concedes) require the practical virtues as well and won't the practical life be enhanced and given perspective by the contemplation? Though Aristotle presents the reader with a dichotomy, it is not clear that the reader (even if he or she is a good Aristotelian) needs to accept it.

Conclusion

I said at the beginning of the chapter that Greek ethical theory reaches its culmination in Aristotle's *Ethics*. This does not mean that Aristotle's system is perfect; there is certainly room for debate about his concept of the good life and the limited role he gives to reason in the life of practical wisdom. One could find fault with the parochialism of many of Aristotle's judgments, with his ready acceptance of Greek attitudes that we no longer share. Yet we ought not to be blind to the accomplishments of his work. He clarifies greatly the role of reason in moral deliberation, he integrates reason with emotion in the moral virtues more closely even than Plato, he presents a much more detailed analysis of the virtues than his predecessors, and he presents a detailed account of the relation between the virtues and the good life which is lacking among his predecessors. Moreover, the virtues of his account are surprisingly independent of its controversial points: one need not accept Aristotle's view about the good life, for instance, to find his account of the moral virtues largely correct. Pervasive throughout his work, of course, is the subtle and deep yet clear Aristotelian intelligence at work, which makes his comments valuable reading even when one chooses to disagree with them. It is both as a great moral philosopher and as the culmination of a tradition that Aristotle's work remains today indispensable reading for the student of ethics.

5

EPICUREANISM AND STOICISM

The Hellenistic world

By the time of Aristotle's death the conquests of Alexander the Great had changed the Greek world. His father Philip had brought mainland Greece under Macedonian rule, ending hundreds of years of independence for the Greek city-states; Alexander, in his brief lifetime, extended the Macedonian Empire to the borders of India in the east and as far as Egypt in the south. He destroyed the Persian Empire and replaced it with his own. In the course of doing so he began the process that made Greek language and civilization the common coin of the Eastern Mediterranean. Though the empire created by Alexander was divided into three parts soon after his death, the cultural influence of Greece on the Mediterranean world was long-lasting. It is common to mark this transition from a Greek civilization made up of independent city-states to that of a far-flung empire by referring to the earlier civilization as "Hellenic," the latter as "Hellenistic."

This transformation and dispersion of Greek civilization affected philosophy in several ways. First, Greek philosophy became much more widely known in the eastern Mediterranean than it had been. Whereas philosophy had previously been the domain of a small elite of native Greeks, it now became available to a much larger group of people from different ethnic groups. One effect of this increased availability of philosophy was the virtual elimination from later philosophy of the distinction between Greek and "barbarian," which plays an important part in the philosophies of Plato and Aristotle. The Greek prejudice against "barbarians" was based not on race but on language. The "barbarians" were not simply non-Greeks, they were people who spoke alien tongues, which sounded to Greek ears like "bar-bar." Once everyone was speaking Greek and was educated in Greek

194

culture, this distinction became idle. It was not unusual in this period for philosophers who wrote in Greek and were part of the Greek philosophical tradition to come from Egypt or other parts of Alexander's empire that were not originally Greek.

A second effect of Alexander's transformation of the Greek world on classical political philosophy was due to the change in the form of government introduced by Philip and Alexander. Plato and Aristotle had written their moral and political philosophy for the world of the *polis*; they thought the city-state the ideal governmental unit for the promotion of human flourishing. Though both were of course aware of larger political entities, such as the Persian Empire, they did not take these seriously as possibilities for Greeks. Philip and Alexander changed all that. In the Hellenistic and, later, in the Roman world, imperial rule was a fact of life. The *polis* continued to exist, but shorn of its autonomy, the center of government shifted from it to the imperial court.

One result of this shift was to make much of what Plato and Aristotle had written about ethics and politics seem obsolete. Philosophers had to form a new notion of their political identities, now that the classical one of "Athenian" or "Spartan" ceased to capture reality. Both because of the change in the form of government and because of the weakening and eventual disappearance of the distinction between Greek and barbarian, philosophers began to see themselves as more similar to others than different, and as part of a single human enterprise. The Stoics used the word "cosmopolitan" (citizen of the world) to reflect this change.

Despite its apparent unsuitability for the new circumstances of the Hellenistic age, the political framework shared and endorsed by Plato and Aristotle had had one important benefit: it had provided an appropriate social setting for the virtues. The classical view of the virtues and of the good life was constructed with the *polis* in mind. People living in small city-states needed courage, temperance, justice and practical wisdom, and the accompanying ability to express that wisdom effectively, both to advance their personal fortunes and to preserve their state. The *polis* was a form of social organization in which the individual could indeed make a difference, by arguing effectively in the assembly or by standing his ground in battle. In the Macedonian Empire this was no longer true. Only those close to the emperor could hope to influence public policy; others could only bear the consequences of decisions they had no role in shaping. Thus, the question naturally arose, of what use are the virtues to an individual in the new age? The new social structure required a new account of the virtues and the good life.

The decline of the *polis* had another effect on philosophy. In the classical age, one's role as a citizen was intimately connected with one's concept of oneself as a person. The *polis* not only provided a setting for the virtues, but it also provided a context in which individuals could shape their lives. Much of the daily activity of a citizen in classical Athens involved the political and social life of the city: there were civic festivals to attend, jury duty and participation in the assembly and military service in time of war. These activities continued in the Hellenistic age, but lost a good deal of their importance with the advent of imperial rule. This created a void, citizenship in a large and remote empire could not play the role in shaping one's identity that citizenship in the *polis* had.

Something was needed to fill this void, to give people a new sense of who they were. In the Hellenistic age, new religions came to play this role to a large degree, but so did philosophy. The traditional civic religion of the Greek *polis* was able to give people a sense of identity only because it was connected to the political life of the city. When the *polis* went into partial eclipse, so did civic religion. Mystery religions and Orphism, which held out the promise of personal salvation, had long supplemented the public worship of the gods of the city and with the advent of the Hellenistic age they were augmented by the importation of similar religions from the east, such as the worship of the Egyptian gods Isis and Osiris. These new religions gave individuals the sense of being part of a larger whole that citizenship in the *polis* could no longer provide. Though this whole was not the local community of the *polis*, but a global community of adherents to a particular faith, people often belonged as well to a local community of believers. Thus, their religious commitment had a concrete aspect that the political allegiance to the empire could not provide.

In this period people often turned to philosophy instead of religion to fill this "gap" in their identities created by the decline of the *polis*. This meant that philosophy had to change in certain ways to accommodate this new desire. Though the Pythagorean brotherhood provided a model for a philosophical school with the aspects of discipleship, doctrine and veneration of a master that were similar to religious organizations, the most famous philosophical schools of the Hellenic period, Plato's Academy and Aristotle's Lyceum, seem to have been schools in a different sense, institutions made up of people with a shared commitment to critical inquiry and the search for truth, rather than to a received set of dogmas or a single philosopher. Philosophy, for Socrates, Plato and Aristotle was more a method of rational thought than a set of specific beliefs.

The "schools" of the Hellenistic period resembled the Pythagorean model more than the Platonic and Aristotelian. For philosophy to fill its new role as a "way of life," certain matters had to be settled, not subject to constant debate. Disciples seeking a means to happiness regarded the doctrines of a school not as hypotheses to be rationally assessed, but as truths to be adopted and, often, committed to memory. Critical reason did not disappear during this period, but it was more often used by adherents of rival schools against each other than as a device for the pursuit of inquiry within a single school.

There was a corresponding burden on philosophers to present complete, intelligible systems of thought which provided disciples with a path to their desired end of happiness, rather than to investigate philosophical problems in a dispassionate, objective way. Both disciples and masters took a partisan, dogmatic stance toward philosophy that discouraged great innovation in thought but provided a sense of security for advocates of a particular view. This was true no less of the two skeptical schools, the Academic and the Pyrrhonist, than of the dogmatic schools, the Stoics and Epicureans, for though the skeptical schools, and the Pyrrhonists in particular, claimed not to be dogmatic, they attracted followers committed to their views about the possibility of knowledge, and excluded those committed to other positions.

In this chapter we shall examine the ethical doctrines of two of the most famous schools of philosophy that arose in this period, Epicureanism and Stoicism. As in preceding chapters, we shall do so by studying specific works, the few surviving writings of Epicurus and the *Encheiridion* (*Manual*) of Epictetus. We shall attempt to understand these philosophies both as developments of the classical themes presented earlier and as responses to the changed political and social conditions of the Hellenistic age.

Epicureanism

Epicurus was born in 341 BC on the island of Samos. His father was an Athenian, however, so he had the rights of Athenian citizenship. He eventually moved to Athens and established there in 307/6 a school, called the "Garden" because it met in the garden of his home. This "school," the beginning of Epicureanism as a philosophy, seems to have been a philosophical community based on Epicurean principles; both women and slaves were among its members. Epicurus lived, wrote and taught there until his death in 271. He is said to have written over 300 scrolls, an extraordinary number; of these, only a tiny portion survives. The Latin poet Lucretius did translate one of Epicurus' works into the epic poem *De Rerum Natura* (*On the Nature of Things*) but unfortunately for our purposes, this work contains little information about Epicurus' ethics. Apart from Epicurus' surviving works, we must rely for information about his views on statements of them by his critics, which is always a risky matter.

Epicurus' philosophy inspired passionate loyalty in his followers and intense dislike among his opponents. Often his views are misrepresented by anti-Epicurean polemicists. It is thought that many of his books were destroyed on the grounds that they were inimical to Christianity, but Christians were hardly Epicurus' only enemies. The most powerful misrepresentation of his thought is the one from which the notion of the "epicure" has been derived: the view of the Epicurean as a vulgar hedonist, a pursuer of sensual pleasure. This is a most unfair caricature of Epicurus' thought, as we shall see.

Like other philosophies of this age, the main aim of Epicureanism was the attainment of happiness. Epicurus thought that the main impediment to happiness was the fear and disquietude produced by religion, specifically the fear of death. His philosophical system was designed to dispel this and related fears by explaining the nature of the universe and teaching how one must live as a result of that nature. Both Epicurus' physics and his ethics, in other words, were responses to a single problem; the ethics, moreover, presupposes the physics. Thus, before we examine the ethics of Epicureanism, we must take a brief look at its theory of nature.

Epicurus borrowed his account of nature from the Greek atomists, Leucippus and Democritus. He modified their atomic theory to suit his own purposes, but did not acknowledge their contributions to his view. Epicurus agreed with Democritus and Leucippus that only atoms and the empty space in which they move exist. Thus, he was a materialist: he rejected formal principles both of the separate, Platonic sort and of the immanent, Aristotelian variety. It seems likely that Epicurus was attracted to atomism because of its denial of divine providence: according to atomic theory, the universe was the result of the chance collision of atoms, rather than of a divine plan as Plato had thought.

The Epicurean theory of atomism differed from that of Leucippus and Democritus in one important respect. The earlier atomists had thought of atoms as being in perpetual motion in all directions. There was no reason why some should move in one direction rather than another, and to that degree randomness or chance entered into the universe. Once atoms collided, however, their new motions resulted from the forces at work in their impact; in other words, given the initial velocity and direction of the atoms, their subsequent career could be determined mechanically. Epicurus rejected this view because it was deterministic. He posited instead that atoms naturally move "down" through infinite space at great velocity, but that they "swerve" at random intervals, with the result that they collide with each other and produce larger bodies. Though Epicurus has been rightly criticized for speaking of "up" and "down" inappropriately in a universe that is infinite in all directions, the doctrine of the swerve allowed him to avoid the deterministic consequences of earlier atomism. Since swerves can occur at any point, it is impossible to predict the future state of the universe from any set of initial conditions. Epicurus regarded this swerve as necessary for the existence of human free will, in which he believed, but how one gets from randomness at the atomic level to human freedom in his system remains a mystery.

As I have noted, Epicurus did not believe in divine providence, but he did not deny the existence of the gods. In general, he held that the impressions of the senses are the result of contact between a sense organ and a film of atoms streaming off the surface of a physical object. Although he allowed that these films could become damaged in their flight from object to sense organ, he held that the impressions themselves were infallible. Since, as he believed, all people received impressions of the gods directly into their minds in dreams, the gods must exist as causes of these impressions. Further, he thought, they must be immortal and supremely happy. The popular conception of the gods was wrong in ascribing to them concern with our lives; the gods live in bliss so perfect that they have no interest in meddling with us.

By removing the fear of divine intervention in human affairs Epicurus thought he had removed a major source of our anxiety about the future. Another feature of atomism allowed him to remove what he thought to be the other major source, our fear of death. Epicurus taught that the human soul was material, composed of atoms as was the body. At death, the atoms that composed the soul dissolved, and as a result the person ceased to exist. Therefore, no one should fear death: "Death is nothing to us; for the body, when it has been resolved into its elements, has no feeling, and that which has no feeling is nothing to us" (*Principal Doctrines*, 2).

Since the gods do not plague us in this life and there is no worry that they shall do so after death, our happiness depends on ourselves and our circumstances. The attainment of happiness is, of course, the object of Epicurus' ethics, to which we now turn. Epicurus held that the good, the end of human existence, was pleasure and that pain, correspondingly, was evil

> Pleasure is our first and kindred good. It is the starting point of every choice and of every aversion, and to it we come back, inasmuch as we make feeling the rule by which to judge of every good thing. (*Letter to Menoeceus*, 129)

He recognized two sorts of pain: physical pain and psychological distress. He regarded physical pain as easily dealt with. The common pains of hunger and thirst could be satisfied by simple food and drink and as for other sorts of pain, such as those that accompany illness

> Continuous pain does not last long in the flesh; on the contrary, pain, if extreme, is present a very short time, and even that degree of pain which barely outweighs pleasure in the flesh does not last for many days together. Illnesses of long

duration even permit an excess of pleasure over pain in the flesh. (*Principal Doctrines*, 4)

The aim of human existence, then, the "sum and end of a blessed life," is "health of the body and tranquillity [*ataraxia*] of mind" (*Letter to Menoeceus*, 128). Of the two ends, it seems clear that Epicurus valued mental tranquility above bodily health, as he says, "the end of all our actions is to be free from pain and fear, and, when we have attained all this, the tempest of the soul is laid" (ibid.).

Thus, Epicurus did not endorse a life of wild debauchery, as he is often misinterpreted as doing. He is quite explicit about this

When we say, then, that pleasure is the end and aim, we do not mean the pleasures of the prodigal or the pleasures of sensuality, as we are understood to do by some through ignorance, prejudice, or wilful misrepresentation. By pleasure we mean the absence of pain in the body and of trouble in the soul. It is not an unbroken succession of drinking bouts and of revelry, not sexual love, not the enjoyment of the fish and other delicacies of a luxurious table, which produce a pleasant life; it is sober reasoning, searching out the grounds of every choice and avoidance, and banishing those beliefs through which the greatest tumults take possession of the soul. (*Letter to Menoeceus*, 131—2)

It is his insistence on reason's role in the attainment of happiness that places Epicurus in the classical tradition of Greek ethics, as we shall see.

Epicurus is not opposed in principle to the pleasures mentioned above, he does not think they are intrinsically evil. "No pleasure is in itself evil," he states (*Principal Doctrines*, 8). Why, then, does he not recommend their pursuit? There seem to be two reasons. First, they are not sufficient to bring about the end of tranquility

If the objects which are productive of pleasures to profligate persons really freed them from fears of the mind . . . if, further, they taught them to limit their desires, we should never have any fault to find with such persons. (ibid., 10)

Physical pleasure does not, however, eliminate mental anxiety

> It would be impossible to banish fear on matters of the highest
> importance, if a man did not know the nature of the whole
> universe but lived in dread of what the legend tells us. Hence
> without the study of nature there was no enjoyment of
> unmixed pleasures. (ibid., 12)

In addition to the philosophical study of nature, practical
wisdom or prudence (*phronesis*) is also needed for the good life;
this is the moral virtue referred to above as "sober reasoning,
searching out the grounds of every choice and avoidance." Practical
wisdom provides a second reason for the rejection of sensual
pleasures, the fact that they produce more pain than pleasure in
the long run. Practical wisdom seems to function for Epicurus by
calculating the balance of pleasure and pain that each sort of
pleasant activity might produce. This leads the wise individual to
reject certain activities, however pleasant they may be

> we do not choose every pleasure whatsoever, but ofttimes pass
> over many pleasures when a greater annoyance ensues from
> them. And ofttimes we consider pains superior to pleasures
> when submission to the pains for a long time brings us as a
> consequence a greater pleasure. While therefore all pleasure
> because it is naturally akin to us is good, not all pleasure is
> choice-worthy, just as all pain is an evil and yet not all pain is
> to be shunned. It is, however, by measuring one against
> another, and by looking at the conveniences and
> inconveniences, that all these matters must be judged. (*Letter
> to Menoeceus*, 129—30)

In order to see why practical wisdom requires the rejection of
sensual profligacy, we must consider Epicurus' definition of
pleasure, given above: "the absence of pain in the body and of
trouble in the soul." By defining pleasure as the absence of pain
and trouble Epicurus goes against the main currents of ancient
thought. Plato, no friend of hedonism, had carefully distinguished
pleasure from a pain-free "intermediate state" that resulted from
the satisfaction of desire, and other philosophers, such as Aristotle

and the Cyrenaics (who held that sensual pleasure *was* the good) agreed that pleasure was a positive state, not merely the absence of pain. Though Epicurus' equation of pleasure with this intermediate state seems to be a mistake, it is important for his system as a whole. If physical pleasure is the termination of pain, such as that of hunger and thirst, a simple diet can accomplish this end as well as a rich one

> Plain fare gives as much pleasure as a costly diet, when once the pain of want has been removed, while bread and water confer the highest possible pleasure when they are brought to hungry lips. To habituate one's self, therefore, to simple and inexpensive diet supplies all that is needful for health, and enables a man to meet the necessary requirements of life without shrinking, and it places us in a better condition when we approach a costly fare and renders us fearless of fortune.
>
> (*Letter to Menoeceus,* 130—31)

The person accustomed to a simple diet, in other words, fares as well as the devotee of rich food and wine when both are available in abundance, and suffers far less in times of shortage. This person is also more self-sufficient than one with expensive tastes and Epicurus regarded self-sufficiency as an important ingredient in the good life.

Since Epicurus equates pleasure with the absence of pain, he denies that a rich diet provides *more* pleasure than a simple one, for "The magnitude of pleasure reaches its limit in the removal of all pain" (*Principal Doctrines*, 3). Once pain is removed, pleasure can only be varied, not increased (ibid., 18). Since concentration on varying one's pleasure would distract one from the task of assuring mental tranquility, presumably Epicurus would disapprove of it for that reason too. Thus, the genuine Epicurean does not live for pleasures of the flesh, but for tranquility of the mind.

Tranquility, peace of mind, is, as we have seen above, attained by two means: philosophical understanding and practical wisdom. Philosophical understanding teaches one not to fear death or divine retribution, the chief sources of mental anguish (*Letter to Herodotus*, 81—2); practical wisdom or prudence teaches one to live virtuously. Of the two, Epicurus ranks practical wisdom higher

Prudence (*phronesis*) is a more precious thing even than philosophy; from it spring all the other virtues, for it teaches that we cannot lead a life of pleasure which is not also a life of prudence, honor, and justice; nor lead a life of prudence, honor and justice, which is not also a life of pleasure. For the virtues have grown into one with a pleasant life, and a pleasant life is inseparable from them. (*Letter to Menoeceus*, 132—3)

Thus, though Epicurus' view of the good life is somewhat different from his classical predecessors, he is led to a doctrine of virtue very similar to theirs. The possession of virtue is necessary and sufficient for happiness, and *phronesis* is the chief virtue. We have already seen that *phronesis* leads to temperance through a careful calculation of the pleasure and pain that results from a profligate life. It also leads to friendship, justice and nobility or honor, as we shall see.

One principle of practical wisdom that leads to specific judgments about the attainment of tranquility is Epicurus' classification of kinds of desire: "Of our desires some are natural and necessary; others are natural, but not necessary; others, again, are neither natural nor necessary" (*Principal Doctrines*, 29). An ancient commentator illustrated this classification as follows

Epicurus regards as natural and necessary desires which bring relief from pain, as *e.g.* drink when we are thirsty; while by natural but not necessary he means those which merely diversify the pleasure without removing the pain, as *e.g.* costly viands; by neither natural nor necessary he means desires for crowns and the erection of statues in one's honor. (ibid.)

Unnecessary desires, both of the natural and unnatural variety, are those which "lead to no pain when they remain ungratified"; Epicurus regards them as "easily got rid of" (ibid., 26). Since pleasure does not increase once pain is eliminated, it is clear that the unnecessary desires should be got rid of, for their satisfaction cannot increase the pleasantness of life. Moreover, these desires are unlimited, insatiable, whereas the natural and necessary desires are limited and easily satisfied (ibid., 15). Thus, confining one's desires to the natural and necessary enables one to satisfy them and live happily, whereas the person with unnecessary desires can never satisfy them (ibid., 21). Among the natural but unnecessary desires to be given up, incidentally, are those of sex: "the pleasures of sexual love never benefited anyone; one should be content if they do no harm" (*Vatican Sayings*, 51). Because the wise person has such easily satisfied desires, he or she is largely immune to misfortune, another source of anxiety (*Principal Doctrines*, 16).

The kind of life Epicurus recommends for a person who has learned these lessons in the limitation of desire is "a quiet private life withdrawn from the multitude" (ibid., 14). This was of course the life lived by Epicurus himself and his followers in the Garden. Political involvement played no role in it, but friendship did: "Of all the means which are procured by wisdom to ensure happiness throughout the whole of life, by far the most important is the acquisition of friends" (ibid., 27). It is worth noting that the pleasure and tranquility Epicurus thinks each of us should seek is our own, and his ethical system is thus an egoistic one, like that of Socrates. Epicurus is to be distinguished in this respect from the classical utilitarian philosophers of the modern era, Bentham and Mill, who otherwise resemble him. Thus, to justify having friends as part of the good life, Epicurus has to argue that friends are a means for the procurement of our own happiness. Specifically, friends enhance our security (ibid., 28). This does not mean that Epicurean friendship involves the mere use of our friends as a means to our own security, we are not forbidden to enjoy the company of our friends for their own sake, and in fact Epicurus expects us to do so: "All friendship is choiceworthy for itself, though in the beginning it has been chosen for its benefits" (*Vatican Sayings*, 23). It does mean, though, that the justification of the practice of friendship is for Epicurus egoistic, as we saw earlier that it was for Aristotle.

Epicurus' justification of the practice of justice is similar to his justification of friendship. Epicurus' account of justice is in fact remarkably like that put forward by Glaucon in Book II of Plato's *Republic*: justice is a matter of convention, a social contract entered into by people to protect themselves from being harmed by others. This protection from harm Epicurus sees as a natural good, but the requirements of justice are those rules which ensure this protection in particular circumstances

There never was an absolute justice, but only an agreement

made in reciprocal intercourse in whatever localities now and again from time to time, providing against the infliction or suffering of harm. (*Principal Doctrines*, 33)

And

Taken generally, justice is the same for all, to wit, something found expedient in mutual intercourse; but in its application to particular cases of locality or conditions of whatever kind, it varies under different circumstances. (ibid., 36)

Where there is no agreement, there is neither justice nor injustice

Those animals which are incapable of making covenants with one another, to the end that they may neither inflict nor suffer harm, are without either justice or injustice. And those tribes which either could not or would not form mutual covenants to the same end are in like case. (ibid., 32)

It is clear that it is bad for someone to suffer injustice at the hands of another, for this would be to suffer harm, but why is it bad to inflict injustice on another, given that justice is a conventional rather than a natural good? Epicurus' answer to this question also resembles Glaucon's: unjust behavior leads to bad consequences

Injustice is not in itself an evil, but only in its consequence, viz. the terror which is excited by apprehension that those appointed to punish such offenses will discover the injustice.
It is impossible for the man who secretly violates any article of the social contract to feel confident that he will remain undiscovered, even if he has already escaped ten thousand times; for right on to the end of his life he is never sure he will not be detected. (ibid., 34—5)

It is this fear of apprehension that makes performance of unjust acts undesirable, for fear of any sort disrupts the tranquility of a good life. "The just man," says Epicurus, "enjoys the greatest peace of mind, while the unjust is full of the utmost disquietude" (ibid., 17). The wise individual, then will enter into just agreements for the sake of personal security, and will live by those agreements because of the good psychological consequences of doing so.

So far we have seen that Epicurus' view of the good life requires the virtues of practical wisdom, temperance, friendship and justice. What, though, of courage? It is not a virtue he discusses in his surviving works. Aristotle defined the courageous person as "a man who fearlessly faces a noble death and any situations that bring about a sudden death" (*Nicomachean Ethics* III.6, 1115a 33—4). Aristotle also noted that, "Such eventualities are usually brought about by war. But of course a courageous man is also fearless at sea and in illness" (III.6, 1115a 35—b 1). The whole aim of Epicurus' philosophy was to make his disciples fearless concerning death, which Aristotle regards as the most fearful of events, so in this respect Epicurus is a proponent of courage in Aristotle's sense of the term. Epicurus himself died of a painful illness, which he bore with equanimity by all accounts, so we know that fearlessly facing death due to illness was an important part of the good life for him. The reason he does not praise courage, I suspect, is that, as Aristotle notes, this virtue was closely connected with warfare, and war was an activity Epicurus surely would have rejected as the pursuit of vain (unnatural and unnecessary) pleasures. Participation in war, like participation in civic affairs in general, had no place in Epicurus' life of quiet withdrawal.

In summation, Epicurus seems to have constructed a justification of most, if not quite all of the classical virtues, despite the fact that his concept of the good life differs somewhat from that of Plato and Aristotle. He succeeded in answering the question I raised earlier in the chapter: of what use are the virtues in a world where the *polis* is no longer the central structure for human existence? I shall defer critical evaluation of his ethical theory until we have had a chance to examine the Stoic alternative, but it is easy to see the charms of a view which states that "We must laugh and philosophize at the same time" (*Vatican Sayings*, 41).

Stoicism

The Stoic school was founded by Zeno of Citium, who lived from about 333 to about 261 BC. Zeno began his teaching at the *stoa poikile* or "painted porch," in Athens, hence the name of the school. Unlike Epicureanism, which was essentially the work of a single philosopher, the Stoic system developed over a long period of time, and several philosophers contributed to its character. Zeno was succeeded as head of the school by Cleanthes, who was in turn followed by Chrysippus; later in the history of Stoicism Posidonius blended Stoic with Platonic doctrines. The works of these early Stoics survive only in fragments, which makes it difficult to know in many cases who the originator of a particular Stoic doctrine was. Like Epicurus, the Stoics seem to have borrowed freely from earlier philosophers, including the Pre-Socratics (especially Heraclitus) and the Megarians. Their ethics were influenced by Diogenes the Cynic, who made a great point of flouting convention and living "according to nature." The life according to nature became in fact the Stoic ethical ideal.

The Stoic philosophers who are best known today lived long after Zeno and Chrysippus. They are the Roman Emperor, Marcus Aurelius (AD 121—180) and Epictetus (c. AD 60—c. 138), who was born a slave. The different circumstances of their lives testify to the universality of the appeal of Stoic philosophy. Unlike the philosophers mentioned above, they wrote works which have survived: Marcus Aurelius' *Meditations* and Epictetus' *Discourses* and *Manual* (actually transcribed from conversation by his disciple Arrian) are still read today. Epictetus and Marcus Aurelius were more practically oriented than their predecessors: their major contribution to Stoicism lay in presenting its moral philosophy in popular form, rather than in developing its metaphysics and epistemology. In this chapter we shall be examining in detail Epictetus' brief *Encheiridion* (the word means "hand-book," or "manual"). Though Epictetus certainly represents in this book a Stoic view of ethics, we need to remember that it was intended as an introduction to Stoic ethics, and not as a work of theoretical philosophy. We must also be aware that, though other Stoics would have accepted the main outlines of his view, they would not necessarily have agreed with every detail of his exposition of it.

As was the case with Epicureanism, Stoic ethics is heavily influenced by Stoic metaphysics. The Stoics, like the Epicureans, were materialists, though their materialism was less restrictive than that of their rivals (they accepted abstract objects, such as propositions, as mental entities, and adapted Aristotle's form-matter distinction to their own purposes). Unlike the Epicureans, however, the Stoics accepted determinism. They thought that everything that happened was pre-determined to happen by previously existing causes. They accepted the result that Epicurus had sought to avoid by his "swerve": the possibility of predicting all future events given a complete list of antecedent causes. Determinism was not the blind working out of mechanical forces that Epicurus feared, however: the Stoics believed that the active power that determined the future of the universe was God. Thus, they accepted another doctrine that Epicurus rejected: divine providence. The Stoics, because they were materialists, conceived of God as a cosmic fire, constantly at work in the universe but they also thought of God as reason personified, as *logos*. Because the material that caused all the motion in the universe was supremely rational, everything that happened in the universe was rational too and, because rational, good. Thus, the Stoics believed that whatever happened had a rational explanation, and was for the best.

Stoic metaphysics entailed that any attempt to change the future was both futile and foolish: futile, because whatever happened had been pre-destined, and foolish, because whatever happened was controlled by divine reason, which always acted for the best, and who would want to act in opposition to divine reason? Evil, according to this view, is non-existent (*Manual*, 27): the universe is perfect, because governed by divine reason. Now at this point someone is sure to object that this is not the way the universe appears to be: there seem to be plenty of evils, both natural (such as diseases and disasters) and moral (such as bad people and bad actions). Stoic ethics sought to explain and to correct the mental attitude that gives rise to this objection. Its aim was not to change the external world, for that was impossible, but to accommodate the individual intellect and will to the nature of that world.

Epictetus addresses this question at the very start of his *Manual*. He begins by distinguishing two sorts of things

Of all existing things some are in our power, and others are not in our power. In our power are thought, impulse, will to get and will to avoid, and, in a word, everything which is our own doing. Things not in our power include the body, property, reputation, office, and, in a word, everything which is not our own doing. Things in our power are by nature free, unhindered, untrammelled; things not in our power are weak, servile, subject to hindrance, dependent on others. (*Manual*, 1)

This is a metaphysical distinction, and a consequence of the Stoic acceptance of determinism discussed above. Things not in our power include both the attitudes of others (which determine our reputation and office) and physical objects (body and property). The former are in the power of someone, but not us; the latter are controlled by God.

It may seem strange to have one's body and property described as "not in our power": normally, we think, we control our bodies and our property. A moment's reflection will reveal, though, that even from the standpoint of common sense our bodies and our property are not completely under our control: though my arm may go up when I desire it to, and though I may invest my money where and when I like, things may go wrong with my nerves that make it impossible for me to raise my arm and my money may be stolen or lost on the stock market. The Stoic insists on more than this, however: my own bodily movements, being part of the divinely governed cosmos, must be really controlled by God. Epictetus illustrates the point by comparing life to a part in a play

Remember that you are an actor in a play, and the Playwright chooses the manner of it: if he wants it short, it is short; if long, it is long. If he wants you to act a poor man you must act the part with all your powers; and so if your part be a cripple or a magistrate or a plain man. For your business is to act the character that is given you and act it well; the choice of the cast is Another's. (*Manual*, 17)

Appearances to the contrary, then, it cannot be my own decision that causes my arm to go up; it would go up, if that were best for the universe as a whole, whether I willed it to do so or not. Thus Epictetus' view of what is in our power differs only by degree from that of common sense, but the degree of difference is considerable, and has a great impact on Stoic ethics. One might wish to modify Stoic doctrine by replacing Epictetus' sharp dichotomy between what is in our power and what is not with a continuum, at one end of which stand our thoughts (completely in our power), and at the other end, things like the weather or the price of tea in China (completely out of the control at least of most of us), with bodily movements somewhere in the middle. Epictetus, however, insists on the sharp division.

As the passage above indicates, the Stoics used the distinction between what is and what is not in our power to delimit the scope of human freedom. Though the Stoics were fatalists, their fatalism was limited to events in the external world. When it came to mental events, they believed in free will. Epictetus, incidentally, does not justify this belief, rather, he treats it as an unquestioned presupposition of his system. Though Stoic fatalism destroys the distinction between what happens to me and what I do when one considers only physical acts, it restores that distinction for mental events. In fact, the view of Epictetus is that, while physical events happen to me, I perform mental acts: the natural world is the world of determinism; the mental world, that of freedom. (Epictetus doesn't always adhere to this distinction himself, we find him, for instance in *Manual* 33 and 46, recommending that we act in certain ways, and not just with certain attitudes). Thus, Stoicism is able to avoid, to some degree, the sense of helplessness that usually follows from deterministic philosophies, for if the course of the world is fixed, I can at least control my attitude toward it.

How then, given the unalterable course of the future, should I alter my attitudes to attain happiness? Here is Epictetus' advice: "Ask not that events should happen as you will, but let your will be that events should happen as they do, and you shall have peace" (*Manual*, 8). In other words, I must make my will conform to events, and not try to make events conform to my will. This is what the Stoics meant by "life in accordance with nature." This requires, first of all, a change in my attitudes toward good and evil. I must understand that

> What disturbs men's minds is not events but their judgments on events. For instance, death is nothing dreadful, or else Socrates would have thought it so. No, the only dreadful thing about it is men's judgment that it is dreadful. (*Manual*, 5)

As with death, so with dishonor

> Remember that foul words or blows in themselves are no outrage, but your judgment that they are so. So when any one

makes you angry, know that it is your own thought that has angered you. Wherefore make it your first endeavor not to let your impressions carry you away. (*Manual*, 20)

In general, we ought to be indifferent to external events, whether they are of great or small importance; we ought not to judge them good or evil in themselves. (This seems inconsistent with Epictetus' belief in a benevolent, rational God controlling everything; for if such a God causes these events, shouldn't we regard them as good?) This advice seems easier to follow in the case of some events than others. When Epictetus urges that we be unconcerned with honors or slights from others (as at *Manual* 25), this seems good, if familiar advice (and it is familiar largely because of the influence of philosophers like the Stoics); but what are we to make of the following recommendation

When anything, from the meanest thing upwards, is attractive or serviceable or an object of affection, remember always to say to yourself, 'What is its nature?' If you are fond of a jug, say you are fond of a jug; then you will not be disturbed if it be broken. If you kiss your child or your wife, say to yourself that you are kissing a human being, for then if death strikes it you will not be disturbed. (*Manual*, 3; cf. 7, 11, 14)

Though Epictetus does not say that one's wife or child are worth no more than a jug, the comparison indicates that our attitude toward the death of a child should be the same as our attitude toward a jug that has been broken. The reasons for this are that death is not a bad thing; that what God has ordained must be good; that human beings don't live forever; and, perhaps most importantly, that one must strive to reach a status of *apatheia*, of insusceptibility to the passions or emotions. This Stoic ideal contrasts sharply with the view of Plato and Aristotle that the emotions require proper expression, though under rational control. Another passage illustrates this ideal in action

When you see a man shedding tears in sorrow for a child abroad or dead, or for loss of property, beware that you are not carried away by the impression that it is outward ills that make him miserable. Keep this thought by you: 'What distresses him is not the event, for that does not distress another, but his judgement on the event.' Therefore do not hesitate to sympathize with him so far as words go, and if it so chance, even to groan with him; *but take heed that you do not also groan in your inner being.* (*Manual*, 16; italics mine)

What Epictetus suggests here sounds like hypocrisy but this indicates the degree to which the Stoics were willing to go to uphold their ideal of inner tranquility or *apatheia*.

Part of the Stoic distrust of the emotions was based on the idea that they made individuals partial to their own situation

when another man's slave has broken the wine-cup we are very ready to say at once, 'Such things must happen'. Know then that when your own cup is broken, you ought to behave in the same way as when your neighbour's was broken. Apply the same principle to higher matters. Is another's child or wife dead? not one of us but would say, 'Such is the lot of man'; but when one's own dies, straightway one cries, 'Alas! miserable am I'. But we ought to remember what our feelings are when we hear it of another. (*Manual*, 26)

All previous Greek moral philosophers had accepted the egocentric nature of human motivation and had built their ethics on a concept of enlightened self-interest but the Stoics strike a more modern note by insisting on a strict impartiality between my interests and those of others. Partiality to one's own fate, they thought, was the major source of our failure to realize the rationality and goodness of all that occurs. We feel that something is bad for ourselves, and thus fail to see that it is good for the universe as a whole.

Since the time of the Stoics, most moral philosophers have stressed the impartiality of ethical action, and so has Christianity. The commandment, "Love your neighbor as you love yourself," Kant's categorical imperative, and the utilitarian requirement that we seek the greatest happiness of the greatest number, all have at their core the requirement that one think of others in the same way as one thinks of oneself. The Stoic principle is similar to these others, but there is also a difference worth noting. The commandment to love our neighbor as ourselves asks us to elevate the interests of others so that they equal our own, and the normal interpretation of the Kantian and utilitarian principles is similar: one should think of "third person" interests as if they were first person, and assign the same dignity or worth to others that one would to oneself. The Stoic principle stated above actually asks that we demote our own interests to that of third parties as a means to ethical objectivity. It seeks as an end, not the recognition of the intrinsic worth of individuals, but the subordination of all individuals, including oneself, to the universal reason at work in the cosmos.

The altruism of the Stoics is connected with their commitment to public service. This commitment is one of the features of Stoicism that distinguishes it from Epicureanism: the Epicureans, you will recall, advocated withdrawal from public life. The Romans in particular admired this feature of Stoic philosophy; but we must note that the Stoics did not advocate a life of public service as a means of improving the life of the state as that would be incompatible with their fatalism. Public service was simply one of many roles that might be assigned to one by the playwright of the play one was in; it should be accepted and played out cheerfully, but in a manner consistent with the primary aim of Stoicism, the preservation of one's inner freedom. If you realize this, says Epictetus, "you will not wish to be praetor, or prefect or consul, but to be free; and there is but one way to freedom—to despise what is not in our power" (*Manual*, 19).

In one respect Epictetus departed from the requirement of universal objectivity in ethics. He insisted that one should not judge others by the standards of ethics one accepted oneself

> If a man washes quickly, do not say that he washes badly, but that he washes quickly. If a man drinks much wine, do not say that he drinks badly, but that he drinks much. For till you have decided what judgement prompts him, how do you know that he acts badly? (*Manual*, 45)

It was not simply because he thought it impossible to know whether another was acting badly that Epictetus rejected moral judgment of others. There was in fact plenty of behavior he was willing to condemn (cf. e.g. *Manual*, 33). Rather, he was concerned that the practice of judgment diverted one from the task of moral self-improvement. As he states

> The ignorant man's position and character is this: he never
> looks to himself for benefit or harm, but to the world outside
> him. The philosopher's position and character is that he always
> look to himself for benefit and harm. (*Manual*, 48)

Since Epictetus' position was that good and evil are properties of
our judgments of events, it is easy to see why our concern should be
with our own judgments and not with the actions of others. In *this*
respect, Stoicism was as egocentric as the other classical moral
theories we have studied: the aim of the individual is self-
improvement, not the correction of others.

The goal of Stoic moral philosophy, as noted above, is a life of
complete rationality, of *apatheia* or imperturbability. The Stoics
described the person who lived such a life as "the sage." They
thought that philosophy (and in particular Stoic philosophy) was
the only route to this life. Thus, for Epictetus as for the other
philosophers we have examined, the good life was the
philosophical life. The attainment of *apatheia* depended on the
adoption of the correct beliefs about divine providence and the
goodness of the universe, which resulted from philosophical
instruction. Only when one had understood nature could one
attempt to live in accordance with nature.

Never the less, Epictetus regarded the philosophical life as
primarily a practical one

> On no occasion call yourself a philosopher, nor talk at large of
> your principles among the multitude, but act on your
> principles. For instance, at a banquet do not say how one
> ought to eat, but eat as you ought. (*Manual*, 46)

Elsewhere he complains that philosophers focus on abstract
problems, such as proving that it is wrong to lie or proving that an
argument of a certain sort is valid, instead of their primary task,
which is the application of the principles established by these
proofs: "Wherefore we lie, but are ready enough with the
demonstration that lying is wrong" (*Manual*, 52).

The ideal of the sage seemed so removed from ordinary life
that both the Stoics and their critics wondered whether anyone of

the kind had ever lived. Epictetus regards Socrates as an example of the sage; he writes that "Socrates attained perfection, paying heed to nothing but reason, in all that he encountered" (*Manual*, 52). Though other Hellenistic philosophies looked back to Socrates as an ideal philosopher, his selection by Epictetus is somewhat surprising. Though we saw that Socrates was a rationalist and was unafraid of death, he certainly did not share the views of the Stoics on the limits of human power: he was not a fatalist, and his statements on divine providence were far less comprehensive than those of Epictetus. In addition, if we can believe Socrates' own statements, his virtue was not based on knowledge, for he repeatedly and emphatically disclaimed such knowledge. Despite these differences between Socrates and the sage, however, Epictetus clearly regarded him as the best exemplar of the life of wisdom.

Socrates and the ideal of the sage no doubt seemed standards too high for most people to emulate, so what did Stoicism offer them? The early Stoics had been rather hard-nosed on this subject: they regarded all lives other than that of the sage as worthless, corrupt and evil. In this respect Epictetus softened traditional Stoic doctrine, introducing the concept of "making progress." "If you are not yet Socrates," he writes, "yet ought you to live as one who would wish to be a Socrates" (*Manual*, 51). One who is making progress toward the ideal of the sage acts in a manner approximating the sage

> he blames none, praises none, complains of none, accuses none, never speaks of himself as if he were somebody, or as if he knew anything. And if any one compliments him he laughs in himself at his compliment; and if one blames him, he makes no defence. He goes about like a convalescent, careful not to disturb his constitution on its road to recovery, until it has got firm hold. (*Manual*, 48)

What is the difference between the one who is "making progress" and the sage? Perhaps this passage illustrates it best

> Remember that you must behave in life as you would at a banquet. A dish is handed round and comes to you; put out your hand and take it politely. It passes you; do not stop it. It

has not reached you; do not be impatient to get it, but wait till your turn comes. Bear yourself thus towards children, wife, office, wealth, and one day you will be worthy to banquet with the gods. But if when they are set before you, you do not take them but despise them, then you shall not only share the gods' banquet but shall share their rule. (*Manual*, 15)

So far we have discussed the Stoic conceptions of the world-order and the good life. What is the role of the virtues in that life? Epictetus discusses the virtues surprisingly little in the *Manual*. At one point he mentions piety

For piety towards the gods know that the most important thing is this: to have right opinions about them—that they exist, and that they govern the universe well and justly—and to have set yourself to obey them, and to give way to all that happens, following events with a free will, in the belief that they are fulfilled by the highest mind. (*Manual*, 31)

In another passage, he discusses situations that require virtue

When anything happens to you, always remember to turn to yourself and ask what faculty you have to deal with it. If you see a beautiful boy or a beautiful woman, you will find continence the faculty to exercise there; if trouble is laid on you, you will find endurance; if ribaldry, you will find patience. And if you train yourself in this habit your impressions will not carry you away. (*Manual*, 10)

In this passage, however, the traits referred to are not the classical virtues of temperance and courage: continence, *engkrateia* is a state of moral strength or strength of will that Aristotle in *Nicomachean Ethics* VII distinguishes from the virtue of temperance.

This might create the impression that the Stoics did not regard virtue as important, but that is emphatically not the case. In fact, Stoic doctrine was that virtue was the only good, and that it was sufficient for the good life. The reason Epictetus does not discuss virtue or the virtues separately is that, for the Stoics, virtue was simply the rationality that made it possible for the sage to attain *apatheia*. In other words, virtue and the good life were indistinguishable, in speaking of one, one spoke of the other also.

The Stoics tended to speak of "virtue" rather than "the virtues," because they accepted the Socratic thesis of the unity of the virtues in a particularly strong form. For the Stoics as for Socrates, the virtues were one because virtue was knowledge. It is possible to distinguish among the virtues for the Stoics as it was for Socrates: courage is the virtue of enduring hardship, temperance is the virtue of withstanding the lure of pleasure, justice is the virtue of resisting the temptation to be partial to one's own case, and so forth. Never the less, these virtues are only formally distinct, in practice, only the sage, who has the wisdom to follow nature, has any of them, and he has them all.

The Stoic doctrine of virtue thus looks like a throwback to an earlier classical conception of virtue, namely that of Socrates. In one respect it differs from that conception, though: the Stoic virtues, unlike the Socratic, are exclusively virtues of endurance, of "bearing with" and accepting hardship, rather than active powers. This is a consequence of Stoic fatalism. They resemble the Socratic virtues, however, in being purely rational states and in this respect the Stoics seem to have ignored or rejected the accounts of virtue developed by Plato and Aristotle. Both Plato and Aristotle sought to give the emotions and appetites their proper role in a full human life, although they placed them under the control of reason. The Stoics, though acknowledging that emotions and appetites were in some sense "natural," strove for a life in which they were entirely supplanted by reason: the *apatheia* of the sage was an imperturbability in the face of troubling emotions. Whether the Stoics intended this or not, this ideal led to a psychological theory in which the emotions and reason were essentially at odds with each other and this theory influenced later moral philosophers, especially Kant. To a very real extent, the picture of a harmonious soul advocated by Plato and Aristotle was replaced by the picture of a soul in inevitable conflict. In part this was due to Christian writers such as Paul, who characterized the conflict in Romans 7 as a war between flesh and spirit but in part it was due to the Stoics.

In addition to the cardinal virtues of the classical tradition, the Stoics were advocates of humility, a fact that led early Christians to admire them. In praising humility and attacking pride, the Stoics actually opposed the mainstream of the classical tradition, and in particular Aristotle, who thought that a proper pride was the mark of the "high-minded" gentleman. Epictetus' *Manual* is filled with warnings against pride and praise of humility: one should not take pride in one's possessions (6); one's eloquence (44); one's ability to interpret philosophical texts (49); or even one's choice of a lifestyle (47). The reasoning behind this seems to be that it is unreasonable to take pride in things such as wealth and status that are not in our power and that taking pride in one's own attitudes, which are in one's power, conflicts with the ideal of detachment.

Stoicism, despite its claims about the intrinsic goodness of everything that happens, is ultimately a pessimistic philosophy, a philosophy of resignation. Again, the rationale behind Stoic pessimism seems to be the ideal of detachment; if one found an abundance of goods in the world, one might become attached to them. Of the several passages in the *Manual* that attest to this pessimism the following is perhaps the best example

> When you go to visit some great man, prepare your mind by thinking that you will not find him in, that you will be shut out, that the doors will be slammed in your face, that he will pay no heed to you. And if in spite of all this you find it fitting for you to go, go and bear what happens and never say to yourself, 'It was not worth all this'; for that shows a vulgar mind and one at odds with outward things. (*Manual*, 33)

Here Epictetus practices the strategy of pessimists everywhere to avoid disappointment, that of lowering one's expectations so that disappointment becomes impossible, or (one might say) experiencing one's disappointment in advance, by way of anticipation, so that one may be inured to it in the event itself. This is one respect in which the early Christians did not follow the Stoics and their optimism was probably one of the reasons Christianity succeeded in supplanting philosophies such as Stoicism and Epicureanism throughout the Roman Empire.

Stoicism, Epicureanism and the classical tradition

Stoicism and Epicureanism were extremely influential in the Hellenistic and Roman world: in some respects, they have been more influential on subsequent Western civilization than the classical views of Socrates, Plato and Aristotle. They were in their time rival claimants to the legacy of classical Greek moral philosophy. The Stoics have proved more influential, largely due to the similarity between some of their views and Christian doctrine (their belief in submission to God's will, their altruism and belief in service, and their distrust of physical pleasure, in particular), but can either school truly claim to be the heir of the classical tradition in ethics?

Though the differences between the schools are more obvious than their similarities, those are real, too. Each school developed its view in response to the changed environment of the Hellenistic world, described above. For both, the arena of human life is not the friendly world of the *polis* but an alien and, one might say, indifferent world of nature. (The Stoics would quarrel with the word "indifferent," but it is a fact that the God of Stoicism was indifferent to individual interests, and considered only the welfare of the whole.) Both philosophies attempted to describe a path to happiness in such a world, both offered comfort to people who found themselves trapped in it. Both based their ethical views on metaphysical ones, but the metaphysical views were chosen with an eye toward the end of providing comfort. Finally, both preached a life of withdrawal and detachment: the Epicureans sought to withdraw from public life, whereas the Stoics sought detachment even from personal relationships.

One of the difficulties with both philosophies is the degree to which their ethical principles depend on their metaphysics. If the metaphysics is wrong, the ethics is likely to be mistaken also. Consider the Epicurean views about death and providence: if we do survive death, or if God does intervene in our lives, it would be foolish to ignore these facts in our moral reasoning but Epicurus urges us to do just that. Or consider the Stoic doctrine of fatalism: if it is true that we can alter the course of external events by our actions, so that more is in our power than the Stoics allow, then their entire system of ethics would seem to be based on a mistaken view of human agency. Now all ethical systems require some metaphysical assumptions but few are as closely tied to unproven and perhaps unprovable metaphysical world-views as are Stoicism and Epicureanism.

Of the two philosophies, Epicureanism seems to be the more humane, Stoicism the nobler. Epicureanism, like Stoicism, teaches calm forbearance in the face of death but it emphasizes the gentler aspects of life, such as the pleasures of friendship, while Stoicism wears a sterner face. Which is more attractive is perhaps a matter of personal preference. Another matter of personal preference is the degree of comfort afforded by each metaphysical system: some people may be consoled by the thought that all the world is only matter in space, arranged by chance, whereas others may find this vision repugnant, and the same may be said for the view that every event in the world is determined by divine providence.

Stoicism, with its emphasis on virtue and rationality, has seemed to some interpreters to be closer to the spirit of classical thought than Epicureanism. I think that this is not the case. Stoicism departs radically from the classical tradition in at least two respects: its severe restriction of free will to our inner attitudes and its denigration of pleasure. The views of the Epicureans on causation and agency (that some things happen according to natural law, some by chance, and some as a result of human choice) are much closer both to common sense and to previous philosophy than are those of the Stoics. Moreover, the Stoics went further than any of their predecessors in denying any role for pleasure in the good life. Because they thought virtue alone sufficient for happiness, and because they identified virtue with rationality and placed pleasure among the lower, non-rational human capacities, they denied that pleasure contributed in any way to the good life. They did not claim it was evil (though they were suspicious of the ability of pleasure to distract reason from its proper ends), but described it as "indifferent." Not even Socrates had given pleasure so small a role in the good life, indeed, in the *Protagoras*, Plato has Socrates at least toy with the idea that pleasure is the good. Though neither Plato nor Aristotle endorsed that view, both gave at least the pleasures of thought a central place in their characterization of the happy life.

In fact, both Stoicism and Epicureanism emphasize aspects of the vision of the good life that we saw developed by Plato and Aristotle, and both fail to unify these aspects into a coherent whole. The defects of each can be seen by comparing their views with the position of Aristotle, which I have described above as the culmination of the classical tradition (though much of what I say about Aristotle may be attributed to Plato as well). I believe Epicureanism actually captures more of Aristotle's insight than does Stoicism but both are more to be faulted for what they exclude than praised for what they include.

Aristotle had described the life of reason as both the most rational and the most pleasant form of life, and had noted that the activity of thought and the pleasure that completes it are so linked that it is both impossible and unnecessary to determine which is our intended end (*Nicomachean Ethics* X.4, 1175a 11—21). It is impossible, because both are essential aspects of the best life. It is unnecessary, because pleasure is never found apart from activity, and pleasant activity never occurs without producing pleasure. Now the Stoics and Epicureans attempted to bring about the very separation Aristotle had thought impossible. Though the Epicureans valued *phronesis*, practical wisdom, and philosophy, theoretical wisdom, as we have seen, they valued both merely as a means to the separate goal of a pleasant life; they answered the question Aristotle had said needn't be answered by deciding in favor of pleasure. The Stoics on the other hand, attempted to banish pleasure altogether from the good life, as I have noted, in favor of rationality.

Aristotle would find both positions unintelligible. He would, of course, reject the Epicurean view that pleasure is the absence of pain but he would also deny that one can live a life of pleasure that is not a life of pleasant activity. He would accept the Stoic view that rational activity is the basis of a good life, but would argue that at least part of the value of such activity lies in the pleasure it produces. This pleasure, he would say, is an inseparable part of the activity but even if the two could be separated, who would prefer the activity alone to the activity accompanied by its appropriate pleasure? Some pleasures, he would concede to the Stoics, impede rational activity but the pleasures appropriate to reason only enhance it. Whether or not Aristotle's doctrine of pleasure is correct (as I think it is), both the Stoics and Epicureans have omitted an important aspect of the good life in formulating their own positions.

Not only do the Stoics and Epicureans bifurcate the Aristotelian picture of the good life and keep different elements of it for their own view, they each omit a central aspect of the Aristotelian picture of the good life: the view of this life as an activity. Both hold views of the good life that are essentially passive. The Epicurean view at least allows for the possibility of change through human action, and in this respect is closer to

Aristotle's vision than is Stoicism but the essential nature of the good life in Epicurean philosophy is tranquility, peace, and this peace is purchased at the cost of withdrawal from the public world and acquiescence in all that goes on there. The Stoics, of course, remove from their philosophy the very idea of acting in the world, and limit the realm of human action to the soul, but even here their goal of *apatheia*, imperturbability, is a negative one. Both the schools see the good life not in terms of its characteristic activities but in terms of its freedom from certain external disruptions.

The cost of this disintegration of the classical, Aristotelian, vision of the good life was a corresponding disintegration of the soul. In lieu of the Platonic and Aristotelian picture of the human psyche as a combination of rational and non-rational elements, the Stoics returned to the earlier Socratic picture of the soul as rational mind. The Epicureans did not explicitly abandon the view of the soul as a complex of different elements, but their treatment of pleasure as the good caused them to treat the intellect as subservient at least to certain desires. As the classical view derived much of its power from its ability to integrate appetite, emotion and reason into a unified whole, loss of this unification is a significant drawback to Stoicism and Epicureanism.

Despite these failings, Stoicism and Epicureanism remain popular philosophies. Indeed, they might be described as permanent possibilities for human existence. The reason for this, I think, is that each philosophy enables us to deal in some way with events that are beyond our control. The Stoics may draw the line between what is and what is not in our power in the wrong place, but some things that happen to us surely are beyond our power. If the weakness of Stoicism (and to a lesser degree of Epicureanism) is that it leads us to acquiesce in matters which are not inevitable, its strength (and the strength of Epicureanism) is that it teaches us how to bear with dignity those events which truly are beyond our control.

The classical views of Plato and Aristotle place more emphasis on the active life and less on endurance in the face of inevitable fate because Plato and Aristotle had an arena of action, the *polis*, in which activity seemed more likely to succeed than did the Stoics and Epicureans. As I noted above, the decline of the *polis* in the Hellenistic age made the moral philosophy of Plato and Aristotle seem obsolete. Though the ethical views of the Stoics and

Epicureans provide a less attractive account of human flourishing than do those of Plato and Aristotle, they may be more suitable views for ages in which institutions like the *polis* do not exist. Our age is certainly more similar to that of the Alexandrian and Roman Empires than it is to the age of classical Athens and this may explain the contemporary appeal of Epicureanism and Stoicism. If, on the other hand, we are dissatisfied with the best that these Hellenistic philosophies can offer, and wish to revive the classical ideal of human flourishing, it might prove necessary to revive the classical form of human society in which it was formulated. Perhaps the *polis* is, as Plato and Aristotle thought, the only form of community in which human beings can flourish, rather than merely endure.

FURTHER READING

I offer below a guide for readers who are interested in pursuing further the topics raised in this book. It is by no means a complete bibliography of any of these issues; my only aim is to enable the reader of this book to take the next step in the study of them. In making up this guide I limited myself to books rather than journal articles, in the belief that such articles are normally not helpful to the general reader. The more extensive bibliographies in the books I suggest will direct the interested reader to these articles. Most of the books I mention should be accessible to the beginner in this field, when I mention on occasion more advanced works of special relevance to the themes of this book, I label them as such. In some cases the items I list have gone through many editions, I cite in each case the most recent of which I am aware.

On the history of Greek philosophy in general: A. H. Armstrong, *An Introduction to Ancient Philosophy* (Rowman & Allanheld; 3rd edition, 1983) is a useful one-volume survey, if a little dated. Terence Irwin, *Classical Thought* (Oxford University Press, 1989) has recently appeared. W. K. C. Guthrie, *A History of Greek Philosophy*, six volumes (Cambridge University Press, 1962—1981) offers a much more detailed treatment of the history of Greek philosophy through Aristotle. Though Guthrie's work is lengthy, it is clearly written and usually accessible to the general reader. A. H. Armstrong, ed., *The Cambridge History of Later Greek and Early Medieval Philosophy* (Cambridge University Press, 1967) covers the period after Aristotle.

On Greek ethics: Alasdair MacIntyre, *A Short History of Ethics* (MacMillan, 1966) contains eight valuable chapters on Greek ethics. Pamela Huby, *Greek Ethics* (St Martin's Press, 1967) and Christopher Rowe, *An Introduction to Greek Ethics* (Barnes & Noble, 1976) are written for the same audience as this book. Martha Nussbaum, *The Fragility of Goodness* (Cambridge University Press, 1986) aims at a more advanced readership.

Alasdair MacIntyre, *After Virtue* (Notre Dame University Press, 2nd edition, 1984) has several chapters on Greek ethics. It is more difficult for beginners than his *Short History of Ethics*, but those who persevere will be richly rewarded.

On Homer: The *Iliad* and the *Odyssey* have been well translated into both poety and prose. The versions quoted in this work are by Richmond Lattimore: *The Iliad of Homer* (University of Chicago Press, 1951) and *The Odyssey of Homer* (Harper & Row, 1967). The introduction to Lattimore's translation of the *Iliad* is the best brief account of Homeric poetry I know. Jasper Griffin's *Homer* (Oxford University Press, 1980) is an excellent introductory study of both the poems; his *Homer on Life and Death* (Oxford University Press, 1980) is more advanced but still accessible to a non-scholarly reader. Two more advanced works that focus on the *Iliad* are Seth L. Schein's *The Mortal Hero* (University of California Press, 1984) and James M. Redfield, *Nature and Culture in the* Iliad: *The Tragedy of Hector* (University of Chicago Press, 1975). M. I. Finley's *The World of Odysseus* (Viking Press, 2nd revised edition, 1978) is outstanding, and easily accessible to the general reader.

On Sophocles and Greek tragedy: The *Antigone* and *Oedipus Tyrannos* of Sophocles can also be found in numerous translations. The translations used in the quotations in this book are those in *The Complete Greek Tragedies*, four volumes (University of Chicago Press, 1959). There are several good books on Greek tragedy that include discussions of Sophocles. H.D.F. Kitto's *Greek Tragedy: A Literary Study* (Methuen, 3rd edition, 1961) is widely available; so also is Albin Lesky, *Greek Tragedy* (Barnes & Noble, 3rd edition, 1978). John Jones, *On Aristotle and Greek Tragedy* (Chatto & Windus, 1967) discusses the great Greek tragedies in light of the *Poetics*. Each of these books contains suggestions for further reading. Bernard M. W. Knox, *The Heroic Temper: Studies in Sophoclean Tragedy* (University of California Press, 1966) is a good book length study of Sophocles for somewhat more advanced readers.

On Socrates and the Sophists: A valuable collection of the Platonic dialogues in English translation is Edith Hamilton & Huntington Cairns, eds, *Plato: The Collected Dialogues* (Princeton

University Press, 1961). G. B. Kerferd, *The Sophistic Movement* (Cambridge University Press, 1981) covers the Sophists; Laslo Versenyi, *Socratic Humanism* (Greenwood Press, 1979) compares Sophistic and Socratic thought. Norman Gulley, *The Philosophy of Socrates* (St. Martin's Press, 1968) is a good general study of Socrates' thought. Michael J. O'Brien, *The Socratic Paradoxes and the Greek Mind* (University of North Carolina Press, 1967) covers both the early and middle Platonic dialogues. Thomas C. Brickhouse and Nicholas Smith, *Socrates on Trial* (Princeton University Press, 1989) offers a very thorough study of the *Apology*. For a radically different view of Socrates than that provided by Brickhouse and Smith and in this volume, see I. F. Stone, *The Trial of Socrates* (Little, Brown and Company, 1988). Richard Kraut, *Socrates and the State* (Princeton University Press, 1984) is an in-depth study of the *Crito*. A classic work that covers the philosophical methodology of both the early and middle Platonic dialogues is Richard Robinson, *Plato's Earlier Dialectic* (Oxford University Press, 2nd edition, 1953). Terence Irwin, *Plato's Moral Theory* (Oxford University Press, 1977) also covers the early and middle dialogues. Several of these works, and Irwin in particular, pose challenges to the beginning reader but none of them should be completely inaccessible.

On Plato: There are many good general introductions to Plato's thought. Two recent books with up-to-date bibliographies are C. J. Rowe, *Plato* (St Martin's Press, 1984), and David J. Melling, *Understanding Plato* (Oxford University Press, 1987). Among works devoted specifically to the *Republic*, Julia Annas, *An Introduction to Plato's* Republic (Oxford University Press, 1981) is particularly lively and accessible to the general reader. C. D. C. Reeve, *Philosopher-Kings: the Argument of Plato's* Republic (Princeton University Press, 1988) has also recently appeared. Note also Hamilton & Cairns, Irwin and Robinson under the previous heading.

On Aristotle: Aristotle's surviving works can be found in English translation in Jonathan Barnes, ed., *The Complete Works of Aristotle*, 2 volumes (Princeton University Press, 1984). A handy selection of his works is J. L. Ackrill, ed., *A New Aristotle Reader* (Princeton University Press, 1987). As in the case of Plato, there are several good general accounts of Aristotle's thought: two recent examples are J. L. Ackrill, *Aristotle the Philosopher* (Oxford University Press, 1981) and J. D. G. Evans, *Aristotle* (St Martin's Press, 1987). Both contain bibliographies. Among works specifically on the *Ethics*, J. O. Urmson, *Aristotle's Ethics* (Basil Blackwell Ltd, 1988) which has recently appeared, is aimed at the general reader. So is Roger J. Sullivan, *Morality and the Good Life* (Memphis State University Press, 1977). More advanced readers will appreciate W. F. R. Hardie, *Aristotle's Ethical Theory* (Oxford University Press, 2nd edition, 1980) and Amelie O. Rorty, ed., *Essays on Aristotle's Ethics* (University of California Press, 1980).

On the Stoics and Epicureans: A. A. Long, *Hellenistic Philosophy* (University of California Press, 2nd edition, 1986) contains useful material on both schools, as does Armstrong, ed., *The Cambridge History of Later Greek and Early Medieval Philosophy*, mentioned above. J. N. Rist, *Epicurus: an Introduction* (Cambridge University Press, 1972) offers a general account of Epicureanism. Rist, *Stoic Philosophy* (Cambridge University Press, 1969) and F. H. Sandbach, *The Stoics* (W. W. Norton & Company, Inc., 1975) are recent general accounts of Stoicism.

INDEX OF PASSAGES CITED

Aeschylus

Agamemnon, 744-54, 22

Aristotle

Metaphysics I.6, 987b 1-4, 78

Nicomachean Ethics
  I.1
    1094a 1-2, 148
    1094a 6-8, 148
  I.2
    1094a 28-b 2, 149
    1094b 8-10, 149
  I.3
    1094b 14-22, 147
  I.4
    1095a 17-20, 149
  I.5
    1095b 19-20, 150
    1095b 24-9, 151
    1095b 32-1096a 2, 151
    1096a 6-7, 151
  I.6
    1096b 33-5, 147
    1097a 3-11, 148
  I.7
    1097b 25-30, 152
    1097b 33-1098a 4, 152
    1097b 8-15, 191
    1098a 15, 154
    1098a 16-18, 154

    1098a 18, 155
  I.13
    1102b 30, 155
    1102b 30-1, 155
    1102b 33-1103a 1, 156
    1103a 3-7, 156
  II.1
    1103a 17, 156
    1103a 23-6, 157
    1103b 23-5, 157
  II.2
    1104a 27-1104b 3, 158
    1105a 28-34, 158
  II.4
    1105b 5-9, 157
  II.6
    1106a 16-17, 159
    1106a 29-1106b 4, 160
    1106b 16-23, 161
    1106b 36-1107a 3, 159
    1107a 6-8, 162
    1107a 8-15, 162
  II.7
    1107b 7, 164
  III.1
    1111a 22-4, 175
    1111b 5-6, 176
    1111b 27-9, 176
    1112a 15-16, 176
  III.3
    1112b 15-27, 177
    1113a 2-5, 177

III.6
    1115a 32-b 4, 164
    1115a 33-4, 207
    1115a 35-b 1, 207
III.8
    1116b 4-5, 166
    1117a 4-5, 166
III.11
    1118b 11-12, 166
    1118b 16, 166
    1119a 6, 166
    1119a 16-18, 167
V.1
    1129b 17-20, 168
    1129b 24-5, 168
    1129b 26-1130a 9, 169
V.2
    1130a 24-8, 170
V.3
    1131a 27-9, 170
V.4
    1132a 2-10, 170
V.6
    1134a 25-7, 171
VI.1
    1138b 27-30, 162
    1139a 6-8, 178
    1139a 12-13, 179
    1139a 23, 177
VI.2
    1139a 31-4, 177
    1139b 4-5, 177
    1141a 20-2, 179
VI.5
    1140a 25-8, 180
    1140a 31, 179
VI.7
    1141a 20, 179
    1141b 9-10, 179

VI.8
    1142a 24-7, 178
    1144a 8-9, 180
VI.12
    1144a 23-b 1, 180
    1144a 34-6, 182
VI.13
    1144b 17-25, 110
    1145a 5-6, 180
VII.1
    1145a 20, 184
VII.2
    1145b 21-6, 185
    1145b 27-8, 185
VII.3
    1146b 31-5, 185
    1147a 7, 185
    1147a 10-11, 186
    1147a 12-18, 186
    1147a 21-2, 186
    1147a 31-1147b 3, 186
    1147b 14-17, 187
VII.5
    1148b 18, 184
    1148b 34-1149a 1, 184
VII.6
    1150a 1-2, 184
    1150a 6-7, 184
VII.9
    1151b 34- 1152a 3, 184
VIII.1
    1155a 22-7, 172
VIII.2
    1155b 18-19, 172
VIII.3
    1156a 10-14, 172
    1156b 7-9, 172
VIII.5
    1157b 28-9, 172

IX.4
    1166a 10-11, 173
    1166a 31-2, 173
IX.8
    1168b 15-28, 174
    1169a 2-4, 174
X.4
    1175a 11-21, 222
X.6
    1176b 27-1177a 1, 189
X.7
    1177a 20-1, 189
    1177a 21-2, 189
    1177a 25-6, 189
    1177a 32-b 1, 190
    1177b 1-2, 190
    1177b 26-7, 190
    1177b 31-4, 190
X.8
    1178a 7, 190
    1178a 9, 190
    1178b 8-21, 190
    1178a 14-22, 191

Epictetus

Manual
    1, 210
    3, 212
    5, 211
    6, 219
    7, 212
    8, 211
    10, 217
    11, 212
    14, 212
    15, 217
    16, 213
    17, 210
    19, 214

    20, 212
    25, 212
    26, 213
    27, 209
    31, 217
    33, 211, 214, 219
    44, 219
    45, 214
    46, 211, 215
    47, 219
    48, 215, 216
    49, 219
    51, 216
    52, 215, 216

Epicurus

Letter to Herodotus
    81-2, 203

Letter to Menoeceus
    128, 201
    129, 200
    129-30, 202
    130-31, 203
    131-2, 201
    132-3, 204

Principal Doctrines
    2, 200
    3, 203
    4, 201
    8, 201
    10, 201
    12, 202
    14, 205
    15, 204
    16, 205
    17, 206
    18, 203

21, 205
26, 204
27, 205
28, 205
29, 204
32, 206
33, 206
34, 206
36, 206

Vatican Sayings
23, 205
41, 207
51, 205

Homer

Iliad
IX
    312-13, 19
    317-22, 12
    340-3, 11
    378, 11
    443, 16
    632-8, 11
    644-8, 11
XII
    310-12, 9
    322-8, 9
XXII
    345-54, 13
XXIV
    525-33, 14

Odyssey
IV
    271-89,, 18
    280-8, 18
IX
    105 to end, 18

V
    215-24, 16
VI
    182-4, 20
VIII
    186-229, 16
    492-520, 18
XX
    17, 107, 137
    18-21, 19

Plato

Apology
18b, 52
18c, 53
19b-c, 52
19c, 53
19c-d, 53
19d-e, 54
21b, 60
21b-c, 60
21d, 60
22a, 60
22a, 59
23a, 59, 60
23b, 59
24a, 65
24b, 49
26b, 57
26d, 52, 57
26d-e, 57
28b, 62, 68
28b-d, 67
28b-29b, 71
28d-29a, 64
29a, 63, 68
29d, 62
29d, 74
30a, 59

30c-d, 71
30c-d, 68
30d, 63
30d-31a, 62
31b-c, 54
31d, 63
31d-e, 64
31e-32a, 64
32b-d, 64
33a-b, 54
33c-d, 56
33d-34a , 52
34b, 57
34b ff., 59
34b-35d, 64
36a, 65
37a-b, 65
37e, 61
40a-b, 63, 68
40c-d, 63, 68
41a-b, 67
41c, 63
41d, 68

Crito
47d-e, 70
47e, 70
48a, 69
48b, 70
48b8, 70
48c-d, 69
49b-c, 72
49e, 73
50a, 73
50d-51c, 73
51e, 73
54b, 69

Euthydemus 278e-282a, 87

Euthyphro
4e-5a, 76
5c-d, 76
5d-e, 76
5e-6a, 135
6a-c, 61
6d, 79
6e, 79
6d-e, 77
6e-7a, 77
9d, 77
10e-11b, 77
11b, 77
12d, 77
12e, 77
15e, 77

Gorgias
481b-c, 72
491a, 45

Laches
187e-188a, 75
198b ff., 85

Meno
72b-c, 78
72c, 79
77b-78b, 85
79e-80b, 80
80d, 80
81a-b, 81
81c-d, 81
84a-b, 82
85c-d, 82
86a, 83
87c, 83
87c ff., 86
87d, 86
88a, 86

88c-d, 87
89d, 88
92e, 88
94e, 88
96d, 88
97b-c, 89
98a, 89
99e-100a, 89

Phaedo 64c ff., 87

Protagoras
327e-328a, 55
347c-e, 134
361e, 45

Republic

I
331e, 93
334a-b, 93
335, 93
335e, 94
336b-d, 46
336c-d, 94
337a, 97
338c, 94
338e-339a, 95
343a, 46, 95
350d-e, 96
354a, 96
354b, 97

II
357a, 92
357a-b, 96
358a, 98
359a, 98
359d-360b, 98
361e-362a, 99

367a-b, 99
368e-369a, 100
369b, 100
369d, 101
370c, 101
371e, 101
372a, 101
372a-c, 101
372d, 101
372e-373a, 102
373c, 102, 105
373e, 102
375, 102
376c-412a, 102
377a, 135
378b, 135
379a, 136
379c, 136
381c, 136
382c, 136

III
386b-c, 136
387a, 135
387d-e, 137
390d, 137
392a-c, 138
412c-e, 102
414b, 104
415a, 103
416a, 104
416d-e, 104

IV
420b-421c, 104
421d-422a, 112
428c-429a, 104
429b-430b, 104
429c-d, 109
430a, 109
430c, 110
431c-d, 104

431e-432a, 104
432d, 105
433a, 105
434a-c, 105
435b-c, 105
435e, 110
436a-b, 106
436b, 106
439d, 106
441b, 137
441b, 107
441c, 107
441d, 107
441e, 107
442a-b, 107
442c-d, 107
442e-443a, 107, 111
443c-d, 100, 111
443d-444a, 108
444b, 108
445a-b, 108

V

449c-d, 115
457c-461e, 112
472c, 115
473a, 115
473d-e, 115
473e-74a, 115
475d, 117
476a, 116
476b, 116
476c-d, 116
477b, 118
482c-486d, 46

VI

504d-505b, 120
505b-c, 120
506c, 120
507b, 120
508a, 120

508e, 120
509b, 120, 121
510a, 121
510b, 122
510d-511a, 122
511b, 122
511e, 121

VII

514a-b, 123
515b, 123
515c-516a, 123
516a-e, 123
516e-517a, 123
517b-c, 124
520c-d, 124
531d-534d, 122
536e-537a, 125

VIII

544c, 126, 127
545b, 126
547b-c, 127
547e-548c, 126
550c-d, 127
551c, 127
554a-d, 127
557a, 128
557b, 128
557e, 128
558a, 128
558c, 128
561b-c, 128
561c-d, 128
567c, 130

IX

571c-d, 130
572b, 130
576c-580c, 131
582a, 131
585b, 132
586a-b, 132

588e- 589b, 133

X

596a-b, 139
597e, 139
599b, 139
599b-601a, 139
604d, 140
606b, 140
606d, 140
607b, 66
607c-e, 141
615a-616a, 142
617d-e, 142
618b, 142
620c-d, 142

Symposium 215d-216a, 46

Protagoras
Fragment 1, 40
Fragment 4, 40

Sophocles

Antigone
48, 26
59-64, 26
99, 26
182-3, 26
187-91, 27
211-14, 27
279, 27
323, 28
362-72, 27
450-7, 28
461-2, 31
484-5, 28
523, 31
559-60, 31
693-5, 28

699, 28
756, 28
761-2, 29
849-51, 31
852-4, 31
1023-8, 29
1111-14, 29
1167, 29
1242-3, 30
1342, 30
1347-52, 30

Oedipus the King
30-31, 32
44-5, 32
133, 33
135-6, 33
137-41, 33
774, 33
794, 33
1076, 34
1170, 35
1177-81, 36
1182, 34
1283, 36
1329-32, 35

Thucydides

History of the Peloponnesian War
II.37, 113
II.65, 129

GENERAL INDEX

Achilles, 5, 6, 9, 10-17, 19, 20, 30, 31, 37, 67, 68, 134, 137, 140, 142
Aeschylus, 21-3, 39, 68
Alexander the Great, 144-5, 194, 195
Antigone, 25-31, 34, 36, 37, 67-8
Antigone, the (*see also* **Index of passages cited**), 23, 25-31, 32
Apology, the (*see also* **Index of passages cited**), 44, 47-68, 71, 73, 74, 80, 82, 87, 88, 90, 94, 134, 136, 139, 141
arete (*see also* virtue), 2-3, 146, 155, 168
Aristotle, Chapter 4, passim; 23, 32, 72, 78, 96, 110, 111, 143, 194-5, 197, 202, 205, 207, 208, 212, 217-18, 219, 221-4
Aristophanes, 42, 44, 49-50, 53, 54, 64
Athens, 6, 21, 23-5, 39, 43-6, 49, 50, 51, 54, 55, 56, 61, 66, 67, 69, 73, 88, 92, 102, 112, 113, 129, 144, 145, 172, 196, 198, 207, 224

belief (*see also doxa* and opinion), 83, 87, 109, 121, 122, 139

Charmides, the 51, 75
city-state (*see also polis*), 5, 25, 100, 127, 144, 195
Clouds, the, 42, 44, 49, 50, 51, 53, 54
courage, 3, 9, 10, 15, 20, 26, 31, 36, 44, 48, 64, 74, 75, 85, 86, 87, 90, 104, 107, 109-10, 125, 127, 136, 147, 158, 163, 164, 166, 167, 195, 207, 217, 218
Crito, the (*see also* **Index of passages cited**), 67-74, 76, 90, 113

doxa (*see also* belief and opinion), 85, 89, 116, 118, 119

elenchus, 75-84, 90, 91, 97, 98
Epictetus, 197, 208-17, 219
Epicureans, 72, 197, 208, 214, 220-24
Epicurus, 132, 197-209, 220
episteme (*see also* knowledge), 3, 79, 116, 118, 119, 179
eudaimonia (*see also* happiness and good life, the), 2, 3, 146, 148-55, 159, 167, 168, 171, 181, 188, 192
Euripides, 21-3
Euthydemus, the (*see also* **Index of passages cited**), 87

Euthyphro, the (*see also* **Index of passages cited**), 61, 75-7, 79, 90, 135

friendship, 146, 167-8, 171-5, 204, 205, 207, 221

good, the, 120-6, 147, 148-55, 168, 169, 172, 173, 184, 185, 203
good life, the (*see also eudaimonia* and happiness) 2, 4-5, 15, 21, 37, 41, 43, 68, 70-2, 74-5, 90, 91, 134, 146, 148-55, 156, 167, 168, 171, 180, 182, 192, 193, 195, 196, 202-5, 207, 215, 217, 221-3
Gorgias, the (*see also* **Index of passages cited**), 45, 46, 72, 141

happiness (*see also eudaimonia* and good life, the), 2, 21, 29, 36, 37, 70-2, 86, 134, 146, 149-50, 167, 168, 189, 191, 197, 198, 200-1, 204-5, 211, 213, 220, 221
Hector, 6, 8-15, 20
Herodotus, 24, 38
Homer, 6-8, 14-17, 20-22, 36, 37, 40, 89, 99, 107, 136, 138, 139, 140, 141
Homeric hero, the, 2, 7-10, 12, 16, 18, 19, 20, 23, 37
Homeric poems, 5-8, 21-3, 37
Homeric society, 7, 8, 16, 17, 20, 36
honor, 8, 11, 12, 126, 131, 151, 166, 168, 169, 204

Iliad, the (*see also* **Index of passages cited**), 5-20, 36, 141, 142

justice, 3-4, 23, 31, 39-43, 48, 50, 66, 69-70, 75, 77, 78, 85, 86, 87, 92-114, 115, 116, 119, 122, 125, 133-4, 138, 143, 153, 156, 163, 167-72, 174, 175, 190, 195, 204, 205-7, 218

knowledge, 3-4, 5, 14, 30, 35, 38, 40, 53, 55, 56, 63, 69, 70-1, 74, 79, 81-90, 91, 93, 96, 97, 108-11, 114-26, 131, 134, 139, 141, 147, 157, 166, 175, 178-9, 181, 182, 184-8, 189, 197, 216, 218

Laches, the (*see also* **Index of passages cited**) 75, 85, 87
Laws, the 48, 92

Meno, the (*see also* **Index of passages cited**), 48, 71, 78-90, 109
moral weakness, 86-7, 91, 109, 146, 182-8

Nicomachean Ethics, the (*see also* **Index of passages cited**), Chapter 4, passim; 96, 110, 207, 217, 222

Odysseus, 5-7, 9, 11, 15-22, 30, 37, 107, 137, 142
Odyssey, the (*see also* **Index of passages cited**), 5-8, 15-20, 39, 107, 137

Oedipus, 25, 32-7, 140
Oedipus the King (*see also*
     Index of passages cited), 23,
     32-6, 40, 141
opinion (*see also* belief and
     doxa), 70, 78, 85, 89, 91,
     108, 109-10, 116, 118-19,
     186

Peloponnesian War, 24, 32, 38,
     43, 44, 49, 50, 51, 112, 129
Persian Wars, 24, 68
Phaedo, the (*see also* Index of
     passages cited), 45, 47, 67,
     68, 87, 109, 141
Phaedrus, the, 141
philosopher-king, the, 2, 89, 114-
     26, 129, 134, 142
phronesis (*see also* practical
     wisdom and wisdom), 3, 69,
     146, 171, 179, 190, 192, 202,
     204, 222
piety, 60-1, 75-9, 85, 163, 217
Plato, Chapters 2 and 3,
     passim; 144-5, 147-8, 153,
     155, 163, 166, 169, 173,
     181-2, 188, 193, 194, 195,
     197, 199, 202, 205, 207,
     212, 218, 219, 221, 223-4
pleasure, 2, 43, 86, 120, 128,
     130-2, 145, 146, 149, 150-1,
     161, 164, 166, 172, 183, 186,
     188-9, 198, 200-5, 218, 220,
     221-3
polis (*see also* city-state), 5, 25,
     100-1, 107, 110, 112, 144,
     195-6, 207, 220, 223-4
practical wisdom (*see also*
     knowledge, *phronesis* and
     wisdom), 3, 14-17, 19-21,

72, 132, 146, 153, 156, 159,
     161, 163, 167, 171, 175, 177,
     178-82, 188-92, 195, 202-4,
     207, 222
Pre-Socratic philosophers, 40,
     42, 44, 49, 50, 52, 58, 208
Protagoras, 39, 40-1, 42, 43, 45,
     55, 75, 85
Protagoras, the (*see also* Index
     of passages cited), 45, 55,
     72, 85, 86, 87, 134 , 221

recollection, Platonic doctrine
     of, 80-84, 89, 90, 91, 116
Republic, the (*see also* Index of
     passages cited), Chapter 3,
     passim; 41, 66, 72, 75, 78,
     79, 80, 84, 87, 88, 89, 90,
     147, 153, 155, 166, 169,
     173, 181, 182, 205

sage, the, 2, 215-18
self-control (*see also*
     temperance), 19, 137, 156,
     158, 166, 174, 183
Socrates, Chapters 2 and 3,
     passim; 3, 30, 37, 145, 147,
     163, 166, 181, 184-5, 187,
     197, 205, 211, 216, 218,
     219, 221
Socratic paradoxes, 56, 71, 84-
     90, 108, 109
sophia (*see also* wisdom), 3,
     178
Sophists, the, 38-44, 46, 48, 49,
     50, 53, 54, 58, 66, 71, 72,
     88, 95, 99
Sophocles, 21, 22, 23, 25, 31,
     32, 36, 37, 43, 44, 67

soul, the, 63, 70-2, 74, 81-3, 85, 86-8, 96, 105-11, 113, 114, 122, 124, 125, 126, 127, 130, 131, 133, 134, 138, 140, 142, 150, 154, 155-6, 163, 178-9, 192, 200, 201, 202, 223

Sparta, 6, 24, 44, 49, 126, 129

Stoics, the, 2, 72, 195, 197, 208, 209, 211-23

Symposium, the (*see also* **Index of passages cited**), 44, 46, 50, 51

temperance, 3, 4, 75, 86, 87, 104, 107, 109-10, 113, 125, 154, 163-4, 166-7, 183, 195, 204, 207, 217-218

Theaetetus, the, 40, 44

theoretical wisdom, 156, 178, 179, 189, 222

theory of forms, Platonic, 79, 111, 117-122, 124, 132, 138, 148

Thucydides, 24, 38, 113, 129

Trojan War, the, 6, 7, 8, 67

virtue, 2-3, 5, 9, 15, 23, 31, 36, 37, 38, 39, 41, 43, 48, 55, 61, 70-2, 74-5, 78-9, 81, 83-90, 91, 94, 96, 99, 109-10, 132, 134, 144, 146, 147, 151, 154, 155-63, 164, 167, 168-9, 172, 174, 176, 179-84, 190, 204, 216, 217-18, 221

virtues, the, 2-4, 9-10, 15, 20, 23, 37, 41, 43, 70, 78, 84, 85, 90, 104, 107-11, 114, 126, 134, 143, 146, 156, 158, 159, 163, 164, 167, 169, 178, 181, 182, 191, 192-3, 195, 196, 204, 207, 217-18

wisdom, 3-4, 9-10, 14, 20-1, 23, 29-30, 34, 36, 37, 45-6, 55, 60-1, 69, 70-2, 86-7, 97, 98, 104, 107-10, 114, 125, 126, 127, 131, 134, 142, 163, 181, 205, 216, 218